The
Schools
in
Contemporary
Society

The Schools in Contemporary Society

An Analysis of
Social Currents,
Issues, and Forces

John Jarolimek
University of Washington, Seattle

Macmillan Publishing Co., Inc.
New York
Collier Macmillan Publishers
London

MACMILLAN PUBLISHING CO., INC.
866 THIRD AVENUE, NEW YORK, NEW YORK 10022

COLLIER MACMILLAN CANADA, LTD.

Library of Congress Cataloging in Publication Data

Jarolimek, John.
    The schools in contemporary society.

    Includes bibliographies and index.
    1. Educational sociology—United States.
2. Minorities—Education—United States. 3. Educational
equalization—United States. 4. Education—Economic
aspects—United States. 5. Teachers' unions—United
States. I. Title.
LC191.4.J37   370.19'0973   79-26129
ISBN 0-02-360430-1

Printing: 1 2 3 4 5 6 7 8   Year: 1 2 3 4 5 6 7

Preface

Today's teachers are relatively free of the pettiness and injustice of local regulations and attitudes that once characterized the public life of their predecessors. In the past, strict and often unreasonable norms of personal conduct were imposed on teachers. Classroom procedures were to be conducted along the lines of establishment expectations. Political activity of teachers was strictly curtailed. Negative attitudes toward collective bargaining in salary and employment conditions were institutionalized to the extent that teachers themselves were reluctant to engage in them. Activism to secure "teacher rights" was perceived as "rocking the boat" and failure as a "good team member." Participation in these activities and others of this type could, and often did, lead to the teacher's dismissal, tenure protection and contracted agreements notwithstanding.

The teacher today is a politically active person who is exercising a great deal of power in decision making at the local, state, and national levels. This has transformed the traditional impotent image of the teaching profession to one of vibrant strength. Teachers have become tough in their bargaining with local authorities. Through their professional organizations, they are demanding—and getting—more to say about their wages and benefits, the conditions of their employment, job entitlements, their own placement in schools, the selection of their administrators, the selection of instructional materials, and the curriculum. Teacher associations have become powerful lobbyists in influencing legislation in state government and in Congress. These recently gained rights in decision making carry with them the additional obligation of teachers to be informed about issues, to be accountable for decisions that were arrived at collaboratively, and to deliberate prudently, in good faith, and in professionally responsible ways.

The political and status gains described in the foregoing paragraph have not, however, made the life of the teacher any easier. Indeed, quite the reverse is the case. Public education today finds itself enmeshed in a bureaucratic system of rules and regulations issuing from state and federal sources that siphon off the creative energy of teachers, stifle much innovative educational effort, and make the teacher legally accountable for professional actions. Today's teacher must know a whole lot of things, quite apart from the subject matter of the curriculum area in which he or she teaches. Increasingly, schools are becoming more legalistic in their day-to-day operation. What a teacher can or cannot do regarding pupil conduct, in classroom presentations, in promotion or failure of students, in the use of certain instructional materials and books, in conducting classroom activities, and in most of what else the teacher does during the school day, is governed by legal requirements. Almost every decision at all levels is subject to a legal challenge, and it matters little if the issue has to do with admission to kindergarten or admission to the graduate school! Student learning objectives, education of the handicapped, sex equity, implied or overt discrimination practices, open meeting requirements, and minimum competency mandates are just a few of the growing list of complex issues that in all states are strictly governed by state and federal regulations.

There can be no doubt that it is in and around the institution of the school that many social problems of the community converge. It is in the affairs of the school that conflicts take shape between community power groups. This drama of community-school-state-federal relations combined with personal striving for power, equity, or social justice in a social structure of enormous complexity, makes a fascinating subject of study for anyone interested in today's education. But for the teacher, this subject matter is essential background knowledge if he or she is to have an understanding of how schools and communities relate to each other and how the teacher, as a professional person, fits into that mix of school-society relationships. This text is designed to provide such a background for the practicing teacher and/or the student preparing to enter the teaching field. The book addresses several of the most significant social currents, issues, and trends in contemporary education. The topics are dealt with analytically, with several points of view presented. The reader is then encouraged to make up his or her own mind on the problem or issue being discussed in the text. The first six chapters deal with the dynamics of school-society relationships; the last six chapters focus on power and decision making in the schools.

It is with a sense of sincere thanks and appreciation that I acknowledge that I am much in debt to my wife, Mildred Fleming Jarolimek, for encouraging me to undertake this project, and for her competent assistance with all aspects of the book's authorship and production.

JOHN JAROLIMEK

Contents

chapter 3

chapter 4

chapter 5

chapter 9

Economic Influences on School Decision Making

chapter 10

Political Influences on School Decision Making

chapter 11

The Influence of Organized Teacher Groups on School Decision Making   271

chapter 12

Managing Educational Change   295

Index   315

chapter 1

The Dynamics of School-Society Relationships

In the time that it takes the average reader to complete reading this sentence—about nine seconds—a baby will have been born somewhere in the United States. The fact that this child was born of human parents, however, does not ensure that it has, or ever will have, those qualities associated with "humanness." The child's parents and the society in which he or she was born will have a great deal to do with shaping the kind of person he or she will eventually become. The development of human beings is greatly dependent on learning, and as such it is totally different from the development of other life forms, whose behavior is largely guided by instinct. For instance, it is not necessary for a salmon to learn anything about being a fish from its parents or from other salmon. Once the female salmon deposits her eggs and they are fertilized, a whole series of events is put in motion that will take place without any intervention by the parents. From the instant of fertilization, the salmon eggs are programmed to lead their life cycle just as all salmon have done for thousands of years.

The dissimilarities between human beings and other creatures are, of course, astounding. Yet there is much that can be learned in con-

1

trasting the lives of animals that are guided mainly by instinct with the lives of human beings, whose behavior is governed by what is learned. For instance, in all life forms there is a strong force that works to assure survival of the species. The parents of the approximately thirty-three and one-third million children who will be born in the United States during the decade of the 1980s will be engaging in one of the essential requirements of the survival of human beings, namely, the literal production of new persons. But most of those mothers, like nearly all human mothers, will have just one child at a time, and if those new human beings are to survive to adulthood, they will have to be adequately fed, protected, and sheltered from the elements for several years.

Among mammals it is characteristic of mothers to protect and care for their young. Human beings are not unique in this respect. What sets human beings apart from all other living creatures is the *extent to which they must learn to become who and what they are.* That is, physical care, feeding, sheltering, and protecting human infants are not enough to assure the survival of human societies. A second critical requirement is that the young are taught the things they need to know—those social and cultural imperatives—that will ensure the perpetuation of the society from one generation to the next. All societies make provisions for such education of the young.

In preliterate societies, learning takes place informally in the family and by direct participation in the life of the group. Young males learn food-gathering and hunting skills from their elders. Young females learn skills associated with the role of women in the culture by working with their mothers and with other women in the extended family, the clan, or the tribe. This is akin to what we would call "on-the-job training." But as the economic, political, and social structures of a society become more complex, it becomes impossible for children to learn all they need to know in this way. The risk of omission of needed instruction on critical knowledge and skills becomes so great that other means must be established to ensure that such material is learned. Just the sheer amount to be learned in a modern industrial society is more than parents and elders could be expected to know. Much of what needs to be learned is technical, abstract, specialized knowledge that requires carefully sequenced instruction over a period of several years if it is to be learned. The widespread use of written forms of communication contributes greatly to the need for institutionalized modes of tuition of the young. Modern societies, therefore, establish school systems that are expected to assume some responsibility for the education of young people. In nearly all cases, this is a responsibility that is shared with the family and other institutions in the community.

THE CONCEPT OF HUMAN POTENTIAL

One of the truly remarkable qualities of human beings is their potential for development. Throughout the animal and plant kingdoms, there are countless examples of living things that have made morphological adaptations that allow them to live in a particular environment. Creatures and plants that have made such physical adaptations to a specific set of conditions often are not able to survive elsewhere. Thus, a world map shows the locations of the native homes of various animals, and, in most cases, it is possible to associate conditions of those environments with the adjustment mechanisms of the creatures found there.

Not so with human beings. If we take the same world map and indicate those places inhabited by human beings, we notice that they are found almost everywhere. Because an area is extremely hot or cold or is agriculturally unproductive or because its elevation is over 10,000 feet or any of several other adverse conditions, we cannot predict that it will not be inhabited by human beings. Even the most hostile environments on earth are places where people have settled, developed cultures, and managed to attend to the basic requirements of social life.

Of course, the reason that human beings are so versatile in their ability to adapt and adjust is because they do so through their cultures. Human beings make cultural adaptations rather than depend on the slow process of physical evolution to accommodate new surroundings. Thus, except for some superficial differences in appearances of people from one place to another, they are basically the same everywhere. A normal child at the moment of birth has the potential to learn to live in any of the several cultures of the world. The evidence we have suggests that the basic physical and mental characteristics of human beings have changed very little from the dawn of human history. If a "time machine" could in some way take a child at the moment of birth from any early Homo sapiens couple and transplant it into the home of an American family in the twentieth century, we have no reason to believe that such a child would

3

be very much different from other American children as it grew to maturity.

What an individual is or who he or she becomes, therefore, depends almost entirely on circumstances of birth. For example, at the turn of the century, a large Ukrainian family south of Kiev broke up, with part of the family emigrating to Canada, settling eventually in the Red Deer area of Alberta Province. Another part of the family came to the United States and established themselves in central Kansas. A third group went to Brazil and located in São Paülo. The rest of the family remained in the Ukraine. Had they all stayed in the Ukraine, their descendants would to-day be citizens of the USSR, they would speak the Ukrainian and Russian languages, and their values and life-styles would be those of the Soviet Union. Instead, few of the descendants of those who emigrated speak Ukrainian fluently, and none speaks Russian. These people have been completely assimilated by their host cultures—Canadian, American, Brazilian. Their languages, lifeways, and values are those of the societies in which they live. Moreover, the host societies promoted the process of acculturation of these immigrant families by requiring their children to attend schools and by exposing them to a school curriculum that would shape the individual to the culture.

Much of the psychological literature of development speaks to the concept of "actualization" of the individual, meaning that the fulfilled person maximizes his or her potential. Although human beings may be long on potential, they may be short on actualizing that potential. The extent to which individuals actually achieve their potential depends on many factors, including personality variables such as motivation, in-terest, drive, and so forth. Critically important in developing individual potential is the opportunity to learn. The case of language learning pro-vides a good example of this point. Any person has the potential to learn any one or more of the more than 3,000 languages and dialects spoken in the world, but most of us learn only the one or two spoken in our own society.

Because the infant human being has the innate potential for great diversity in development, the society in which he or she is born takes great care to mold the individual—through teaching and condition-ing—to behave and act the way others in his or her society behave and act. This process is called *socialization* or *enculturation*. According to Basil Bernstein, "Socialisation [*sic*] refers to the process whereby the

4

biological is transformed into a specific cultural being."[1] Through socialization, the individual becomes familiar with the mainstream or common culture. It teaches the person what the society knows and values. It teaches the person critical survival skills and, most particularly, communication skills. It transmits important myths, rituals, traditions, and protocols. Such learnings make communication and interaction possible between and among individuals and are essential prerequisites for group life. Socialization produces a degree of similarity in the behavior patterns of all individuals in the group, and it provides the criteria for defining deviant behavior.

SOCIALIZATION OR SOCIAL CHANGE?

There is not agreement—even among experts—regarding the relative importance of two central missions of the schools, namely, socializing the young on the one hand and promoting social change on the other. The issue is not so much that the school should do one and not the other; but, rather, deciding what the *main thrust* should be. It is clear enough that schools are expected to engage in the socialization of young children because of the relationship of socialization to societal continuity. What is less clear is whether the schools should transmit the culture uncritically to each oncoming generation of schoolchildren or should seek to teach in ways that will change society for the betterment of individual and group life.

This issue, like so many in education, cannot be resolved on the basis of empirical studies or even on the basis of expertise because it is basically a question of values. No one can say for certain which thrust is the better alternative to follow. All we can do is to try to predict the effects that are likely to flow from each choice.

There is little doubt that, through the years, schools have been less concerned with promoting social change than with socializing children into the existing lifeways. This has branded schools as conservative institutions that are usually reactive in their posture, that lag behind social

---

[1] Basil Bernstein, "Social Class, Language and Socialisation," *Power and Ideology in Education*, ed. Jerome Karabel and A. H. Halsey (New York: Oxford University Press, 1977), p. 476.

trends and movements, and that will not change unless forced to do so by some external intervention. Some apologists for the school would not deny this; indeed, they would claim this to be an appropriate posture for the schools. They see the school as an important bastion in the preservation of the cultural heritage from the onslaught of the modernists and revisionists who "want to change everything." They would take the position that conservative school policies provide a balancing mechanism for society. Such schools prevent society from taking off on tangents that may be unproductive. If schools are slow to change, contemporary developments and trends can play themselves out in the larger social arena, with the residual effects eventually becoming a part of public policy. At that point, such policies would be institutionalized by being incorporated in the school curriculum.

Advocates of social change, on the other hand, would say that the school cannot ignore social injustice, the flaunting of human rights, misuse of the earth's resources, environmental contamination, overpopulation, inequitable distribution of wealth, and a whole host of similar social issues. They would urge that the school take an activist position in helping society to come to grips with these complex issues. To do less would indicate that the school is simply an arm of the affluent elite who are the major decision makers in society, for whom the system works well, and who want to keep it that way.

Although it is true that schools have in practice been on the conservative end of the continuum of change, it is also true that there has been a consistently recurring faith in the capability of schools to resolve baffling social issues. One must conclude that hope does, indeed, spring eternal insofar as the school's solving society's problems is concerned! Elaborate and costly programs have been proposed—and in some cases have even been implemented—that would have the school build a new social order, engage in a war on poverty, eliminate racism, help win the space race, teach for peace and global understanding, reduce traffic fatalities through driver training, rescue the inner cities from further deterioration, and so on and on through a long litany of social concerns that "schools should *do* something about." In making an objective assessment of how well schools have contributed to the resolution of such complex social problems as appear on this wish list, one would be forced to conclude that the schools have been long on promises and short on delivery.

This is not to say that schools have not been successful in much of what they have done. It is rather to suggest that in many instances the schools are given the impossible task of doing something about problems that are indigenous to the larger society. They are chronic ailments of society, and the school is not likely to be very effective in alleviating them without some basic realignments in the larger society. So-called school problems such as racism, vandalism, racial segregation, and inequality of opportunity are not only school problems; they are problems of society. But because of the close relationship between society and school, the schools become a convenient scapegoat for many of society's ills.

It is often said that schools mirror the society in which they are found. What this means is that the major values and concerns of the society are reflected in the schools. For instance, a society that is highly centralized is likely to have a centralized school system. A society that is strictly stratified according to social classes is likely to have special educational programs for children of the elite and other programs for the non-elite. If a society is racially segregated in its residential housing patterns, the schools are likely to reflect such segregation. When the larger society is not clear about its values or is uncertain about its priorities, these same uncertainties often show up in schools.

If it is true that schools mirror the larger society, it is doubtful that they can be effective proactive agents of change where deeply held social values are at stake. For example, a high school social studies class might become involved in a social action project to promote legislation that would benefit the elderly. It might even be successful in lobbying the state legislature to the extent that such a measure is enacted into law. This is a humanitarian concern that, it could be expected, would get widespread support in the larger society outside of school. Such an event might be picked up by the wire services and carried as a news story nationally, thereby winning for the school public acclaim and commendation for teaching young citizens the skills associated with social action and by doing so "through regular channels."

Now let us suppose the same class became involved in a study of income differentials in the local community. Let us assume, further, that they found that, in a significant number of families in the community, the head of the household worked full eight-hour days for five days a week throughout the year, but that his or her income was still not high enough to keep the family above the poverty line. Moreover, the class

7

found that many young persons who were sufficiently well educated to be employed simply could not find jobs. The problem, they found, was especially critical if the young person happened to be a member of a visible minority group. Armed with these data, the class now begins a campaign to seek reforms in the social conditions that produce these inequities. As this social action project proceeds, there is growing resentment on the part of the community toward the school for "meddling in things that are none of its damn business." "The school should stick to basics instead of filling our kids' heads with all this socialist nonsense." The school authorities are taken to task for permitting such matters to be a part of the curriculum. The social studies teacher is accused of being a Marxist and a Communist, and only the state tenure law prevents his or her out-and-out dismissal.

The two foregoing examples illustrate the parameters within which the school can function in promoting social change. In those areas and on those issues where there is public readiness to accept change, the school can be a potent instrument in promoting reforms. In those areas and on those issues where there is firm public resistance to a proposed change, the school will be relatively ineffective in promoting reforms. In the latter case, the school's role will be limited to building awareness of the problems that surround such "closed areas." That is to say, social changes for which there is not now general public support must be perceived as cross-generation goals, if they are to be achieved at all.

What should be apparent, yet is often overlooked by school authorities, is that much of the decision making that affects schools most profoundly is influenced by social, political, and economic forces that the school as an institution is powerless to control. For instance, what a school can or cannot do is often affected by the amount of money it has to spend. Fiscal decisions are usually made by the state legislature and/or by local taxpayers, not by local school leadership. Nor can school leaders do very much about components of the curriculum that are mandated by state law or by local regulations. Likewise, conditions of employment are increasingly coming under the control of teachers' unions and are not determined entirely by local school officials. Thus, the school as an institution is compelled to operate within such constraints over which it has no control. It is not an island set apart from the rest of the social reality that surrounds it.

EDUCATION FOR ALL

The English word *school* is derived from the Greek word ςχολ~η, (Scholé) whose root meaning is "leisure."[2] One must interpret this to mean that, among the ancient Greeks, schooling was pursued during one's leisure. It can be inferred that this required a level of economic independence that permitted one to engage in leisure-time pursuits. This reminds us that, historically, formal schooling went to those who could afford it—afford it not only in terms of money but, just as importantly, in terms of time. Those persons who had to spend most of their waking hours meeting their basic needs of food, clothing, and shelter had little money or time to engage in leisure or schooling.

Thus, institutions such as schools that would educate all the children of all the people and be supported by public funds were unheard of until in relatively recent times. Similarly, the concept of compulsory schooling is one of recent origin. More typical forms of education consisted of schools for children of the affluent elite paid for by those families or the use of governesses or tutors. Until the middle of the nineteenth century, children of working people or peasants throughout the world were hardly schooled at all. It was not until the education of everyone became a social necessity that we saw the opportunity for an education extended to all.

The heritage of American education can be traced to those early English Protestant colonists who settled the eastern seaboard in the seventeenth century. Because of their religious conviction that *Bible* reading was essential to salvation, they sowed the seeds of the American system of education. By the time of the American independence, numerous leaders spoke out on the importance of education to the new republic. The often cited statement of Jefferson is a case in point:

> If a nation expects to be ignorant and free, it expects what never was and never will be. Enlighten the people generally and tyranny and oppression will vanish like evil spirits at the dawn of day.

The recorded public utterances of men like George Washington, Thomas

[2] John S. Brubacker, *A History of the Problems of Education* (New York: McGraw-Hill Book Co., Inc., 1947), p. 359.

Jefferson, Benjamin Franklin, and Benjamin Rush show clearly that they saw education as vital in shaping the minds and hearts of the people of the new nation.

Even though education figured prominently in the rhetoric of the post-Revolutionary period, significant changes did not occur in American education until the beginning of the Common School Movement after 1820. Dramatic changes were beginning to take place in the country at that time, and these developments were giving rise to new social, political, and economic problems. Industrial development was beginning to take shape in the New England area. The country's population was moving in two directions—to the West and to the nation's cities. Whereas the country as a whole was growing at an average rate of 34 per cent during the decades of 1820 to 1860, the nation's cities were growing on the order of 71 per cent.[3] National leadership and political influence that had long resided in the hands of Eastern influentials were beginning to move to the West. Communities throughout the land were becoming more heterogeneous with respect to wealth, religions, ethnicity, and national origin. Reformers of the time demanded that the common schools be established in order to equip the young people of the nation to deal with these emerging developments. One of the major goals of this movement was to provide a free education to all white children living in the United States:

> The common school was common because it taught the common subjects and common values and it was common because it was to enroll every single child in the United States in order to socialize him. Reformers hoped the common school would carry out all the socialization functions that the traditional community had performed with a stable and homogeneous population.[4]

The reformers who promoted the growth of the common school were convinced that if the opportunity for education were made available, most would take advantage of it. To them the values of an education to the individual seemed so obvious that the notion hardly needed defending. So strongly was that idea held that even to this day equality of opportunity in education is often interpreted to mean equal *access* to education. Of course, the reformers were disappointed to find that many

---

[3] David Ward, *Cities and Immigrants* (New York: Oxford University Press, 1971), p. 6.

[4] Robert L. Church and Michael W. Sedlak, *Education in the United States* (New York: The Free Press, 1976), p. 80.

children attended school on an irregular basis, and some did not attend at all. Many children did not attend out of economic necessity. In rural areas, particularly, children attended school only during the winter months when they were not needed to help with the farm work. Indeed, the traditional school year beginning in the fall and terminating in the spring is a legacy of our rural life heritage.

After 1865 it became clear that the failure of children to attend school was becoming a serious problem. The nation became more aware of the importance of simple literacy and of the deficiencies in knowledge, values, and skills relating to citizenship among black children and children of immigrant families. In the latter part of the nineteenth century, immigrants were pouring into the country by the hundreds of thousands, most of them of peasant stock from non-English-speaking countries of eastern and southern Europe. Consequently, there seemed to be a need to force children to attend school. Massachusetts, in 1852, was the first state to pass a compulsory school attendance law. In the latter part of the nineteenth century, state after state enacted compulsory education legislation that required children to attend school, in most cases, through the eighth grade. By the turn of the century, thirty states and Hawaii had such laws. By 1918 all states in the Union had enacted compulsory school attendance laws. It is fair to say, however, that these laws were either largely disregarded or not strictly enforced until after 1920.[5]

The Common School Movement focused on the elementary school, and early compulsory attendance legislation was aimed at the elementary school-age child. By the middle of the nineteenth century, the idea began to emerge that the high school was a natural upward extension of the elementary school and that it should also be a part of the common school. This was a hotly contested issue, particularly as the establishment of these schools called for support from public funds collected through taxes levied at the local level. The issue came to a head and eventual resolution by a challenge in a taxpayers' suit in Michigan that would have prevented the use of public funds for the support of high schools. The Kalamazoo case of 1874 resulted in a precedent-setting judicial action. The Michigan Supreme Court was persuaded that the high school was an integral part

[5] Following judicial mandates relating to school desegregation, Virginia, Mississippi, and South Carolina repealed their compulsory attendance laws. Alabama, Arkansas, Georgia, Louisiana, and North Carolina modified their compulsory attendance statutes in order to waive such requirements under certain conditions.

of the common school system and said so in a decision by Justice Thomas Cooley. The court rejected the Kalamazoo taxpayers' suit that would have prohibited the use of public funds for the support of the high school in that city.

The Kalamazoo case clearly contributed to the growth of secondary education in America, but its early growth did not occur without serious problems. The eighth grade was solidly established as the terminal grade for the common school. Students encountered both a physical and psychological gap between the eighth grade and the high school. First of all, the elementary school was relatively close to where the child lived. Many could walk to school. This was not true of the high school. High schools were located in cities, towns, and villages. Children from rural areas who wanted to attend high school had either to live away from home or transport themselves back and forth at their own expense, using their own vehicles. The busing of schoolchildren to high schools at public expense was not widespread until after World War II. The problem of accessibility of the high school was so severe for many children in rural areas that they simply could not attend.

The second obstacle that discouraged many children from continuing on to high school was the psychological breach between the elementary and high schools. Today it is assumed that when children finish the elementary school, they continue on in the next school up the ladder. Only a small fraction of pupils terminate their educations at the end of the eighth grade, and almost none do so at the end of the sixth grade. It is hard to believe that no longer than fifty years ago almost the reverse assumption obtained.

Shortly after the turn of the century, it became clear that something had to be done to entice more students to continue their educations beyond the elementary school. Some new organizational pattern was needed to bridge the gap between the elementary school and the high school—one that would have strong holding power on students. In part, it was for the purpose of filling this need that the junior high school concept emerged. The first junior high school became operational in 1910. Once a student was in junior high school, there was little to discourage him or her from completing the ninth grade. That made it possible for students to hurdle the traditional, terminal eighth grade and to complete one of the four years of the traditional high school in junior high school. Successful completion of the junior high school, along with peer pressure to stay with one's class, provided strong motivation for the teenager to continue into the high school program. The growth of junior and senior high schools was much more rapid in the larger urban areas than it was in rural regions.

The relationship between the early high schools and the colleges and universities remained unclear for many years. High schools were not accredited as they are today, nor was the high school curriculum in any sense standardized. Prior to 1906, high school graduation was not regarded as a requirement for admission to colleges and universities. High school curricula were so diverse that it was impossible to interpret the meaning of high school graduation. In 1909 the Carnegie Foundation for the Advancement of Teaching helped to establish order in an otherwise chaotic situation by establishing the "Carnegie Unit," a standardized unit representing one-fourth of one year's work in a high school subject. Thus, when colleges required sixteen Carnegie Units for admission, they were assured that the students had devoted a standardized amount of time to those subjects.

Even though high school enrollments doubled every decade from 1880 to 1930, by 1920 only about one-third of the nation's fourteen- to seventeen-year-olds were in high schools. Of those who were in school, three out of four were preparing for entrance to college. Clearly, these schools were serving the needs of college-bound students, and the curricula reflected that thrust. But with the enormously expanding student populations, the high school was about to undergo an institutional transformation. For many who were attending—in some cases, unwillingly because of compulsory attendance—the college-bound curriculum made no sense. Nor did high school teachers particularly like the idea of having to teach young people who presented new challenges, new needs, and who were not perceived as being "high school material."

In 1918 the National Education Association's (NEA) Commission on the Reorganization of Secondary Education issued a report entitled *Cardinal Principles of Secondary Education*. The report called attention to extant changing social forces and called for a secondary school curriculum based on broad goals associated with effective and fulfilled living: sound health knowledge and habits; command of the fundamental processes (reading, writing, computation, and oral and written expression); worthy home membership; education for a vocation; education for good citizenship; worthy use of leisure; and ethical character.[6] These

[6] Commission on the Reorganization of Secondary Education, *Cardinal Principles of Secondary Education*, U.S. Bureau of Education, Bulletin No. 35 (Washington, D.C., 1918).

13

"seven cardinal principles" received widespread attention and had a profound effect on the leaders who would shape the American comprehensive high school in the five decades that followed the issuance of the report.

By the end of World War II, it was apparent that universal secondary education was accepted in principle and would before long become a reality. In the years that followed, the high school dropout became a matter of concern for educators. As a result, numerous proposals surfaced to deal with the problem of presenting a relevant high school experience for the masses of students now in the nation's secondary schools. What finally resulted in the 1960s was the securing of the comprehensive high school as the institutional model of American secondary education. The comprehensive high school would provide on one campus a diversity of educational programs to accommodate the needs of all the children of all the people. The idea of the comprehensive high school had been around at least since the early part of the century, but its place in the educational structure of American education was made secure largely through the efforts of the late Dr. James B. Conant and his study of the American high school, a nationwide survey underwritten by the Carnegie Foundation.

Today the high school is firmly established as a part of the common public school system of this nation. In the decade of the 1960s, the dropout problem was no longer as prevalent as it was earlier. In 1970 nearly 93 per cent of the population between the ages of fourteen and seventeen were enrolled in secondary schools. Now that nearly all children attend high school, the challenge facing educators and teachers is to design an educational program at the secondary school level that is in tune with the educational requirements of all of America's youth.

In recent years our notions about who is to be educated have undergone important changes. "Education for all" has usually been interpreted to mean "education for all who are educable," that is, for those who do not have mental or physical handicaps that interfere with or impede learning. The term *educable* has almost disappeared from the educational literature except when used in the historical sense as it is used here. Today *all* children are considered educable, no matter what their mental or physical impairments may be. Besides, many handicapped children who would formerly have been placed in separate classes or special schools are today a part of the regular stream of students passing through the schools. The practice of "mainstreaming" or placing children in the "least restrictive environment" has gained very wide acceptance in

14

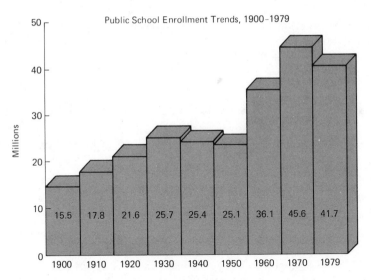

Public School Enrollment Trends, 1900-1979

	1900	1910	1920	1930	1940	1950	1960	1970	1979
Millions	15.5	17.8	21.6	25.7	25.4	25.1	36.1	45.6	41.7

FIGURE 1. Numbers of students in public elementary and secondary schools combined at 10-year intervals from 1900 to the present. How do you explain the large increase during the 1960 and 1970 years? (SOURCE: U.S. Office of Education, Department of Health, Education, and Welfare.)

American education. This means that children with a wide range of physical and mental handicaps are found in increasing numbers in the regular classrooms of the nation's schools, seated side by side and participating on an equal basis with their nonhandicapped cohorts. In 1975, with the passage of PL94–142, the Education for All Handicapped Children Act, these policies became a part of the law of the land.

America does not yet provide equality of educational opportunity for all its children. Perhaps it will never achieve that goal. But neither does any other country provide education equally for all its children. Nevertheless, the United States has moved a long way toward achieving the goal of *education for all the children of all the people* since the Common School Movement began in the early part of the nineteenth century. This goal—the dream of educational reformers for 125 years—clearly became national policy as a result of the ruling of the Supreme Court in the 1954 case *Brown* v. *The Board of Education of Topeka:*

> Today, schooling is a principal instrument in awakening the child to cultural values, in preparing him for later professional training, and in help-

15

ing him to adjust normally to his environment. In these days, it is doubtful that any child may reasonably be expected to succeed in life if he is denied the opportunity of an education.

EDUCATION IN A CHANGING AMERICA

Significant school policies and trends are fashioned by political, social, and economic conditions external to the school. Therefore, over a period of time, there will be consistency between school practices and policies and the values of the major political, economic, and social institutions. Henry M. Levin and other authors have referred to this relationship between schools and society as the "correspondence principle." He states that "all educational systems serve their respective societies such that the social, economic, and political relationships of the educational sector will mirror closely those of the society of which they are a part."[7] This suggests that if one wants to understand school policies and trends, one must examine the social context within which they are found. In the remainder of this chapter we will examine some of the areas in which changes are particularly apposite to the schools.

The Pluralistic Ideology

The use of the melting pot as a figurative representation of America made its appearance at the turn of the century when the country was being inundated with immigrant people, largely from eastern and southern Europe. Seven or eight decades later it is easy to ridicule the idea of a melting pot; but for those who were concerned about the future of the nation, as it was absorbing some twenty million immigrants in a period of three or four decades, the melting pot notion made sense. Somehow those immigrant people and their children had to be acculturated into the values and lifeways of the nation that was to be their new home. This was not an easy task considering that even as late as 1920, 40 per cent of the people living in the United States were of "foreign stock," meaning that they or their parents were born outside the country.

[7] Henry M. Levin, "Educational Reform: Its Meaning?" in Martin Carnoy and Henry M. Levin, *The Limits of Educational Reform* (New York: David McKay Company, Inc., 1976), p. 26.

Consistent with the idea of rapid assimilation, immigrant groups were encouraged to become Americans as quickly as possible and usually took great pride in doing so. Thus, the melting pot concept was surrounded by a romantic aura that concealed its true character. Visible minorities, even if they wanted to—and many did *not* want to—could never be "melted" in the sense that they would be indistinguishable from other Americans. It may be true that in Brazil "money bleaches,"[8] but that was certainly not the case in the United States. The melting pot did not prevent blatant discrimination, prejudice, bigotry, and racism from flourishing in the land, no matter how financially successful the victim might have become. Nowhere did the gap between the ideal and the actual seem so wide as in the area of human relations between the people of America on such variables as race, ethnicity, and religion.

The term *cultural pluralism* was first used by Horace M. Kallen in 1924, but it has only recently come into widespread use. In the decades since World War II, this society has moved more and more toward a conception of itself along the lines of pluralism. The pluralistic ideology stems from the ethnic diversity that characterizes this country. No nation on earth can trace the origins of its people to so many of the world's cultures. As a nation we speak all of the world's languages and dialects, we eat the world's favorite culinary creations, we dance their dances and play their music, we embrace their religious traditions, and we have accepted ethnic holidays as our own.

In the latter half of this century, Americans have displayed a renaissance of interest in their ethnic heritages. This was epitomized in the enormous popularity of the Alex Haley book *Roots* and the television program based on it. But several years before *Roots* appeared, many third and fourth generation Americans, now psychologically and financially secure, were searching the little peasant villages and graveyards of eastern and southern Europe for traces of their forebears. The support for the pluralistic ideology comes, at least in part, from a deep desire of Americans to know more fully who they are—individually and as a nation.

The pluralistic conception of society has had and will continue to have many implications for schools. School desegregation and integra-

[8] Pierre L. van den Berge, *Race and Racism* (New York: John Wiley & Sons, Inc., 1967), p. 10.

17

tion, bilingual education, curriculum reform, intergroup education, and equality of educational opportunity are just a few of the educational concerns that flow from this development. In recent years there has been a significant reversal in the attitudes of Americans toward race and ethnicity, and the rate of intermarriages among groups is rising.[9]

An Expanded Student Population

More people are being schooled in America than ever before. This is true whether we use absolute numbers or percentages. As has already been noted, this nation has been amazingly successful in getting its adolescents into secondary schools. It is significant to note that at the turn of the century only a fraction over 11 per cent of the fourteen- to seventeen-year-old youth was in school.

The increased numbers of youngsters attending school has, of course, been reflected in a decline of those same individuals in the work world. At the turn of the century, a high percentage of youths—especially males—who would today be enrolled in school were already employed in the work world. School attendance has had the effect of removing individuals below the age of eighteen from the labor market. Those who are below eighteen years of age and who are employed typically hold part-time, low-paying jobs that provide little opportunity to learn valuable work skills.

Traditionally, we have thought of schoolchildren as those between the ages of six and sixteen (or eighteen) and of college-age students as those between the ages of eighteen and twenty-two. That is no longer true. In recent years we have seen greatly expanded school attendance at both ends of this traditional school-attending group. Growth has been very great in preschool programs as well as in the postsecondary school group. In fact, one might accurately say that a "college-age" student might be anyone between the ages of fourteen and eighty!

The most common preschool experience for children is the kindergarten. The first American kindergarten was established in Watertown, Wisconsin, in 1855. The kindergarten was and continues to be designed in accordance with ideas developed by Friedrich Froebel, a German

[9] Thomas Sowell, "Ethnicity in a Changing America," *Daedalus* 107 (Winter 1978), p. 213.

educator, who is universally recognized as the father of the kindergarten. By 1930, three quarters of a million children were enrolled in kindergartens. Kindergarten attendance has increased very rapidly in the decades since 1950, and today over three million children attend them. Typically the kindergarten experience is limited to the year immediately prior to entry into the first grade (age five) and is ordinarily a half-day in length.

The increasing number of one-parent families, the liberation of women, and the massive growth of women in the labor market have resulted in expanded numbers of day-care centers for children between the ages of two and five. These preschool establishments are not ordinarily a part of the public school enterprise but are operated by churches, colleges, community agencies, or private entrepreneurs. There have been some efforts to extend the public school responsibility to include four-year-olds, but there has been considerable resistance to this for political and financial reasons.

Preschool education received national financial and psychological support with the advent of Head Start. This program was authorized and funded under the Economic Opportunity Act passed by Congress in 1964 as a part of President Lyndon Johnson's War on Poverty. The target population of the Head Start effort was the socioeconomically disadvantaged preschoolers. The program was intended to provide intervention experiences that would make it possible for the disadvantaged child to begin school, if not on a par with, at least with a "leg up" on, his or her more advantaged cohorts. To date, the success of these programs has been spotty and, for the most part, disappointing. The Head Start effort, however, has focused national attention on the importance of the education of the preschool child.

At the other end of the spectrum, the most spectacular growth has been in the public community and junior colleges. These institutions have played a significant role in extending the opportunity for higher education to the large masses of Americans. Typically two years in length, they offer programs of traditional lower-division work that can be transferred to four-year institutions and also occupational programs for entry to the job market upon graduation. Community colleges also may be involved in adult basic education whereby individuals can complete high school requirements. They often provide courses for leisure-time activities, for cultural enrichment, and for community service. They are designed to provide postsecondary education that fulfills the needs of the people of the community in which the college is situated. Consequently, they have

19

been popular institutions with their constituents. In fact, the community college idea caught on so quickly and was so well received that by the mid-1960s new community colleges were being opened at the rate of one per week.

The GI Bill of Rights following World War II had a profound impact on American higher education. Not only did it enormously enlarge the population of students pursuing higher education; it had the effect of transforming the institutions themselves. Both of these developments were altogether unanticipated effects of the legislation. Millions of returning veterans, most of whom were elementary and secondary school students during the Great Depression, descended on the nation's campuses. These mature, self-directed, and highly motivated students made demands on colleges and universities the likes of which were unheard of in academe. The institutions were forced to inaugurate reforms in admission requirements, curricula, counseling services, and administrative practices. The veterans of World War II did much to institutionalize the concept that colleges and universities should be flexible enough to accommodate the varying needs of students rather than have students adjust to the anachronistic rigidities of institutions. These experiences of college and university faculties and administrators were to bespeak the kinds of adjustments that were demanded—and received—by visible minorities in the 1960s.

The consequences that flow from an expanding student population are many, varied, and complex. For several decades there has been a continuing trend toward escalating educational requirements way beyond what is required by most jobs. If it is true that 80 per cent of all jobs in the American economy can be learned in three weeks or less by someone with a high school education,[10] then clearly advanced education is superfluous in terms of job requirements.

If advanced education is not really needed for job skills, then it must obviously serve other goals or values. Such goals may deal with personal development and growth, cultural enrichment, social prestige, power, status, and others. When the achievement of such goals through education becomes a criterion of preference in establishing a social class hierarchy, there is a strong—one might even say an *unavoidable*—ten-

[10] Stephen K. Bailey, *The Purposes of Education* (Bloomington, Indiana: Phi Delta Kappa, 1976).

20

dency to associate individual worthwhileness with educational success. This is another way of saying that success in school enhances one's self-esteem; failure in school destroys it. Moreover, these same values affect the way an individual is perceived by others. The child who does poorly in school is evaluated negatively *as a human being,* a regrettable but predictable consequence of our persistent concern for successful school achievement. Little wonder, then, that the "highest grade attained in school" becomes a summarizing variable from which one is able to infer much about the social role, occupational status, social class, and income of an individual.

A Changing Marketplace

Until the time of the Great Depression, people in this nation did not really face the problem of unemployment as we know it today. This does not mean that everyone was happily employed all of the time. Far from it. Wages were low, hours were long, and workers had no job security. Fringe benefits, health and safety requirements, and unemployment benefits did not exist. Employers could use whatever arbitrary methods they wished in dealing with workers, and some did just that. Nonetheless, if one really wanted to work, he or she could usually find something to do. In the last third of the nineteenth century, America moved rapidly into the Industrial Age, and hundreds of thousands of workers were needed to meet the nation's growing manpower needs. Indeed, the country could not produce a sufficient number of laborers and thus welcomed the willing hands of immigrants so eager to establish themselves in this land of opportunity.

In times of economic distress in the cities, there was always the back country that beckoned the person who was willing to clear the land, break the sod, and till the soil. The Homestead Act of 1862 made it possible for a person over twenty-one years of age who was head of a family and a citizen (or an alien intending to become a citizen) to secure 160 acres of land free of charge if he lived on that land for five years and improved it. In place of the residence requirement, the person could pay $1.25 an acre for the land. This legislation was passed to encourage settlement of the Western lands. Although the Homestead Act did not prove to be as effective as its promoters had hoped, it did attract thousands of settlers to the West. From the time it was passed until the turn of the century, some half million or more families were provided new homes by the Homestead Act.

Routine factory labor and farm life did not make great educational demands on the worker. Even simple literacy was not essential in order to perform many jobs. Indeed, factories and mines often preferred the immigrant precisely because he or she was illiterate and, therefore, presented less of a threat to the company in terms of unionization. Educational requirements for jobs did not become widespread until a surplus of laborers developed and the competition for jobs became more acute. This was beginning to be apparent after the turn of the century and contributed to the legislation restricting immigration in 1924. In 1938 the Fair Labor Standards Act was passed, which set age sixteen as the minimum age for employment in work that involved interstate commerce and age eighteen as the minimum age for employment in hazardous occupations. This act had the effect of virtually excluding anyone under eighteen from manufacturing and mining industries. During and since the Great Depression there has been a growing interdependent relationship between the nation's manpower requirements and formal education.

Sophisticated technology and mechanization have greatly reduced the need for manpower in the traditional sense. The percentage of self-employed persons has steadily declined for several years and now stands at about 10 per cent. The number of persons employed by local, state, and federal governments has risen sharply. Today some seventy out of every one hundred workers are employed in *service* occupations such as medical and health care, education, social welfare, technical services, research, merchandising, personal services, and so on. All of these occupations require a constant stream of competently trained people who require higher and higher levels of education. These changing conditions in the economic and social systems of the nation have brought us to what some authors have referred to as the "post-industrial society."[11] In the postindustrial society, education becomes the "coin of the realm" that converts into an "investment" in "human capital."

Thus, education in the postindustrial society is the prerequisite to survival. To cut an individual off from an education freezes that person out of economic opportunity, social mobility, and an independent

---

[11] Daniel Bell, *The Coming of Post-Industrial Society* (New York: Basic Books, 1973).

livelihood. The level of education becomes related to social prestige and occupational status. Because the economy cannot provide enough jobs to absorb all of the trained workers, unemployment becomes an increasingly serious problem. The problem is particularly severe among youth, especially minority youth, among whom the level of unemployment may be four or five times what it is among white adults.

Young people secure additional postsecondary education in order to become employable, believing that the additional education and acquired skills will make them more competitive in the job market. This accounts in part for the rapid growth in community college programs and for the attractiveness of vocational education programs. It also explains why minorities have been so insistent that the schools equip their children with practical, job-related skills. Regrettably, unemployment and job competition have the effect of driving educational requirements for jobs higher and higher, making the employment possibilities of the undereducated even more severe.

An International Perspective

The decade of the 1960s was an unfortunate one for the United States in many ways, but especially so in the international arena. The Vietnam War, plus the sale of arms to nations all over the world, badly tarnished America's image as a nation of people devoted to the pursuit of peace. In the latter part of the 1970s, the United States was showing the world once again that it aspired to a position of moral leadership among nations and that it desired to have cordial relations with all nations. Fairminded people everywhere knew that the United States in this century had demonstrated its concern for the dignity of people around the globe countless numbers of times. The basic values implied in the concept "human rights" were and are values that the American people strongly embrace.

Because of international relations during the past forty years, large sections of the world have been closed areas for study. The most obvious example is, of course, the People's Republic of China, but to some extent this is also true of the Soviet Union and all of Eastern Europe. At least a full generation of Americans have received nothing but the most superficial instruction about that vast part of the world that begins with the Iron Curtain and stretches eastward through *twelve* time zones to the

Pacific Ocean. Much of this area is occupied by people who are non-white; most are non-Christian. Africa and South America have not been closed areas in the same sense as some other parts of the world have been, but they, too, are places that too few Americans know very much about.

In all of these areas of the world are found nations that have developed or are developing modern technologies. This means that they, along with the United States and other developed nations, are linked to a worldwide system of resources, energy, technology, markets, and politics. It seems clear that the world is on the threshold of a whole new set of relationships in which each nation will be tied even more closely to the international community. Our own nation is absolutely dependent on interrelated systems that are international in scope and that we ourselves do not control.

American education at all levels will be greatly affected by these new developments in international relations. Americans in increasing numbers will be spending part of their lives outside the States not only as tourists and in military assignments but as civilians in job-related activities or as students. Likewise, we can expect to see more people from other countries visiting the United States as tourists or conducting business here or studying at schools and colleges in the States. Simply out of necessity, American education will become global in its perspective.

New Views of Social Power

The term *social power* is used here to mean the capacity to influence or control the behavior of others. Thus, an individual or group of individuals who has power is able to shape the outcome of social policy decisions in accordance with their views. There is considerable evidence that through the years social power has resided in the hands of a relatively few persons.[12] In recent years there have been massive assaults on the traditional strongholds of social power resulting in increased participation in decision making in matters concerning the schools. This subject is developed in greater detail in Chapter 7, but it is presented here as an advance organizer because it so profoundly affects school-society policy.

[12] G. William Domhoff, *Who Really Rules? New Haven and Community Power Reexamined* (New Brunswick, New Jersey: Transaction Books, 1978); idem, *The Higher Circles: The Governing Class in America* (New York: Random House, 1970).

It is important for our purposes now to focus on the use of power by legally constituted groups who govern schools. These groups ordinarily are school boards, trustees, commissioners, or regents. They may be elected, as is the usual case with school board members, or they may be appointed by an official who is elected. For example, the governor of the state often appoints members of the board of regents of the state colleges and universities. The administrative officers such as school superintendents and college and university presidents and their administrative staffs are extensions of these governing boards and are charged with the responsibility of implementing policies established by the boards.

The American system of governance of public educational institutions is unique among the nations of the world in that it is in the hands of laypersons from the local area.[13] The principle of local lay governance of educational institutions is derived from a long tradition and a deeply held conviction that "the schools belong to the people." It is a highly coveted prerogative.

In addition to being governed by local laypersons, school governing boards are typically autonomous, independent political units. That is to say, they are not legally subordinate to other political bodies or officers. For example, the superintendent of schools of a large city is not accountable to, and does not take orders from, the mayor of the city. The city council cannot legally dictate school policy to school boards, nor can the governor of a state tell the board of regents how it should run its colleges and universities.

Although school board members are composed of locally elected laypersons and although school officials are accountable to such boards, it does not mean that all constituents of the school are served equally well. There have been several studies of the socioeconomic and educational backgrounds of American school board members. Typically, they are persons whose level of education and income are better than average, and most of them are white males who are drawn from such occupations as proprietors, business executives, and the professions. Quite naturally, the policies that they set for schools are consistent with the values that guide their own lives. There is not anything wrong with that except that schools operating under such policies often do not serve the needs of large numbers of children who come from a vastly different socioeconomic-ethnic-racial background.

[13] Geraldine J. Clifford, *The Shape of American Education* (Englewood Cliffs, New Jersey: Prentice-Hall, Inc., 1975), p. 1.

Until recent years those who were not well served by the schools accepted their school failure with an attitude of resigned acquiescence:

School is o.k. for you guys, but I never was much for books and figgers.

I was too dumb; school never made no sense to me.

I flunked four times before I quit the eighth grade. The teachers couldn't learn me nuthin'.

The prevailing attitude was that there was nothing really wrong with the school and its program; the fault lay with the learners if they did not learn: poor background of language and experience, lack of motivation, ineffective study habits, inability to concentrate, and low IQ. Until the 1960s this attitude was completely institutionalized. Even the victims of poor schooling believed it.

But in the decade of the 1960s some new views concerning social power began to emerge. There was a nationwide movement toward participatory democracy, a type of "do it yourself" populist attitude, along with a growing suspicion and distrust of officials and experts. Social movements of the 1960s sowed seeds of distrust of officialdom at all levels. Voices never before heard were saying, "We *demand* that you provide a decent education for our children, and if you do not, we will throw you out and do it ourselves. Moreover, we *demand* a voice in decisions concerning the education of our children." Also in the sixties, the poor, the disenfranchised, and, most importantly, the minorities found a powerful advocate and ally in the leadership in high levels of government.

This brings us to the important concept of *legitimacy* of authority, authority being the legal exercise of power. Insofar as school decision making is concerned, whether or not a person or a group has the *authority* to take some action is less important than whether or not it is perceived as legitimate. That is to say, people ask, "Does that authority really represent me?" "Were democratic procedures followed so that my views or those of my group could be heard?" "Are there due process provisions so that I can appeal decisions that are perceived to be capricious, arbitrary, or discriminatory?" Individuals are not likely to afford legitimacy to decisions if they have not been a party to them, no matter how sound they may be from a substantive standpoint. Unless the decision-making *procedure* involves them, the decision and decision makers will lack credibility and, therefore, will not constitute legitimate authority.

These new views of social power that have emerged in the past two decades have and will continue to have many implications for schools. Decisions that school authorities could at one time make behind closed doors must now be made out in the open. Adequate provisions must be made for the solicitation of ideas from all parties involved. Grievance and appeal procedures must be provided in order to guard against arbitrary and capricious actions. Policies and procedures must be published and be equally accessible to all. Discretionary powers of school officials are carefully specified and circumscribed. School policies, procedures, personnel, and curricula can no longer serve only the needs of the dominant, decision-making group. Increasingly, American schools are serving "all of the children of all of the people" because the people themselves now have the social power to convert that dream to reality.

STUDY AND DISCUSSION

1. Much has been said and written urging schools to serve as agents of social change. Yet schools were created by society to transmit the cultural heritage. These two missions appear to be in conflict with each other. Can you provide some insights as to how—or if—schools can function in these two roles? Explain.

2. Show by example how societal trends affect school policies and procedures. What social forces have contributed to the growth of American education?

3. From what is known about present social trends, what are likely to be the most crucial problems facing American education in the next two decades? Write down your list, and check it again at the end of the course to note whether or not you still perceive the same problems as "most crucial."

4. What social conditions are creating a demand for increased education?

5. Explain the interrelationship between various social goals and the role of the schools in achieving those goals. Provide ex-

amples of how schools have assisted in the attainment of social goals.

6. Explain how the school serves as a major economic institution in many American communities, that is, as a major producer and consumer of goods and services.

7. Identify practices in child rearing in the home that enhance the child's success in school.

8. What are the key agents in the socialization of children in American society? How do each of these agents define the boundaries of their influence and responsibility?

9. List five consequences that come about as a result of the fact that human beings are capable of adapting to the physical environment through their culture. What implications are there in this for the education of the young?

10. What are some of the emerging alternative family structures apparent in American life today?

SELECTED BIBLIOGRAPHY

A New America? Entire volume (Winter 1978) of *Daedalus,* Journal of the American Academy of Arts and Sciences.

BELL, DANIEL. *The Coming of Post-Industrial Society.* New York: Basic Books, Inc., 1973.

CHURCH, ROBERT L., and MICHAEL W. SEDLAK. *Education in the United States: An Interpretive History.* New York: The Free Press (Macmillan), 1976.

CREMIN, LAWRENCE A. *The Transformation of the School: Progressivism in American Education 1876–1957.* New York: Alfred A. Knopf Company, Inc., 1961.

KARABEL, JEROME, and A. H. HALSEY, eds. *Power and Ideology in Education,* Part 1: "Education and Social Structure." New York: Oxford University Press, 1977.

OVERLY, NORMAN V., ed. *Lifelong Learning: A Human Agenda.* 1979 Yearbook Association For Supervision and Curriculum Development. Alexandria, Va.: Association for Supervision and Curriculum Development, 1979.

SCHIMAHARA, NOBUO KENNETH, and ADAM SCRUPSKI. *Social Forces and Schooling: An Anthropological and Sociological Perspective,* Part 1: "Contemporary Social and Cultural Perspective." New York: David McKay Company, Inc., 1975.

SCHWARTZ, AUDREY JAMES. *The Schools and Socialization.* New York: Harper and Row, Publishers, 1975.

SCIMECCA, JOSEPH A. *Education and Society*. New York: Holt, Rinehart and Winston, Inc., 1980.

SMITH, B. OTHANEL, and DONALD ORLOSKY. *Socialization and Schooling: The Basics of Reform*. Bloomington, Indiana: Phi Delta Kappa, Inc., 1975.

TYACK, DAVID B. *The One Best System: A History of American Urban Education*. Cambridge, Massachusetts: Harvard University Press, 1974.

Critics
of the Schools

The criticism of American schools since 1950 has been so pervasive that all levels—from preschool to the graduate school—have felt its sting. The concerns of the critics have ranged from such matters as textbook content, anti-intellectualism, excessive school costs, and sex education to equal time for the creation theory when the theory of evolution is discussed and to busing of students. Much of the criticism of schools—and of education in general—has been cynical, rancorous, and bitter, often conveying strong feelings of enmity.

Perhaps it is inevitable that people should have strong feelings of resentment when they believe the schools have failed them or their children. Especially is this so when one considers how critically important an education is in forecasting the future status roles of individuals. Imagine the hopes, dreams, and aspirations that many—perhaps even most—parents have for their young ones. Then think of what happens to them when their child's school experience is characterized by frustration, disappointment, and failure. What happens to them when they see dreams shattered and hope turned to despair and have a memory bank filled with unfulfilled aspirations?

There can be no question that the assessment of American schools weighs heavily on the negative side. Part of this can be accounted for by publications of popular books and articles that have exploited the disappointments and frustrations of parents and patrons of the schools. These opportunists have fanned the flames of dissatisfaction with the schools and have found the process a handsomely rewarding one. Their nostrums for the ailments of the schools have enjoyed a degree of credibility among laypersons and, surprisingly, even among certain segments of the professional community. This widespread negative appraisal presents a distorted picture of American education and tends to overlook its achievements, which have been substantial.

Whatever one chooses to say or write about schools in the way of criticism, the chances are that examples of such practices or conditions can be found somewhere in the country. Moreover, observers of schools often engage in a fair amount of selective perception simply because of their own values and predispositions toward education. This is not to say that schools are faultless, but only to suggest that the picture is far from clear. There are many thousands of schools in the country that are first-rate. They serve their constituents well, they enjoy strong community support, and they have competent faculties. Doubtless there are many other thousands that have the potential for being first-rate but have some few easily correctable deficiencies that prevent them from becoming as strong as they might otherwise be. Surely, we have thousands of schools in this country that are mediocre and many that are downright poor. Perhaps the truth about American education can be found somewhere midway between what the apologists claim for it and the position of its most severe critics. In this chapter we will be examining a broad spectrum of comments concerning American schools.

AMERICAN EDUCATION—ITS SUCCESSES

The contemporary educational literature has much more to say about the failures of American education than it does of its successes. Nevertheless, it could be argued that American education has been amazingly successful, particularly because it has often worked under such handicaps as skimpy budgets, political interference, unclear social policies, large class sizes, and, for many years, minimally prepared teachers. This country does not have a national system of education, and, therefore, we have not had clearly articulated nationwide educational policies that carry the imprimatur of an official or government agency at the national level. There have been significant judicial decisions that speak to educational matters, but these are directed toward specific issues rather than constituting a coordinated set of policies. In spite of these limitations, American education has, on the whole, served the nation in ways worthy of the nation's confidence.

Availability of Education

The term *ladder* is sometimes used figuratively to describe American education because it is intended that students begin at the bottom "rungs" and climb as high as they want to or are able to. With some obvious and unfortunate exceptions, it has been a system that is open and available to all. Availability of schooling is not denied anyone because of economic, political, or social reasons, and the United States enrolls more students today than it ever has. Equality of opportunity has been thought of in terms of access to schooling, and one of the great strengths of American education is that it is easily accessible to all.

Historically, the obstacles to access to a good education have been financial, geographical, and social. Financial deterrents to educational access were both private and public. As was noted in Chapter 1, education has traditionally gone to those who could afford to pay for it. With the advent of *public* education supported at *public* expense, access to education depended less on the individual's personal wealth but more on the taxable wealth of the area in which he or she lived. Because much of the money for school support came from the tax moneys collected on local property, it was obvious that areas with highly valued property would have more money available for schools than areas in which property carried a low value. Naturally, there is still a relationship between personal wealth and quality of education because persons with high income tend to live in areas with highly valued property. In order to mitigate these disparities, states instituted a policy of "equalizing" school support statewide. By providing state financial aid to local school districts according to a formula that takes into account these property value differences, states have been able to reduce the severity of differences between school districts. These efforts have assisted in making schooling *available;* they

33

have not been as successful in equalizing the *quality* of education that takes place within those schools.

Geographical obstacles to access to education have been virtually removed with the extensive use of school busing. Today children throughout the land have, for all practical purposes, a schoolhouse as close as the driveway to their home. Huge fleets of buses are operated by or are contracted for by nearly all districts that enroll more than a couple of hundred students. Today only the most remote and inaccessible places in the country do not have educational facilities available to the children who live there. At the adult level, the growth of the community colleges and vocational-technical schools has made it possible for hundreds of thousands of students to live at home, work at income-producing jobs, and pursue their college educations on a full- or part-time basis.

The most difficult obstacle to educational access has its roots in social relationships. Prior to the outlawing of the "separate but equal" principle, it was not unusual for black students in the South to have a shorter school year in the number of days attended than did white students. This meant, of course, that even though all students had *access* to education, not all of them had access to school in the same amount. Although there have been enormous steps taken in recent years to rectify inequity of access to education, this problem continues to dog American education. Children of visible minorities—particularly blacks, Chicanos, Native Americans, and *some* Asians—do not enjoy access to education in the same way that white children do. Similarly, women and girls continue to have their educations affected by social attitudes toward the role of females in society. It is fair to say, however, that there has been a narrowing of differences between and among these groups in recent years with respect to accessibility to education.

The Schools and Social Mobility

It is commonplace for Americans to change the social class into which they were born. The movement of persons to another social class occurs at the rate of about 33 per cent; about one person in three moves to a different social class during his or her lifetime. Most of this movement is in an upward direction. There is also a downward mobility, but with a greatly reduced frequency, about one in ten. This society's class structure is flexible enough to allow a fair amount of social mobility to occur.

Sociologists are careful to point out that education per se does not cause social mobility. To be educated does not mean that one will move to a higher social class. Yet it is clear that there is a relationship between social mobility and schooling. No doubt, availability of education has had a great deal to do with keeping our social class structure fluid and the boundaries between social classes reasonably penetrable. For millions of children of this land, the door to opportunity was, quite literally, the school door. Through education the individual was and is able not only to acquire knowledge and skills that enhanced his or her occupational status, but, just as importantly, to learn the behavior associated with educated persons. In other words, the school experience was and still is a powerful force in socializing lower social class children into the lifeways, language, and culture of the middle and upper classes. Schooling, therefore, is a major means of promoting social mobility. Upward social mobility is often the result of—the effects of—one's education. Considering the high rate of social mobility in this country, one must conclude that schools have made a substantial contribution to that process.

The School as a Culture Bearer

Much of what schools concern themselves with most centrally can be described as components of the mainstream culture—basic literacy, the arts and humanities, sources of the American heritage, the economic system, the systems of law and justice, the political system, and a set of core values for which there is general support. This by no means is a complete list—these are simply examples of learnings that might be described as basic to the common or mainstream culture. Commitment to the core values of the common culture provides the basis for social cohesiveness. Knowledge of the common culture makes it possible for an individual to live and participate in it.

How is the mainstream culture transmitted to each new generation of children, and how do they learn it? There are several ways this occurs, of course, but the family and the community are usually regarded as important contributors to the process. But what about those American children whose families and communities are not themselves a part of the mainstream culture? How do they learn about the American heritage when adults around them are not able to share that knowledge with them? How do those children learn to speak, read, and write English if no one around them speaks the language? It becomes obvious that the public schools of the country is where much of this learning takes place, even in the case of those children who come from families who are familiar with the mainstream culture.

The most dramatic example of the schools' serving as culture bearers —and one of American education's biggest success stories—is the acculturation of millions of immigrant children and their parents during the period of huge immigration from 1870 to 1924. Considering the diversity of the immigrant groups and the cultural gulf that separated them from the American mainstream culture, the magnitude of this task staggers the imagination even today. Between 1870 and 1910 alone, nearly twenty-one million immigrants came to this country—largely from eastern and southern Europe. For the most part they were non-English-speaking and of peasant background. The immigration of non-native people to the shores of the United States represents the largest transplantation of human beings in the entire history of the world.

But not all of the immigrants came from Europe, and not all of them settled on the mainland. Here we have an example of what the McKinley High School in Honolulu was doing in the 1920s to acquaint the children of Asian extraction with the mainstream culture:

> In 1959, the year of statehood, more than half the classmates, many relatives and friends, and some faculty members of McKinley's class of 1924 met at the Hawaiian Village Hotel Long House for their thirty-fifth reunion. Among these sons and daughters of plantation laborers were medical doctors, dentists, lawyers, professors, and brilliantly successful businessmen. From Berkeley, California, came Dr. Rebecca Lee Proctor, who, thirty years before, had been a small Korean girl determined to go into medicine. Also present was Masaji Marumoto, then associate justice of the territorial Supreme Court and soon to be appointed associate justice of the Supreme Court of the fiftieth state. There, too, were Hung Wai Ching, son of an illiterate cook, now president of several corporations and member of the Board of Regents of the University of Hawaii; Chinn Ho, multimillionaire entrepreneur; Modesto Salve, a former plantation laborer and the first Filipino to graduate from a high school in Hawaii, now a successful

businessman and civic leader; the former Kimiko Pearl Kawasaki, wife of Hawaii's most distinguished agricultural extension specialist, Baron Goto; and Stephen Kanda, one of the first nisei to be appointed principal of an Island high school. Perhaps the most illustrious of the 233 graduates of the class of 1924 was Hiram Fong, president of Finance Factors, former speaker of the House in the territorial legislature, and, within a year, to be elected to the U.S. Senate. A message of *aloha* was sent from the class of 1924 to Miles Cary, at the University of Virginia. Cary was to live only a few more months, just long enough to know that Hawaii had been accepted as a state by the U.S. Congress and, more importantly, that his boys and girls had learned their lessons well.[1]

The United States has the longest continuous record of democratic government of any modern nation. This would not be possible without an educated electorate, which, in turn, would not be possible without a sophisticated educational system. The schools *have* been able to take people of diverse backgrounds and develop in them a strong commitment to those core values that have contributed to the strength of the republic. In so doing, the schools *have* been able to help the nation convert its pluralistic strength into a genuine national human resource.

The Schools and the National Interest

There is considerable evidence that the schools of this country have served the national interest well in times of peace as well as in times of war. Indeed, critics of the schools would claim that the schools have served the nation's interest too well, that the relationship and the financial involvements that schools, colleges, and universities have with corporate-industrial-military components of society are not desirable in terms of broad humanitarian, social, and research goals. This is a legitimate concern, but these relationships probably cannot be avoided altogether. Therefore, a more acceptable plan of action is to control the relationships, not let them get out-of-hand, and to maximize the public benefits from such relationships.

There are many examples that could be cited to illustrate how the

[1] Lawrence H. Fuchs, *Hawaii Pono: A Social History* (New York: Harcourt, Brace & World, Inc., 1961), pp. 297–298.

schools have served the national interest. The virtual elimination of illiteracy in the early part of this century could be one. Medical research and the development of allied health services could be another. The school's response to the late President Kennedy's challenge in the space race could be still another. But the story of American agriculture provides one of the best examples of any. It is no accident that American agricultural technology and practice for mass production are unmatched in the entire world. The capacity to produce efficiently is such that today less than 8 per cent of our population can produce enough food to feed the entire nation and have a large surplus for export. In addition to the direct benefits of adequate food supply at reasonable costs to consumers, American society has enjoyed secondary and tertiary benefits as a result of the development of agriculture. For example, agribusiness provides jobs for hundreds of thousands of Americans who make their living manufacturing, wholesaling, retailing, and merchandising farm machinery, fertilizers, irrigation equipment, plant seeds, insecticides, and a long list of goods and services associated with agriculture.

The success story of American agriculture begins with the Morrill Act of 1862, which granted 30,000 acres of federal land for each senator and member of the House of Representatives that a state had in Congress. This land was to be sold and the money used as a permanent endowment for the establishment in each state of at least one college where "the leading object shall be, without excluding other scientific and classical studies and including military tactics, to teach such branches of learning as related to agriculture and the mechanic arts." This legislation bears the name of its sponsor, Justin Smith Morrill, then a member of Congress, later a senator from Vermont. The Morrill Act of 1862 is doubtless one of the most significant pieces of educational legislation in the history of the country. A second Morrill Act of 1890 provided additional funding for the support of instructional programs at these colleges and universities, now known as "land-grant" institutions.

The establishment of schools and colleges of agriculture ensured the application of scientific thought to farming practices. Naturally, there were many problems for these institutions in their early years, but by the turn of the century agricultural education was firmly established. Institutions were preparing scientists and specialists to assist farmers. Model farms were established, as were experimental farms where research proceeded at a rapid pace. As the scientific base for agricultural education was established, the curriculum became more diversified and more specialized. No aspect of agriculture escaped the researcher's interest—soil chemistry, animal and plant breeding, development of new varieties and strains of seed, hybrid technology, growing conditions, dry farming technology, soil erosion control, and an endless list of variables that relate to efficient farm production.

Developing new agricultural practices on a college-run experimental farm is one thing; having those practices adopted by the rank and file farmer is something else. Some type of dissemination strategy was needed in order to get those ideas into practice on the nation's farms. The Smith-Lever Act of 1914 established the Cooperative Extension Service in agriculture and in home economics. Its purpose was to diffuse the scientific knowledge being generated to the farmers of the nation. Thus, a dissemination network developed in states that brought the farmers, the agricultural colleges and research stations, and the United States Department of Agriculture into close contact with each other. To extend the dissemination program into the high schools, the Smith-Hughes Act was passed in 1917, which subsidized high school agriculture and home economics programs and had the effect of bringing agricultural education to virtually every community in the country. Today this network extends to the entire world, for nearly every country has some type of relationship with one or more American land-grant universities. These institutions have been the chief source of technical knowledge and high-level specialists in American assistance programs abroad.

American agriculture could not possibly be as highly developed as it is today without the involvement of education in the process. And we have all benefited from this effort whether we work in agricultural activities or not. Critics of education tend to forget that the United States is the world's leading nation in science, medicine, economic output, and industry and technology and that the individuals responsible for those achievements are, for the most part, products of our public educational system. America's contributions, not only to its own citizens but to all of humankind, have been phenomenal in health, science, medicine, arts, business and industry, and agriculture. In 1930 only 5 per cent of the Nobel Prizes were held by Americans. Today Americans claim more than 40 per cent of them. Significantly, more than half of the living American Nobel Prize winners earned one or more of their degrees at land-grant colleges or universities.

The Schools as Flexible Institutions

In spite of all that is said and written about the schools' tendency to be conservative institutions, American schools have been relatively flexible in being able to accommodate to changing conditions and changing requirements. Those who seek changes quickly are often impatient with the schools' seeming inability to respond to social changes. But the fact is that schools are probably more responsive than most social institutions. To a remarkable degree, schools have been able to respond to the educational needs of the times.

The following are examples of changing social conditions that have required major shifts in emphasis in American education:

- the change from a rural nation to an urban nation.
- education of immigrant children.
- science and mathematics emphasis of the 1950s and 1960s.
- changing lifestyles, later entry into the world of work, more leisure time, and more vocational education needed.
- vast expansion in secondary school enrollments.
- intergroup and ethnic concerns of the 1960s and 1970s.
- international and global relationships of the United States since 1945.
- increased attention to the education and employment of handicapped persons.
- extension of education to the preschool years and to the postsecondary level.
- the racial desegregation of American society.

AMERICAN EDUCATION—ITS CRITICS

The critics of American education may or may not be more numerous than its apologists, but they are certainly more vocal. There has not been a single book-length publication in the popular press lauding American education in the past fifty years that has enjoyed a wide sale, but there have been several best sellers that have been critical of it. Newspaper articles, editorials, articles in widely read journals, and other publications—even the *Congressional Record*—have had much to say about what is wrong with American education. It is an ironic paradox that those who are most critical of education often want to use the schools to promote their own causes. Groups that have not often been well served by the schools are devastating in their criticism of them, yet actively seek greater access to schools. This love-hate relationship takes a variety of forms. We will examine it in terms of five broad categories of critics.

Pressure Groups

In the category of pressure groups, we will place all of those pressure groups and special interest groups that are concerned more or less with a specific matter. They are not necessarily interested in the total school program; they are concerned only that the school is or is not teaching something of particular importance to them—sex education, driver training, law-related education, consumer economics, environmental studies, and so on. In some instances, these groups are relatively benign; indeed, they often represent constructive efforts to improve the school program. The ones that usually come to the attention of the public, however, are those that engage in what can correctly be called attacks on the schools; they are sudden, often vicious, always disrupting. In the past thirty years, hardly any school district has escaped this type of attack. It usually represents an exercise of power to see which group will have the strongest influence on the allocation of resources. A few of these groups are discussed here.

Taxpayer Groups

The American system of financing schools grew out of a rural tradition that called for sizable contributions from the local area. This was done deliberately for at least two reasons: (1) it was presumed there would be more interest in local education if local funds were being spent for it, and (2) school authorities would be accountable for wise expenditures of funds to their local constituents—people they saw and served on a daily basis. In something of a romantic way, schools were expected to reflect in practice those traditional values of thrift, frugality, and economic efficiency that were long associated with colonial America. Much of this thinking becomes linked philosophically to the need for formal education to be tedious and difficult if it is to be effective; that is,

41

good schools are "hard" schools—they impose a demanding discipline not only intellectually but physically as well. One must be careful not to make school environments too comfortable for learners, for this would lead to ineffective education. Some of the residuals of these orientations to education remain imbedded in the public mentality concerning education even today.

Historically, therefore, taxpayers have had a legitimate concern over the expenditure of funds for school support. The system was designed to encourage such concern. But the expectation is that the concern will be shown in responsible ways—in ways that will not be destructive to schools. In recent years we have had numerous examples of taxpayer actions and "revolts" that did not meet these criteria. Such efforts, even though well intentioned, are always disruptive and usually have a detrimental effect on the educational program of the school. Much of the school budget consists of *fixed* costs for services that schools are required by law to provide—salaries, heating, lighting, maintenance, safety, and so on. There is no way of reducing school costs beyond certain limits without making programmatic cuts such as removing the kindergarten program or reducing or eliminating art, music, foreign languages, remedial programs, drama, physical education, and electives at the junior and senior high school levels. Moreover, programmatic reductions have to be severe in order to reduce costs substantially. When this happens, obviously, it has a harmful effect on the quality of the school program.

There should be no argument about the wise and careful use of public funds. Of course, money should not be wasted on unnecessary expenditures. But what is or is not a necessary expenditure has to be decided in terms of present-day norms and values. Those critics who perceive only the three Rs as essential and everything else as "frills" are not being realistic about the kind of education that is needed for life in a postindustrial society such as ours. Children can hardly be expected to leave modern, well-furnished, and well-heated homes to go to schools that are furnished and decorated in nineteenth-century decor. A favorite line of money-conscious critics is, "In my day, by damn, we didn't have such country clubs for schools," as if there were something especially meritorious about school conditions "in my day." Some taxpayers are even resentful of such expenditures as carpeting on the library or classroom floors, even though it can be shown that floor covering is, in the long run, less costly than bare wood or tile floors.

Education still provides the nation and its communities with a good return on their investment dollar, but it is not the bargain that it once was. School costs, like everything else, have risen dramatically in recent years. The salaries of professional personnel—teachers, principals, supervisors, counselors—have markedly increased, and most would agree that such increases are well deserved. Publishing costs have risen, and this is reflected in the price of books, magazines, and other printed matter essential for schools. The cost of paper products, fuel, custodial services, school supplies, and transportation have also skyrocketed. It seems to be unrealistic to expect that school costs will be reduced significantly in the foreseeable future.

"Patriotic" Groups

Because schools are bearers of basic cultural values to young people, they have come under careful scrutiny when teaching such subjects as history, government, political affairs, controversial issues, morality, and citizenship. Americans have always had a fear of political indoctrination, which helps explain why this country has shied away from a single, national system of education. Extremists play on these understandable concerns of parents and often try to make it appear that teachers and college and university professors are politically naïve and idealistic and, therefore, are easily influenced by those who would want schools to espouse and teach socialistic and communistic political and economic ideologies.

It is impossible to monitor completely what goes on behind the closed doors of classrooms. Therefore, educational materials, particularly textbooks, have been targets of the watchful eye of such patriotic organizations as the American Legion, the Daughters of the American Revolution, America's Future, and the John Birch Society. Teaching strategies that stray from the adopted textbooks, especially inquiry, have come under heavy criticism. It follows that if texts are examined and approved, but the teacher does not use them, or if the teacher reinterprets what the text presents, the content and emphasis of the lessons cannot be controlled. Many critics who have an extreme right-wing persuasion object to inquiry because it suggests that there are alternative ways of dealing with social, political, and economic issues. They are inclined to want children taught the *right* facts and ideas about history, government, and the economic system. Although the issue of requiring teachers to take

43

loyalty oaths has been laid to rest by state legislatures and the courts, it was very much alive as late as the 1950s and 1960s.

Thus, the freedom to teach and the freedom to learn are constantly in jeopardy from external forces that have their own ideas about the meaning of patriotism. In elementary and secondary schools, the issue is clouded because of the clear right of the parents to have something to say about the nature of the education their child is to receive. Even today prevailing community attitudes and values, therefore, still threaten the free exchange of ideas in many schools of the country. At the college and university levels, the concept of academic freedom is more firmly established as the right and the obligation to investigate any and all topics and to present all sides of issues no matter how unpopular such views may be. Nonetheless, the pressures from outside groups to restrict what is to be taught and studied is ever present.

The reverse side of this issue is that in some cases teachers and professors have themselves violated principles of academic freedom by presenting a single point of view and by ridiculing those who do not share that view. Intellectuals and college students, for example, have so violently objected to speakers promoting unpopular views that they would not allow the speakers to make presentations on their campus. A case in point being the cancellation of Professor Richard J. Herrnstein's lecture on the campus of an eastern university during the mid-1970s because of his position on interracial differences in intelligence and their potential genetic origins. In other cases, audiences, including college students and so-called intellectuals at some of the nation's most prestigious universities, have shouted down speakers who were expressing politically conservative ideas, making it impossible for their views to be heard. This, too, is a violation of academic freedom and, unfortunately, gives substance to the claim of critics that anti-American values are being promoted by schools and colleges.

Religious Groups

Critics from religious groups are usually Christian fundamentalists whose generalized criticism of the public schools is that they are "godless." These individuals are firmly of the belief that this country was founded on Christian principles, that the Founding Fathers were deeply religious men of the Christian faith with an abiding trust in God, and that these ideas should be included in the public school curriculum. Many would want time set aside for prayers during the school day. Some would want the Biblical story of creation taught, along with, or as an alternative to, the history of evolution in science classes.

Much of what these critics are calling for is clearly illegal under the separation of church and state requirements of the United States Constitution. Thus, it has been proposed that there be a constitutional amendment that would at least make prayers legal in schools, although this proposition has not met with success to date. But even beyond the illegality of these propositions, many parents, including many Christian parents, would find it offensive to have Christian doctrine taught in public schools. Many parents are not Christian but are Jewish, Islamic, Buddhist, or Hindu or may be any one of a number of faiths—or of no faith at all—yet clearly have the right of religious freedom guaranteed by the Constitution. Christian doctrine itself is subject to different interpretations as evidenced by the great number of Christian denominations. Therefore, it is unlikely that there could be any unanimity of thought concerning what religious concepts should be included in a school program.

Special Interest Groups

The schools are bombarded by a vast number of groups that have a single mission: to bring the school program in conformity with their point of view. Often these groups work in concert with school authorities and are involved in developing study guides or new instructional materials for the school curriculum. They may also sponsor workshops for teachers and/or field trips for the pupils. These groups usually represent power groups in society, and their involvement in school affairs gives credence to the claim of collusion between the education and business establishments. Examples of groups of this type are the Joint Council on Economic Education and its state and local affiliates; the American Bar Association promoting law-related education; the National Education Association; consumer advocate groups; Newspaper in the Classroom; National Association of Manufacturers; the American Railway Association; the Milk Foundation; American Telephone and Telegraph Company, and, of course, many, many more.

Advocates of Basic Education and Intellectual Discipline

There is a well-defined group of critics of education who believe that intellectual training was traditionally the primary responsibility of schools and that it should remain so today. Furthermore, they believe that schools in modern times have not lived up to that responsibility. Indeed, their frequent criticism is that schools promote anti-intellectualism. The views of this group are publicized by the Council for Basic Education, a national organization founded in 1956 "by humanistic scholars, scientists, professionals, and other individuals who were concerned about the direction and quality of education in America."[2] The council publishes a bulletin ten times a year plus occasional papers. It also sponsors book-length publications. Because the council attracts competent scholars who are often well known and highly respected, its positions on issues are frequently published in the popular press. Individuals who have been public advocates of basic education and intellectual discipline are Arthur Bestor, Jacques Barzun, George Weber, James D. Koerner, Hyman Rickover, Clifton Fadiman, Maxwell Rafferty, and the late Robert M. Hutchins.

There are deeply rooted philosophical differences over the meaning and purpose of education between those who support the views of the Council for Basic Education and those who set policy for, and implement programs in, the public schools. It follows, therefore, that the educational establishment, the so-called professional educators or "educationists," have come in for harsh criticism by council spokesmen, although this seems to have been softened in recent years. The council's position is that the central purpose of education is the development of the intellect. Whatever the school does that does not serve that goal leads away from true education. Education, in this view, has as its outcome the disciplining of the individual in the intellectual-rational tradition. A good education is a liberal education, and, in the classical sense, the aim of liberal education is wisdom. In the council's own words,

> Basic education for any child requires instruction and demonstrable achievement in the basic disciplines upon which all other forms of education must rest: English, mathematics, science, history, foreign languages and the arts.

[2] From a membership promotion brochure (1978) of the Council for Basic Education, 725 Fifteenth Street, N.W., Washington, D.C. 20005.

It is the Council's position that failure of the schools to insist on the intellectual discipline of these subjects at all levels of instruction produces students who are unable to compete in today's world because they lack the necessary skills to do so . . . young people who cannot read effectively, cannot spell, cannot add, and cannot write three consecutive declarative English sentences.[3]

Notwithstanding the fact that the council's views have not enjoyed wide acceptance among practicing public school educators and teacher trainers, its views as expressed in its publications and by its spokespersons have had a strong influence on American education. It is significant that many of the curriculum reform efforts of the early 1960s were addressed to the very concerns that the council had publicized just a few years earlier. Although not much was heard from the council from the mid-1960s to the mid-1970s, in the late 1970s it once again gained national attention as parents and the public expressed concern about the deficiencies in basic learnings among young people.

The Advocates of Radical Reform and the "New Left"

The rhetoric of the radical group of critics is most closely associated with the social upheavals of the late 1960s and early 1970s. They described schools as oppressive, stifling, boring, grim, joyless, mindless, dull. The school life of the child is overregimented and overregulated. According to this view, children need to be free to make choices, to be involved in planning their own programs, and to be given much more physical freedom than is usually found in conventional classrooms. These critics are strong on "humanizing" the school, although it is not altogether clear what this involves.

Such critics often claim that the school regimen actually works to the disadvantage of the child because it stifles creativity, freedom, and the natural intellectual, social, and emotional growth processes. They are usually strong supporters of open education and are keen on citing the British Infant School as a model. Individuals who have been associated with this view are Edgar Friedenburg, Ivan Illich, Everett Reimer, John Holt, Charles Silberman, and the late Paul Goodman.

There seems to be little doubt that this group of critics was instru-

---

[3] Ibid.

mental in promoting the spread of the alternative school movement. Alternatives to the regular public schools were first formed outside the public school establishment under a variety of labels such as "free" schools, storefront schools, alternative schools, and open schools. In general, these establishments did not enjoy a very long life. In fact, few of them were able to survive more than a year or two. But the idea of providing parents and students with choices caught on and was incorporated within the framework of the public schools. Today it is not uncommon to find open classrooms or alternative programs in many public schools.

The extremists within this group claim that schools, as social institutions, should be done away with altogether. Schools would be replaced by informal and voluntary information networks that would link those who wanted to learn something with those who could teach it. Proposals to "deschool" society or to abolish schools usually come from intellectuals, many of whom hold college and advanced degrees and who have had the advantage of being well schooled. These critics do not bother to explain what the social consequences of abolishing schools would be to a knowledge-based, scientifically oriented, industrially dependent society.

Internal Critics: Professional Educators

Most of the solid curriculum development through the years has come not from fly-by-night critics who capitalize on the mood of the country by making sensational but unworkable proposals, but has come from the educational establishment itself. Some of the most severe, yet constructive criticism of schools has come from educators themselves. These individuals have career commitments to education and are by training and experience well qualified to speak on educational matters. Their views are found in the several educational publications that appear each month. The leadership of such organizations as the Association for Supervision and Curriculum Development are good representatives of the type of critic we are including in this group. A large number of individuals could be cited as examples; a few of the best known are Jack Frymier, John Goodlad, Richard L. Foster, Vito Perrone, B. O. Smith, Larry Cuban, Harry S. Broudy, and Gordon Cawelti.

Individuals in this group have worked within the education system for reforms in the following areas:

Teaching Strategies

For years unimaginative read-recite and/or lecture methods, coupled with an overdependence on textbooks, have dominated classroom teaching procedures. Some of the harshest critics of these limited and often disabling teaching strategies have been from the teaching profession. They have urged wider use of multimedia in teaching and have persistently called for more learner involvement through individual inquiry and activity-type learning experiences. They have stressed the need to make school experiences meaningful for learners, to make careful needs assessments prior to instruction, to state objectives unambiguously, and to evaluate outcomes in terms of objectives. The changes that have come about in school practices have not been as extensive as many would hope, but clearly substantial progress has been made in the past two decades.

Curriculum Content

Educators, with assistance from their colleagues in the various scholarly disciplines, have effected major revisions in curriculum content. Many of these changes reflected additions of new knowledge or the reinterpretation of familiar concepts. This is most evident in such fields as chemistry, biology, physics, mathematics, and geography. Other changes have been necessary because of changing social conditions or values, as, for example, changes in the treatment of minorities and women in history and the social studies curriculum. Still other changes in the curriculum content have been made in order to deal more realistically with the interests and problems of learners, as, for example, emphasis on drug-related health problems, law-related education, sex education, and career information.

Treatment of Learners

In spite of the rhetoric of the "New Left" about the treatment of learners, schoolchildren have had no stronger advocates than educators. There is, for instance, a sizable amount of educational literature that speaks to such topics as the importance of the self-concept in learning, the effects of labeling and the self-fulfilling prophecy, individual differences among learners, the role of interest and motivation in learning, and similar topics. Much of this has resulted in better treatment of youngsters in the classroom. Educators have also been concerned about the stifling effects of school routines, regimentation, and repressive school environments. Although there are still many abuses of learners in schools, there is a greater awareness of the rights of children today than there ever has been. This has come about largely through the efforts of educators who have worked to update, modernize, and improve existing practices.

The Minorities

The voice of the minorities, no louder than a whisper for generations, burst forth with a mighty roar in the decade of the 1960s. Their spokespersons were demanding an increased share in the social and economic rewards of this society. To a large extent, these demands focused on education. Quite clearly, schools had not and still do not adequately serve the needs of a great number of minority-group children. The broadsides that are leveled against the schools usually claim that the schools are racist and totally irrelevant and that they contribute to the problems of the lower-class minority children rather than help them. It is often said that the schools are not helping children of black, Chicano, Indian, and Asian families move into the middle class fast enough. Some of the individuals who have had things to say about the plight of the children of minorities in school are Barbara Sizemore, James A. Banks, Madelon D. Stent, William R. Hazard, Vine DeLoria, Jr., James Baldwin, Art Pearl, Jesse Jackson, and Carlos Cortes. Their criticisms have tended to group themselves around the following issues:

1. The school experience does damage to the self-concept of the minority child.

A minority child may come from a loving, caring family that has taught the child to feel good about himself or herself. These children may reside in a relatively homogeneous community where they live and play with children much like themselves. When they enter school, however, they may be stepping into a new world, a world that does not respect the culture from which they have come. The school program begins to set goals and tasks for them that they are not able to achieve successfully. When this happens time after time, the child quite naturally begins to have self-doubts about his or her ability or even self-worth. Once having sowed the seeds of lowered self-esteem, the process feeds on itself. One failure follows another until hardly anything attempted can be successfully completed. This pattern could, of course, apply to any child, but because the visible minority child is easily identified and often stereotyped negatively, the expectation of failure may be presumed right from the first day of school. Critics say that if the schools cannot do anything to enhance the self-concepts of minority children, at least they should not contribute to a child's lowered self-esteem and self-worth.

2. The school does not do an adequate job of teaching minority children use of the English language.

Many minority children have problems with the English language. For some, English is not their first language; indeed, some do not know English at all. In other cases, the children use a dialectal English, not accepted in the business and work world, as for example, "black" English. In still other cases, the syntax, articulation, and structure used by the child deviate so completely from standard English that the child is hardly able to communicate at all with a standard English speaker.

The critics are not in agreement as to what should be done by the schools in dealing with this problem. For those children who speak a language other than English, bilingual education is usually demanded.

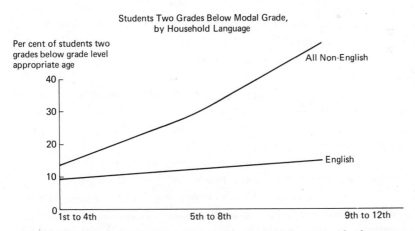

FIGURE 2. Explain why the gap in achievement becomes wider between the two groups as students progress from lower to higher grades. (SOURCE: National Center for Education Statistics, July 1975 Survey of Languages.)

There is not agreement, however, on whether the bilingual program should be used as a transition to the learning of English or as an enrichment program or as a way of teaching equal fluency in both languages. Much controversy surrounds the use of dialectal English as a vehicle of instruction. Whatever one's personal views are on this issue, the reality is that the business and work worlds do not accept it, and the individual who is only able to use dialectal English is going to be handicapped in getting and holding a job and/or in being admitted to a college or vocational training program. If schools are to make these children more employable, their English language skills simply must meet the standards required by the work world.

3. The school does not do enough to expand the life experiences of minority children.

Children of the poor usually have limited life experiences. They have little contact with the world beyond that of their own neighborhood. Because many minority families are also poor, these children frequently lack life experiences that would enhance the learning of abstract concepts in school. Critics insist that schools should actively seek to correct this deficiency by including more field trips and by providing other types of direct experience modes of teaching and learning.

4. The school does not adequately prepare minority children for the world of work.

It is a sad fact that unemployment among minority people is regularly two to three times what it is for whites. Unemployment among young blacks in American cities may be 35 to 40 per cent. In the case of Indian people, the figure is also that high and, at certain times of the year, may be even higher. Likewise, for migrant Chicano labor, during nonharvest seasons unemployment soars. This is a malady of the society in which we live, and it will require a broader effort than that of the school alone if it is to be solved.

Minority parents see these unemployment statistics and demand that the schools make their children more employable. Their claim, not without justification, is that schools do not even acquaint these children with the world of work. The minority children do not know what occupational choices are available to them, so, of course, they cannot make intelligent career choices. These parents want more adequate counseling services available in order to help their children make sensible choices about their life work and thereby be more competitive in the labor market.

Although these critics make a strong case for vocational preparation, they are adamant in their opposition to tracking, again with some justification. Tracking is the practice of placing high school students into particular curricula on the basis of each student's interest, aptitude, intelligence, aspirations, and similar criteria, resulting in a vocational track, college-bound track, terminal track, and so on. Too often they see their children placed in dead-end tracks in junior and senior high schools that do not lead anywhere either vocationally or in terms of meeting requirements for postsecondary education. In the sorting and selecting process that accompanies tracking, they see their children tracked into programs that are not appropriately rewarding career choices.

5. The school does not familiarize minority children with the systems of law and justice.

Because of the negative stereotyping of minorities, the minority person is much more likely to have encounters with the legal system than is the nonminority person. For that reason, if for no other, these children should be heavily schooled in law-related studies. If we assume that ignorance is no excuse for breaking the law, we must also assume that people are given the opportunity to learn about the systems of law and justice. Law-related education should be provided to help the person avoid having encounters with the law and, secondly, to teach the person what action is appropriate if one should have such an encounter; that is, one needs to know both one's rights and one's responsibilities.

6. The school does not do an adequate job of teaching minority children how to use the political system.

Poor people and minorities are often referred to as the "powerless." This is a less apt label today than it once was because minorities, at least, have learned a great deal about the use of political power in recent years. A case in point is the role of black voters in the election of President Carter in 1976. Nonetheless, critics claim that the schools should be much more complete in providing political education to minorities. Why minorities? Because they are the ones who have traditionally been disenfranchised. If pressed on this matter, critics would say that schools should do a good job with the political education of *all* students.

7. The school does not provide minority children with appropriate experiences in decision making.

There are two points of view on this issue. One group of critics claim that schools do not provide low-income and minority children with enough experiences in decision making. Consequently, they never learn these skills and go through life having others make decisions for them. The second group claims that these children come out of environments in which their behavior is highly directed. In order to help them learn most effectively, the school should, therefore, use teaching modes that are highly directive because the children are familiar with them. To ask them to make choices and decisions about their learning simply frustrates them. This latter group is critical of the school for not being assertive enough with minority children. They go on to say that, as a result, these children are left to make their own decisions, which are too often bad ones. It is not clear why this needs to be an either-or issue. The school could use directive strategies at early levels and, over a period of years, teach these children how to use decision-making skills effectively.

8. The school does not provide a multiethnic curriculum.

One of the most commonly heard criticisms from this group is that schools do not teach the realities of the multiethnic character of this society. Their claim is that the schools provide a monocultural emphasis, which is Anglo and Protestant. As a result of this emphasis, the minority child finds little in the curriculum with which to identify. The allegations of inadequate treatment of minorities in the school curriculum is well documented. Numerous analyses of textbooks and other learning resources, as well as district curriculum documents, indicate the absence of a pluralistic emphasis in traditional programs.

It should be said, however, that much of this is being corrected in schools today. There is a high level of awareness among teachers, teacher educators, publishers, and the general public of the need to have more truthful pictures of social reality find their way into the school curriculum. There are big differences in the treatment of minorities in textbooks today from the treatment even a decade ago. This is seen by most as a step in the right direction. Undoubtedly, even more will be done in the years ahead to build programs that accurately teach about the multiethnic composition of this society, thereby no longer making this criticism a valid one.

THE RECONCILIATION OF DIFFERENCES AMONG THE CRITICS

School authorities sometimes attempt to accommodate the demands of their critics, thereby hoping to reduce the amount of conflict associated with the operation of the schools. This effort is, of course, commendable insofar as it does not do violence to sound educational practice and moral and ethical principles. School leaders have a responsibility to be sensitive to the voices of the people who are served by the schools at the local level.

But is it possible to reconcile differences among the critics and have schools operate in ways that satisfy all constituents? Probably not, because to satisfy one group of critics will serve to alienate other groups. Those who expect to design school programs that will please everyone are destined to encounter one disappointment after another. The role of the school is to design curricula that meet the educational needs of the greatest number of persons it serves. The availability of alternative delivery systems can do a great deal to accommodate the varying educational needs of individuals in a community.

The School Attitude Inventory that follows is based on frequently voiced criticisms of schools, all of which have been discussed in this chapter. The use of some such device as this can help to provide school authorities with insights about how local constituent groups perceive the meaning, purpose, and practice of education in schools. The reader is encouraged to complete the School Attitude Inventory in order to gain insights into his or her own perceptions of education, schools, and schooling.

GUIDELINES FOR USING THE SCHOOL ATTITUDE INVENTORY

Responding to the Items

The Attitude Inventory consists of thirty value statements relating to the schools, their purposes, procedures, policies, and practices. These statements are neither right nor wrong but reflect various honest perceptions that persons have of the schools.

In responding to the items, do not dwell at length on any one statement. Simply read each one thoughtfully, register the strength of your feeling, and proceed to the next item. Do not omit any of the items. There is no time limit, but most persons can complete the inventory in about twenty minutes.

Scoring the Responses

When you have completed responding to all of the items in the Inventory, place the *number* you have circled for each item on the score sheet in the space provided for that item. For example, if you were undecided about statement twenty-one, you would have circled number three: 1 2 3 4 5. Accordingly, you would write "3" on the score sheet in the cell labeled "Basic Education" in the space just to the right of number twenty-one. Record your responses to all of the items in this way. Then add your entries in each cell and place the total for each cell in the space provided for that total.

Interpreting the Results

The items are clustered in such a way that one will get high scores in some cells and low scores in others. If one's belief system is in any sense consistent, it is impossible to get high scores *or* low scores in all the cells because the item clusters are contradictory.

The lower your cell total score is, the more your attitudes toward education resemble the group identified in the cell. Contrariwise, the higher your cell total score is, the more unlike your attitudes are when compared with the group identified in the cell. A low score is between six and twelve; a high score between twenty-five and thirty. A profile of your scores can be drawn on the chart provided on the score sheet.

Of course, this inventory represents a very small opinion sample and, therefore, not too much confidence should be placed on the results. Nonetheless, the items do provide opportunities for discussion of your beliefs about education with others, and they do indicate a general trend or direction in which your beliefs tend to lean.

An interesting and worthwhile class project would be to generate several new items, perhaps increasing the total number of items on the inventory to ninety, with eighteen in each cell. Be sure that new items accurately reflect the views of the group identified in the cell for which they are being written. Distribute new items randomly throughout the inventory. Such an instrument could be administered to various constituent groups in the community and the results compared.*

School Attitude Inventory

Directions: Circle the number that corresponds to your attitude toward each statement. (SA: strongly agree; A: agree; U: uncertain; D: disagree; SD: strongly disagree)

		SA	A	U	D	SD
1.	In general, schools do not adequately individualize instruction.	1	2	3	4	5
2.	The school life of most children is overregimented and overregulated.	1	2	3	4	5
3.	It is not too far from the truth that in schools today "the three Rs are being replaced by the three Ts: typing, tap dancing, and tomfoolery."	1	2	3	4	5
4.	Schools do not adequately teach the realities of the multiethnic character of this society; there is a monocultural emphasis that is Anglo, Protestant.	1	2	3	4	5
5.	The school experience often works to the disadvantage of the child because it stifles creativity, freedom, and the natural intellectual, social, and emotional growth processes.	1	2	3	4	5
6.	A significant result of recent efforts to revise the curriculum has been the updating of curriculum content, that is, subject matter.	1	2	3	4	5
7.	Basic education for any child requires instruction and demonstrable achievement in the basic disciplines upon which all other forms of education must rest: English, mathematics, science, history, foreign languages, and the arts.	1	2	3	4	5
8.	Open education designed along the lines of the British Infant School provides a good model of what American schools should be like.	1	2	3	4	5
9.	When the theory of evolution is taught in schools, equal time should be given to the creation theory as another explanation of reality.	1	2	3	4	5
10.	Schools should encourage inquiry strategies in order to develop reflective processes.	1	2	3	4	5
11.	Schools do not do an adequate job of increasing children's facility with the English language.	1	2	3	4	5
12.	Historically, intellectual training was the primary responsibility of the schools and remains so today.	1	2	3	4	5
13.	The best thing that could happen to education in this country would be to abolish schools altogether.	1	2	3	4	5

 * Students and instructors have the author's permission to reproduce this inventory and use it with community groups. Acknowledgment of the source would be appreciated.

	SA	A	U	D	SD

14. Parents and other adults in the community should review the textbooks used in schools to make sure that foreign social, political, and economic ideologies are not being presented in a favorable light.   1   2   3   4   5

15. American schools are generally racist and do not serve the needs of a great number of children of visible minorities.   1   2   3   4   5

16. School instruction is often ineffective because objectives are ambiguously stated or not stated at all.   1   2   3   4   5

17. Schools waste money on such nonessentials as carpeting, expensive decor, media centers, and sophisticated laboratory equipment.   1   2   3   4   5

18. Much of what schools do today promotes anti-intellectualism.   1   2   3   4   5

19. Children should be free to make choices and to be involved in planning their own programs, and they need much more physical freedom than is found in conventional classrooms.   1   2   3   4   5

20. The increased use of multimedia in teaching has been a good development.   1   2   3   4   5

21. Most of what goes on in schools is not really *education* in the true sense but is training in knowledge and skills that are vocationally oriented.   1   2   3   4   5

22. Schools do not do enough to help minority children attain and maintain positive self-concepts.   1   2   3   4   5

23. Schools can best be described as "godless."   1   2   3   4   5

24. Adjectives that best describe conditions in school are these: oppressive, stifling, boring, grim, joyless, mindless, dull.   1   2   3   4   5

25. Schools do not do enough to open the door to the world of work, especially in the case of minority children.   1   2   3   4   5

26. Schools do not adequately teach the advantages of the free enterprise economic system.   1   2   3   4   5

27. In the case of inner city education, it is far more important to address the education of the disadvantaged child than to provide for his or her social adjustment.   1   2   3   4   5

28. Good education should be concerned with the person's *total* development as a fully functioning human being—social, emotional, physical, and intellectual growth.   1   2   3   4   5

29. Schools should provide much more adequate counseling services than they do currently in order to ensure better career choices by minority students.   1   2   3   4   5

30. In all grades K-12 there should be a few minutes of quiet time for pupils to meditate or to pray.   1   2   3   4   5

SCHOOL ATTITUDE INVENTORY

SCORE SHEET

Pressure Groups	Basic Education
9. _____	3. _____
14. _____	7. _____
17. _____	12. _____
23. _____	18. _____
26. _____	21. _____
30. _____ Cell Total _____	27. _____ Cell Total _____

New Left	Educators
2. _____	1. _____
5. _____	6. _____
8. _____	10. _____
13. _____	16. _____
19. _____	20. _____
24. _____ Cell Total _____	28. _____ Cell Total _____

Minorities	Directions:
4. _____	1. Transfer your circled values to the appropriate place on the score sheet.
11. _____	
15. _____	2. Add scores for each cell and record total.
22. _____	3. Use cell totals to prepare your profile.
25. _____	
29. _____ Cell Total _____	

59

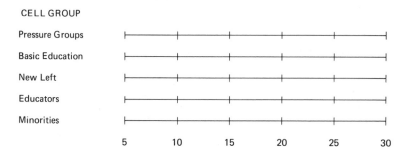

YOUR PROFILE

Mark your cell score total on each line. Connect your scores to show your score profile. Low scores represent similarities; high scores represent dissimilarities with the cell group.

STUDY AND DISCUSSION

1. This chapter has dealt with a number of expressed dissatisfactions with American education. Discuss in some detail the source, nature, and extent of those dissatisfactions.

2. Provide examples of responses the schools have made to the critics of education.

3. How do you explain the fact that so much of the commentary in the popular press regarding public education has been and continues to be negative?

4. Identify ten values embraced by American society. How would you establish the validity of your choices? In what ways do Americans expect to see those values reflected in school programs? Using your list of values, comment on the difference between the *ideal* and the *actual* in behavior based on those values. What can—or should—schools do to lessen the gap between the ideal and the actual in converting value commitments into reality?

5. Cite examples of the successes of American education beyond those discussed in this chapter.

6. Is it a sound policy for school authorities to try to accommodate all of the concerns of critics of the schools? Why or why not?

7. What evidence can you cite to suggest that being a "professional" critic of the schools can be a very lucrative enterprise?

8. After making case studies of communities around the country that had experienced destructive criticism of their schools, one group of researchers noted that in all cases where the critics persisted over a long period of time, they were receiving sympathetic coverage by local newspapers. What does this suggest about the power of the local press? What strategies might school authorities use to combat this kind of one-sided newspaper reporting?

9. Assume you were asked to advise a school district as to what it could do to protect itself from unfair and unwarranted criticism of its programs and practices. What are five specific recommendations you would make?

10. Schools are often intimidated by parents and others who wish to censor instructional material. Should schools remove books from the library (such as *Catcher in the Rye, Native Son, Soul on Ice, Little Black Sambo, Mein Kampf*) that some parents find objectionable? Do the same principles apply in selecting materials for required reading (that is, textbooks) as apply in selecting optional reading, such as library books? How would you resolve the value conflict inherent in the parents' right—and responsibility—to guide the lives of their children *and* the child's right to learn *and* the teacher's right—and responsibility—to teach? Is it possible to have good censorship?

SELECTED BIBLIOGRAPHY

ARMBRUSTER, FRANK E., with PAUL BRACKEN. *Our Children's Crippled Future: How American Education Has Failed.* New York: Quadrangle Books, 1977.

BERG, IVAR. *Education and Jobs: The Great Training Robbery.* New York: Praeger Publishers, Inc., 1970.

BUTTS, R. FREEMAN. *Public Education in the United States: From Revolution to Reform.* New York: Holt, Rinehart and Winston, 1978.

COPPERMAN, PAUL. *The Literacy Hoax: The Decline of Reading, Writing, and Learning in the Public Schools and What We Can Do About It.* New York: William Morrow and Co., Inc., 1978.

HENTOFF, NAT. *Does Anybody Give a Damn?* New York: Alfred A. Knopf, Inc., 1977.

HURN, CHRISTOPHER J. *The Limits and Possibilities of Schooling: An Introduction to the Sociology of Education.* Boston: Allyn & Bacon, Inc., 1978.

61

ILLICH, IVAN. *Deschooling Society*. New York: Harper and Row, Publishers, 1970.

OCHOA, ANNA S. "Censorship: Does Anyone Care?" *Social Education* (April 1979): 304–309.

REIMER, EVERETT. *School Is Dead*. Garden City, New York: Doubleday and Co., Inc., 1970.

RIST, R. C. *The Urban School: A Factory for Failure*. Cambridge, Mass.: The MIT Press, 1973.

SILBERMAN, CHARLES E. *Crisis in the Classroom: The Remaking of American Education*. New York: Random House, Inc., 1970.

chapter 3

Perceptions of the Functions of Schools

Education, like parenting, is a subject on which most adults—especially educated adults—perceive themselves as having some measure of expertise. Everyone seems to have well-formed ideas about what schools should or should not do. Thus, in the United States, we have many disparate views as to what the major purposes and functions of schools should properly be.

In nations that have centralized systems of education, defining the basic purposes of education is less of a problem than it is in the United States. Through their Ministries of Education at the national level such nations are able to issue policy statements that define the nature, purpose, goals, and functions of the schools. In the United States we are not organized to provide such national direction for our system of education. Consequently, our educational efforts lack a singleness of purpose, and, indeed, at times segments of the educational enterprise appear to be working at cross-purposes.

Because we have no official nationally articulated purpose of education, we depend on consensus formation at the grass roots level to give direction to the schools. These beliefs surface in public forums, at school board meetings, in letters to editors, and at community gatherings. Perhaps some particular group feels strongly enough about an issue to petition school officials or state legislators to enact policies consistent with their views. The case of economic education provides us with such an example. Interest groups supporting the free enterprise system have said to the school authorities and state legislatures, "It is important for our people to be economically literate." If such a petition gets support and is institutionalized as a school requirement, it becomes defined as a goal of the schools. Implicitly, it also defines the function of the schools to be one of teaching young people to be socially effective, in this case, competent producers and consumers through their knowledge of how the economic system works.

Often consensus on school purposes is achieved as a result of trends revealed by social statistics or as a result of a social condition believed to be in need of correction. The concern over basic skills during the 1970s is an example of such consensus formation. Test scores on national samples of schoolchildren confirmed what many adults thought they already knew, namely, that there was a deterioration of proficiency in basic skills among the nation's children. This was followed immediately by a ground swell of concern to correct the deficiency. State after state instituted some form of competency examinations. Many made skills mastery a condition of high school graduation. What this tells us, of course, is that basic literacy is perceived as an important national goal of education and that an important function of the school is to provide children with skills they will need in order to live in society.

The examples cited in the foregoing paragraphs are two of a very few goals on which there is a fair amount of accordance among the American people. The components of a person's education for which the school is *totally* responsible are few in number. Similarly, there are only a few areas in which the public school has *no* responsibility—religious education being an obvious example. Generally, there is little problem in gaining consensus in those areas in which the school has either complete or no responsibility. The problems connected with achieving agreement on goals lie in that large gray area in which the school shares responsibility with other agencies such as the home, church, or community. This is the largest component of a person's education and includes most of what schools do.

Arriving at a unity of opinion on the purposes of the schools was less of a problem in earlier times when communities tended to be more homogeneous with respect to social, economic, ethnic, and religious backgrounds than they are today. Even today in homogeneous communities, such as those of the Hutterite colonies in Montana, there is little disagreement about the puposes of the school. But in highly heterogeneous communities—and this means most of them in modern America—it is difficult to gain a consensus on all but a very few purposes. We are products of many cultures, and we have varied social, ethnic, and economic backgrounds. With the amount of diversity that characterizes most communities today, it is little wonder that we cannot agree on what schools are supposed to accomplish.

Schools do, nevertheless, set purposes and build curricula consistent with those purposes. School programs are intended to prepare young people for life in the future. This means that the programs reflect purposes and goals that *someone* believes will be important in the future. These "someones" might be the teacher, the local curriculum director, textbook authors, school boards, state legislators, and so on. But no matter who establishes those purposes and develops a curriculum consistent with them, we can be sure that there will be others who will not be pleased with the curriculum and will not believe that its purposes are valid. These differences in perceptions as to the basic functions of schools explain why schools are almost constantly under fire from some segment of the community served by them.

THE SCHOOLS AS MULTIPURPOSE INSTITUTIONS

An individual's perception of the purposes and functions of schools is developed around a set of abstract beliefs, propositions, and assumptions having to do with the nature of human beings, with the nature of society, with what constitutes the good life, with how individuals relate to the ultimate reality, and with the purpose of life. Out of these beliefs, propositions, and assumptions is generated a statement that describes an educational program based on those beliefs, propositions, and assumptions. The reader should bear in mind that such philosophical positions or "schools of thought" are often intellectual abstractions that may or may not relate very closely to the day-to-day work of public schools. Indeed, it would probably be impossible to find a public school anywhere in the country that represents in practice one of the various philosophical positions in the pure sense.

In most cases, what we see happening in schools is a program representing a series of philosophical compromises regarding goals, purposes, and methods. This does not always result in the best education for those who attend but, from the standpoint of political reality, is probably necessary for schools to operate at all. Thus, as we look at a school, we can say, "Most of the time it seems to reflect this or that purpose." Or, "Most of the time the school is concerned about self-development of children, but that is combined with a concern for basic learnings." Because most schools serve a variety of constituencies, they have to build programs that reflect multidimensional purposes. Of course, schools are concerned—or should be concerned—about the individual development of human beings. This does not mean, however, that they do not at the same time have a responsibility to the larger society to educate children for effective citizenship. Schools can teach learners skills needed to earn a living. They can also teach them to obey the law. It is obvious that schools serve many purposes, some of them of private benefit to the learner, others of more general consequence that become public purposes.

Even though public schools are multipurpose institutions, we can examine what they are doing in terms of their *major* concerns, their *main* emphases, and their *primary* goals. Moreover, in looking at a school, we would expect to see consistency in what was going on there. For instance, we would not expect to see conflicting educational purposes being sought in the same classroom or even in the same school. In practice, however, it is not uncommon to encounter such incongruities. For example, it is not at all unusual for teachers to engage in individualized instruction, yet use the same evaluative instruments for everyone. Or teachers will evaluate ongoing work in the classroom, using criterion-referenced standards, but when report card grades are given, these are based on norm-reference standards. School practice is filled with inconsistent practices that are based on differing perceptions of what schooling is supposed to ac-

knowing, based on reason and the rational process, that are useful in validating knowledge about the nonmaterial domain of values and metaphysical principles. These latter concerns are perceived to be of a higher order and cannot be dealt with appropriately through the application of scientific methodology.

Individuals who embrace this position distinguish between *education* and *training*. Education has to do with developing the intellect in order to be able to deal with abstract ideas. Training, on the other hand, is learning how to do the mundane things associated with day-to-day living—preparing for a job, being a good citizen, consuming wisely, being a responsible marriage partner, being a loving and considerate parent, and so on. These latter elements should not be associated with true education, according to this view. Such a view smacks of intellectual elitism, a charge the advocates of this position would not deny. Of course, education is not for everyone—not everyone has the cognitive capacity to engage in thought of a higher order. The real issue here is the dichotomy between the intellectual on the one hand and the practical on the other.

It would be hard to find a public school today that operates entirely for the purpose of training the minds of students. Nonetheless, vestiges of this point of view remain imbedded in our thinking about the purpose and function of schools. The idea that schools ought to be concerned with intellectual matters is an attractive idea to many persons, especially those who do well at intellectual pursuits. Because those who are the most influential decision makers are persons whose own educations have been largely intellectual, there is little wonder that school programs reflect this bias. The idea of "general education" (as opposed to career education) at the high school level in some measure reflects this point of view. The liberal arts baccalaureate at the college level that does not prepare the person to "do anything" also reflects this position. The extent to which these programs at the high school or college levels portray perennialist ideology would, of course, depend on the composition of the curriculum.

The Council for Basic Education, discussed in connection with the critics of education in the last chapter, promotes the perennialist point of view. The leadership of the council and its board of directors are well-educated intellectuals for whom this kind of education makes sense. They have a faithful following in many communities in the United States, who work to have school programs shaped in accordance with their views. They are often viewed as traditionalists because they press for intensive work on literacy skills at the lower levels and conventional academic sub-

68

jects at upper levels. They talk about maintaining high standards, intellectual discipline, and hard work—values not altogether objectionable to many Americans.

THE TEACHING OF THE BASICS

Another perspective on the purpose of education has to do with the responsibility of the school for the development of learnings essential to the preservation of the culture and the transmission of those essentials to oncoming generations of young citizens. This view of education, quite appropriately, has been called *essentialism;* and its followers, *essentialists.* It has been a strong force in American education in this century. It differs from the point of view discussed in the preceding section in several important ways. First, it does not view education simply as "training the mind"; that is, it does not deal in terms of the mind-body dualism that characterizes the perennialist position. Second, it does not view education as a process reserved for the intellectual elite. Third, it is clearly more closely linked to scientific problem solving as a system of discovering and validating knowledge and would, therefore, place less reliance on the use of reason and the rational process alone as means of securing new knowledge. Fourth, essentialists support a close relationship between the school curriculum and the requirements of living, whereas perennialists do not because they perceive the purpose of education to be the development of the intellect.

The essentialist view gained substantial ground in American education during the last half of the 1970s. The dominant concern of parents and the educational community throughout the nation was to teach the "basics." This means that there are some things that are so fundamental, so basic, so *essential,* that everyone who goes to school should be required to learn them, assuming, of course, that the learners are sufficiently competent intellectually to do so. The concern for mastery learning, for minimum competency testing, for statewide testing, and for national assessment suggest school purposes based on essentialism. What is being communicated is the idea that there are some essential elements of the culture that need to be passed on from one generation to the next if the society is to survive.

It is one thing to get support for the notion of the need to teach

69

essential elements of the culture to all; it is quite another to get agreement as to what those essential elements are. To answer the question, "What is essential?" one needs criteria in order to make an objective judgment as to what qualifies as essential and what does not. If one does not have objective criteria, one person's opinion is about as good as the next person's. If there is no way of assessing what deserves higher priority than something else, then everything must be given equal weight. This is obviously not a desirable plan of action, for, under such an arrangement, a trivial fact would be equated with a major concept. Educators have been struggling with the problem of identifying criteria for selecting essential content of the curriculum long before 1859, when Herbert Spencer published his often cited essay entitled "What Knowledge Is of Most Worth?" They have enjoyed only moderate success in this effort.[1]

Thus, once one gets beyond simple literacy skills such as reading, writing, spelling, and mathematics, there is little agreement, even among experts, as to what is essential or basic. What usually happens, therefore, is that these decisions are made by individuals who are influential within the educational establishment. Such persons are (1) parents in the local community who are perceived by others as opinion shapers; (2) school board members; (3) officials in the state departments of education; (4) curriculum directors, principals, and teachers; (5) leaders in professional associations; (6) textbook authors and standardized test authors and publishers. All of these individuals are drawn from groups of people who have had the advantage of good educations and who, for the most part, have succeeded in school. Schooling has been an important factor in their lives.

The question, of course, is how well do the essentials, as defined by the individuals and groups for whom schooling has been a successful experience, serve those persons who have been traditionally disenfranchised by the school? Are the essentials that are defined by educational elites also essential for that large group of learners—perhaps as many as 40 per cent—who are not academically inclined? Or are there different kinds of "essentials"—some being more essential than others? Many find essentialism to be attractive in defining the purposes of education, but it

---

[1] John Jarolimek, "The Basics in Social Studies: Implications for the Preparation of Teachers," in *Competency Based Teacher Education: Professionalizing Social Studies Teaching*, ed. Del Felder, NCSS Bulletin no. 56 (Washington, D.C.: National Council for the Social Studies, 1978), pp. 17–36.

presents many problems of implementation in a school system that is supposed to serve all of the children of all of the people.

ADJUSTMENT TO SOCIETY

It is possible to view the basic purpose of education as that of teaching students to adjust to the realities of the social world. The major constructs of this point of view, also known as *social realism*, are as follows: There is "out there" in society an objective reality with which every one of us must learn to cope. There are rich people and poor people; educated ones and uneducated ones. Some are white, some are black, others are brown, and still others have different racial and ethnic identities. There are factories out there that belch pollutants into the air we breathe and discharge poisonous wastes into the rivers, streams, and lakes. Many people work for a living, but some do not. Some steal and lie and rape and kill. Most obey the laws, but some do not. There are times when people can experience supreme happiness, but they also fall victim to debilitating and painful diseases. The happy, playful children we see on a kindergarten playground will one day be residents in nursing homes, devastated by the ravages of disease and old age. They will all die. Everyone will die. These are facts—irrefutable, indisputable realities.

Social realists hold that schools cannot, or at least *should* not, be unmindful of those realities of social life. Young people are being prepared for life in that society, and, therefore, what the school should do is to teach them how to adjust to it. In curriculum building, social realists would want to make surveys and analyses of society in order to get a better grasp on the social realities that will confront the school graduate. The curriculum would be modified accordingly. Such programs would be very much concerned about current happenings. For example, if surveys show a growing number of young teenage pregnancies, social realists would want the junior and senior high schools to address themselves to this problem. Driver education presents another example, as does drug-abuse education, law-related education, health and nutrition education, and safety education.

It seems clear that educational programs developed from this point of view would be individualized and might vary considerably from one place to another. The object is not necessarily to improve society but rather to teach the individual to live in the present society, to adust to and to cope with the realities confronted there. There is a heavy emphasis on the selection of learnings that will be practical, useful, functional.

This orientation to the purposes of education has come under considerable criticism in recent years because it does not adequately encourage the *improvement* of social conditions and realities that are unjust or destructive. To "adjust" to social realities suggests a docile acceptance of things as they are. Activists would hold that such an education simply perpetuates unwholesome social conditions that need remediation. Some would perceive such a view of the school's role as racist and sexist because it would encourage traditional racial and sex-role stereotyping. Critics also assert that schools developed along the lines of social realism are designed simply to perpetuate existing social class structure. They allege that the elites implement school programs of this type to keep lower classes and under-classes in their place while, at the same time, maintaining the present power elites in their positions. Nonetheless, this has been a popular point of view, and evidence of it can be seen in the curriculum of almost any public high school in the country.

PROBLEM SOLVING AND CRITICAL THINKING

The main purpose of education as viewed from the perspective of problem solving and critical thinking is to develop persons who are able to apply scientific procedures in a creative way to the problems they encounter in society. The ideas embodied in this position are usually associated with John Dewey and his predecessors, William James and Charles S. Peirce, and have been called *experimentalism, pragmatism,* or *instrumentalism.* Certainly, John Dewey was its most respected and profound spokesman, and William Heard Kilpatrick, its best-known disseminator.

The idea that schools should teach learners to be problem solvers and critical thinkers developed during the time when educational psychology (and particularly measurement) was in ascendancy and at the time when the child study movement was in its heyday. Clearly, both of these movements influenced the thinking of educators who were pondering the basic purpose of education. Psychologists were searching for and measuring those traits that in any way seemed to have an effect on school learning and were applying statistical procedures to analyze individual differences in ability and school achievement. Although the measurement movement and the child study movement both focused on the individual learner, education was viewed as occurring in a social context. Much of the work in the child study movement stressed the importance of social interaction among young children, and this also became a central value in the definition of the broader purposes of education.

If children are to learn critical thinking and problem solving in a social context, they must be placed in an environment that will encourage exploration, curiosity, wonderment, and hypothesis testing. Freedom to explore and encounter problems is an essential characteristic of such an environment. Elementary school classes that are taught in ways consistent with this orientation often engage in "units of work." At the beginning of such units, the teacher prepares or arranges an environment relating to the topic to be studied. Children are then encouraged to explore that environment, handle objects, ask questions, and define problems for study. In this way, children's "needs and purposes" are defined. The child "needs" to get information, and his or her purpose is to get information that will shed light on some problem of study. One methods book describes this process as follows:

> Another efficient and effective way to initiate a unit is through providing a "setting" that will arouse interest and curiosity on the part of the children. This may be done before school begins or as soon as the unit is selected. The teacher will include in the environment stimuli to children's innate drives and urges, which also provide for individual differences. To arouse curiosity he will choose pertinent materials—books, pictures, exhibits, models, maps and globes, and science objects. Because children need physical activity, the teacher will select paints, wood, weaving, art materials, models, costumes, and tools. To provide play stimuli, the environment will include objects which can be moved or worn.[2]

In the earlier edition of this same book, this paragraph followed:

> On the first day that the children come to the room there will be ample opportunity for them to move around it, to look at the books, pictures, and objects, to touch the materials, to try on the clothing, and to manipulate the

[2] Lavone A. Hanna, Gladys L. Potter, and Robert W. Reynolds, *Dynamic Elementary Social Studies: Unit Teaching*, 3d ed. (New York: Holt, Rinehart and Winston, Inc., 1973), p. 95.

models that are in the environment. The teacher will observe the pupils as they explore the materials and he will note which things are of greatest interest. He will follow this short period of exploration with a guided discussion, giving children an opportunity to ask questions and to talk and share things of interest to them. It is of paramount importance that the teacher pick up important leads from the children in order to guide the discussion about worthwhile activities. Their first questions or interests should give impetus, direction, and motion to the emerging, dynamic, and vital experience that will follow. As a result of this discussion, interest will become focused on common concerns, which furnish the leads to get the unit underway.[3]

In these two excerpts we find described many of the fundamental ideas that undergird the experimentalist or progressive point of view: (1) program planning based on pupil interests and needs; (2) the teacher's role as that of a guide and facilitator of learning, who engineers the environment to enhance pupil learning; (3) respect for individual pupil personality; (4) problem-solving, emergent curriculum; (5) a child-centered program; (6) activity-oriented, "doing" type of learning experiences; (7) intellectual and physical freedom to explore; (8) a life-centered curriculum that has meaning and significance to the learners; (9) concern for the total—not only the intellectual—development of learners; (10) an environment that allows and encourages social interaction that leads to democratic group living; (11) integrated learnings.

Programs based on this approach were promoted by prominent educators during the Progressive Education Movement of the decades of the 1930s and 1940s. The movement gained some substantial strength at the elementary school level, where the social studies curriculum was used as the integrating center of the school day. Model programs could be found in some campus laboratory schools such as the one at UCLA under the direction of the late Corrine Seeds and the Lincoln School in New York City operated in connection with Columbia University. Progressive education never established itself as a strong force at the secondary school level. In recent years the programs that are referred to as "open education" and some alternative classrooms are based on similar ideas about the purpose of education and schooling. These movements have never had a wide following among parents and other laypersons because of the pupil permissiveness they require.

Of the many contributions of the advocates of problem solving and

[3] Lavone A. Hanna, Gladys L. Potter, and Neva Hagaman, *Unit Teaching in the Elementary School*, rev. ed. (New York: Holt, Rinehart and Winston, Inc., 1963, p. 152.

critical thinking perhaps none has been so widely applied as the reflective thinking strategy developed by John Dewey. In the book *How We Think*, Dewey defined the following five basic components of problem solving: (1) recognizing that a problem exists, (2) defining and delimiting the problem, (3) forming related hypotheses concerning the problem, (4) gathering data and drawing conclusions based on those data, and (5) testing the conclusions and noting the consequences of the conclusions. In one form or another, these now famous "five steps" have been widely cited in educational literature and have been extensively applied—and misapplied—in many curriculum areas. These steps have served as the basis for inquiry strategies so widely promoted in modern times.

Experimentalism makes a big point of the firsthand experience of learners and has been the source of more than its share of educational clichés based on experience. Because of its reliance on firsthand experience, curricula based on this philosophy are always pupil-involving, activity-oriented. A great deal is made of background experience as a readiness for new learning. When children come to school without adequate life experience, it is the school's responsibility to provide it, according to this view. Learning is defined as a change in behavior as a result of experience. Throughout the theoretical and practical aspects of experimentalist thought, the concept of experience as a prerequisite for learning recurs over and over again.

TEACHING FOR SOCIAL CHANGE

In times of social unrest and stress, society tends to fault its schools for contributing to such conditions, or it turns to its schools to correct social ills. Time after time, schools have been asked to take on new responsibilities or to improve what they are already doing as a way of coping with a specific social problem. Society blames the schools for the disruptive behavior of its young people, for their failure to accept responsibility as young citizens, for the increasing crime in society, and for other facets of social life for which the schools may at best share only partial responsibility. In addition to the idea that schools should respond to such social needs as become apparent through social statistics, there is also the point of view that schools should be proactive in their handling of social problems; that is, that schools should anticipate social changes and build a curriculum in accordance with those anticipated changes.

The belief that schools should be an active force in promoting social change grew in ascendancy during the Great Depression of the 1930s. Educational literature usually refers to this view as *reconstructionism,* although in recent years the term *revisionism* is more commonly used. The latter term is applied to the point of view of those scholars who embrace socialistic, neo-Marxist views, who are critical of the American capitalistic social and economic structures, and who would see the school as playing a major role in revising and reforming that system.

Many authors perceive the beginning of reconstructionism as an off-shoot of experimentalism, which was discussed in the foregoing section. It was spawned during the Great Depression by educators who believed that schools were not dealing in any creative way with the deplorable social conditions of the time. While the entire social fabric was being unraveled by the effects of the Great Depression, schools continued to operate with a seemingly business as usual attitude. Some scholars came to believe that what was needed was a new social order and that the schools had to play a significant part in the creation of that new social order. The most widely cited statement dealing with this point of view was an address by Professor George S. Counts to a national meeting of educators, later published as a document under the title *Dare the School Build A New Social Order?*[4] Although many liberal-minded intellectuals found the idea of the school's becoming a major force in social redirection and regeneration, it did not result in a national movement to reconstruct either the schools or society.

Reconstructionism was kept alive as an educational philosophy through the writings of scholars but remained dormant until the decade of 1960s, when renewed interest in social action and social participation held sway. The social activists of the 1960s railed against the curriculum of the schools for being irrelevant and out of touch with the social realities of the times—social injustice, racism, sexism, exploitation, and so on. Schools were implored to take an active role in redressing these social ailments. It was a significant sign of the times when, in its *Social Studies Curriculum Guidelines* issued in 1971, the National Council for the Social Studies proclaimed activism in the form of social participation as a legitimate and *necessary* part of social studies education:

[4] George S. Counts, *Dare the School Build A New Social Order?* (New York: The John Day Company, 1932).

It is essential that these four curriculum components be viewed as equally important; ignoring any of them weakens a social studies program. The relationship among knowledge, abilities, valuing, and social participation is tight and dynamic. Each interacts with the others. Each nourishes the others.[5]

The National Council for the Social Studies clearly is saying that the school must play an active role in improving society by instilling in young citizens those skills needed to bring about social change. Many persons would give enthusiastic support to such a position.

The American public appears to be somewhat less enthusiastic in its support of the views of some of the revisionist scholars who are calling for radical social change. Revisionists would want the schools to restructure society along socialist lines, but—

educational reform is limited in its ability to produce social change by the inherent structures of corporate capitalism and because the school is geared to fulfilling the needs of corporate capitalism rather than changing it.[6]

Christopher Jencks also calls for social change but is not sanguine about the schools' ability to be an effective force for such change:

As long as egalitarians assume that public policy cannot contribute to economic equality directly but must proceed by ingenious manipulations of marginal institutions like the schools, progress will remain glacial. If we want to move beyond this tradition, we will have to establish political control over the economic institutions that shape our society. This is what other countries usually call socialism. Anything less will end in the same disappointment as the reforms of the 1960s.[7]

The excerpt from Jencks illustrates another reason why many are wary of the views of reconstructionists and revisionists. They are not ready to agree that teachers, educators, and social scientists should deter-

[5] NCSS Task Force (Gary Manson, Gerald Marker, Anna Ochoa, and Jan Tucker), *Social Studies Curriculum Guidelines* (Washington, D.C.: National Council for the Social Studies, 1971), p. 15.

[6] Martin Carnoy and Henry M. Levin, *The Limits of Educational Reform* (New York: David McKay Company, Inc., 1976).

[7] Christopher Jencks, *Inequality: A Reassessment of the Effects of Family and Schooling in America* (New York: Harper Colophon Books, Harper & Row Publishers, 1972), p. 265.

mine the kind of society we need based on the findings of researchers from the social sciences. Quite clearly, many Americans would not accept the values implicit in the solution being presented in the foregoing excerpt from Jencks. The American people are not likely to accept "blueprints of a new society" taught in their schools, least of all blueprints prepared by social scientists whose political views seem often to become enmeshed in their scientific studies.

EDUCATION FOR SELF-ACTUALIZATION

Education for self-actualization combines concepts from existential philosophy, developmental psychology, and the cognitive theory of learning. It is a logical extension of experimentalism and shares many of its concepts. There are, of course, variations in the extent of individual commitment to this point of view ranging from pure existentialism—meaning complete freedom for the individual to choose and to take responsibility for those choices—to individualized instructional programs not much different from what one would see in experimentalist classrooms. In any case, the key concept underlying this point of view regarding the purpose and function of education is the sanctity of the individual person. All else fades into the background; it is the individual human being who creates his or her world, and the educational program should facilitate that process.

In existential philosophy, it is up to the individual human being to make sense of, and to find meaning in, what is essentially an absurd and tragic world. The universe is perceived as purposeless, and, therefore, each individual human being must learn to cope with this basically hostile environment by making wise choices and then leading his or her life in accordance with those choices. The exercise of choice and free will is important to existential thought. The individual must not be persuaded by social pressure to conform to ways of living that he or she has not freely accepted. Of course, the whole range of available knowledge may be useful in clarifying meaning, but, fundamentally, it is up to the individual human being to decide the meaning of his or her own existence and what he or she will do with his or her life. Although few Americans would embrace pure existential philosophy in its nihilistic and pessimistic view of the world, many of its notions have become a part of the stream of consciousness of most of us.

Education for self-actualization places heavy reliance on the modifiability of the human personality. Educators who support this view often talk in terms of a human being's "becoming" and often refer to learning as "growth." They believe that most people do not come close to realizing their potentials as fulfilled human beings. Because self-development has not been a major educational goal, learners are not provided with an opportunity to think creatively about what or who they can become. What is needed are highly differentiated programs of instruction that help all learners to develop self-actualization. Included here are not only those children who have been traditionally perceived as educable, but *all* children, including those with serious physical or mental handicapping disabilities. Programs in self-actualization do not view education as a process concerned only with the intellectual development of persons but as being concerned with the whole person as an integrated, functioning human being.

Teaching for self-actualization necessarily defines the teacher's role as facilitator and guide. Because programs are highly individualized and involve much choice making, the teacher must provide a learning environment that invites the selection of topics and problems that are significant to learners. The teacher is careful not to make too many decisions for pupils; otherwise, the goals of teaching choice making and creative thinking would be short-circuited. The teacher must help pupils make their own decisions and then hold them to the consequences of those choices. The teacher constantly thinks in terms of helping the child maximize his or her potential for growth—intellectually, socially, physically, and emotionally.

Self-actualization thinking is easy for Americans to accept. Indeed, they find it attractive because it seems to be so consistent with traditional American values relating to individualism, self-improvement, and the virtues of being a self-made person. Undoubtedly, this affinity for self-actualization accounts in part for the phenomenal success of so-called self-improvement books in recent years. Americans have a great confidence in the improvability of the human being. Self-actualization thought includes a broad spectrum of beliefs. It covers the tragic, pessimistic views of the existentialist philosophers and, at the same time, includes those optimists who see in every human being the opportunity for self-improvement!

A SYNTHESIS OF VIEWS

With the exception of special schools such as private schools, campus laboratory schools, or experimental schools of one type or another, it would be difficult to find schools operating programs based on a point of view or a single educational philosophy. Most programs represent a mix of views—perhaps a synthesis of several elements from various schools of thought concerning the major purposes and functions of education. There is nothing particularly wrong with this approach; indeed, it is probably necessary in order to serve as diverse a clientele and as many publics as American schools are expected to serve. Problems arise, however, when there are philosophical inconsistencies in programs.

No one can say for certain what qualities of education would receive a high degree of consensus among Americans. But on the basis of practices that have received enthusiastic support from parents and the public generally, it would seem that many Americans would like to see their schools developed along lines somewhat as follows:

1. Although most agree that the *main* concern of schools should be intellectual, educational goals should be broad enough to include the physical, social, emotional, and aesthetic development of young people. Communities value their school athletic programs, their music and art programs. They want schools to help their children become responsible citizens by learning to get along with others, doing what is right, dealing fairly with others, developing a loyalty to basic institutions, and so on.

2. Most Americans expect schools to take into account individual differences between and among learners. They do not want children individually tutored; indeed, they might want most of the instruction to take place in group settings. Nonetheless, they want teachers to recognize differences in talents and abilities and build programs to maximize the capabilities of each child for self-fulfillment.

3. Most Americans want the conduct of instruction to take place in something of a disciplined, orderly setting. Americans simply do not take kindly to educational practices that encourage a high degree of student permissiveness.

4. Most Americans are essentialists in the sense that they expect

schools to teach children certain basic knowledge, skills, and values and expect all to attain a minimum level of mastery.

5. Most Americans want school programs that are relevant to current life in society. They do not want schools to be immune from the society and community in which they are located.

6. Most Americans expect schools to represent what is perceived as good in the culture—to be morally uplifting, to develop aesthetic sensitivities, and to provide children with good role models.

It is to be expected that some of these points will be of more significance in some communities than in others. Some communities may have a greater religious orientation than others, in which case the teaching of values is an implicit expectation even though religious doctrinal teachings are prohibited by law. Educators need to know enough about the many different perceptions of the functions of education in order to understand better the concerns of the parents and communities and thereby be able to build educational programs that have a strong possibility of gaining community support. This probably means a program that represents some mix of the various orientations to the purposes and functions of education that are discussed in this chapter.

STUDY AND DISCUSSION

1. How do you account for the fact that some of the more traditional views of education are the most popular ones with parents and with the public generally?

2. Explain how population growth, urbanization, and industrialization have affected the role of the school in society.

3. How can social statistics be used in deciding new directions for education? Provide specific examples of how this has been done in the past.

4. What are some of the responsibilities and tasks public schools have today that they did not have at the turn of the century?

5. It is often claimed that schools try to do too much and that, as a result, they do a poor job of doing what they are really supposed to do. Another view is that schools as institutions of soci-

ety do not do nearly enough in the way of social service and that they could reasonably be expected to greatly expand their sphere of concern in meeting human needs at the local community level. What are your views on this issue?

6. Explain how graduate school admission requirements affect the curricula of elementary and secondary schools.

7. Can "how to do it" in-service workshops ever be very effective with teachers who do not embrace the educational philosophy on which they are based? Provide examples to illustrate that a knowledge of, and commitment to, a particular philosophy of education on the part of individual teachers are essential to the effectiveness of in-service education.

8. Show by example how practical curriculum problems arise as a result of a lack of agreement about purposes of education between curriculum developers and curriculum implementers, that is, teachers. What does this suggest about the role of teachers in curriculum development?

9. Do you believe that schools should first of all serve the private purposes of individual citizens or give first priority to serving public purposes of society? Provide examples to support your point of view.

10. In 1897, John Dewey published a statement he called, "My Pedagogic Creed." In it he developed his basic beliefs about what education is, what the school is, the role of subject matter, the nature of a teaching method, and the school and social progress. If you were to prepare a statement of *your* "pedagogic creed," list ten beliefs about education, schools, and schooling that you hold so strongly that it is not likely that you could be persuaded to change your mind about them.

SELECTED BIBLIOGRAPHY

BUTTS, H. FREEMAN. "The Public Purpose of the Public School," *Teachers College Record* 75 (December 1975): 207–221.

COMBS, ARTHUR W. *Myths in Education: Beliefs that Hinder Progress and Their Alternatives.* Boston: Allyn & Bacon, Inc., 1979.

CREMIN, LAWRENCE A. *Traditions of American Education.* New York: Basic Books, Inc., 1977.

DELLA-DORA, DELMO, and JAMES E. HOUSE, eds. *Education for an Open Society.* 1974 Yearbook. Part 1: "Movement Toward an Open Society." Washington, D.C.: Association for Supervision and Curriculum Development, 1974.

PARSONS, TALCOTT. "The School Class as a Social System: Some of Its Functions in American Society." *Harvard Educational Review* 29 (Fall 1959): 297–318. (Also included in the Ronald M. Pavalko volume of readings.)

PAVALKO, RONALD M., ed. *Sociology of Education: A Book of Readings.* 2d. ed. Part 2: "Some Functions of Education." Itasca, Illinois: F. E. Peacock Publishers, Inc., 1976.

SIEBER, SAM D., and DAVID E. WILDER, eds. *The School in Society.* Part 1: "Classical Perspectives." New York: The Free Press (Macmillan), 1973.

TYACK, DAVID B. *The One Best System: A History of American Urban Education.* Cambridge, Mass.: Harvard University Press, 1974.

chapter 4

Race, Ethnicity, and Sex and the Schools

In this chapter we concern ourselves with several related concepts: race, racism, institutionalized racism, ethnicity, ethnocentrism, sex-role stereotyping, sexism, and the self-fulfilling prophecy. These concepts have obvious implications for school-society relationships. Indeed, they lie at the heart of some of the most complex and profoundly serious social and, therefore, educational problems of modern times.

RACE AND RACISM

When asked to define the concept "race," most individuals think of groups of people having somewhat similar physical characteristics. They doubtless learned early in life that human beings could be grouped on the basis of common physical attributes. They learned that these groups were labeled Caucasoid (white race), Negroid (black race), Australoid (black race variant), and Mongoloid (yellow race). Some of the traits that have been used for the purpose of placing individuals in racial groups have been skin pigmentation, blood type, sickle cell gene, color and texture of hair, eye color, size and stature, Rh blood group factor, and color blindness. Because people with somewhat similar physical appearances tended to inhabit certain specific parts of the earth, these groups have come to be referred to as *geographical* races. Geographical races have been identified as African, American Indian, Asian, Australian, European, Indian, Melanesian, Micronesian, and Polynesian. Additionally, at points of contact, there are hundreds of local races that are variants of the major groups.

In terms of the phylogenetic tree, all human beings are in the order *primates*, species *Homo sapiens*. When race is conceptualized as described in the foregoing paragraph, it is defined as a subspecies of *Homo sapiens*. This classification works well in theory, but in practice it presents many problems. These problems arise from the fact that individual human beings cannot be reliably categorized by applying the criteria conventionally used for this purpose. The attributes used to make the classification are often not strong enough or distinct enough to enable an observer to make sharp distinctions between individuals.

For several hundred years human beings, for one reason or another, have traversed all areas of the world; and on these expeditions they did not, of course, leave their sex drives at home. Human beings have a propensity to mate and at those moments are not especially concerned about the racial identity or skin complexion of their eligible partner. The offspring that were the result of such trysts and their progeny several generations removed represent every conceivable genetic combination, thereby defying any effort to classify them neatly into easily defined racial groups. In fact, this traditional system of labeling human beings has been so confusing that many anthropologists no longer make use of it.

If we cannot reliably use phenotypical and genotypical traits as the basis of grouping into categories we call races, why do we continue to use this term? Part of the answer can be found in the fact that race has *social* relevance. That is to say, race is a concept that has social meaning and, therefore, social consequences. Many practices having to do with the labeling of people by race have no basis in objective reality. People group themselves and/or group others not necessarily on the basis of objective physical traits but on the basis of subjective judgment of what they *believe* to be true. It is often impossible to identify a person as a black, a Latino, or a native American Indian on the strength of their facial features because they may in every way resemble northern Europeans. Such an individual might move to another part of the country and easily pass as a white if he or she wanted to. But as long as the person maintains an identity as a visible minority, he or she will be treated by others as having that identity. It is clear that *race* must be defined in terms of both physical *and* social characteristics if it is to have meaning as a social phenomenon relevant to schools and schooling.

Professor Pierre L. van den Berghe provides a definition of race that takes both the social and physical dimensions of this concept into account. According to his definition, race is

> a human group that defines itself and/or is defined by other groups as different from other groups by virtue of innate and immutable physical characteristics. These physical characteristics are in turn believed to be intrinsically related to moral, intellectual, and other non-physical attributes or abilities.[1]

The first part of the definition speaks to physical qualities that a group has in common. These are described as being "innate and immutable," meaning that one is born with them and that they cannot be changed. One can join a social or cultural or religious group, but one cannot opt to join a group whose membership is selected on the basis of "innate and immutable" physical characteristics. Needless to say, neither can one opt out of such a group. Notice that this definition includes criteria dealing only with physical attributes; it does not say that the group is defined or defines itself by virtue of "shared history, culture, or religion." Groups that have common cultural origins, shared history, speak the same language, have a common religious tradition, but do not have similar physical qualities based on genetic heritage are *not* racial groups. It is, therefore, inaccurate to speak of the "American race," the "German race," the "Mexican race," or the "Japanese race." These are either national groups or ethnic groups, but they are not racial groups.

One might argue that the second half of the van den Berghe definition really speaks to *racism* rather than race. This is quite correct, and it underscores the fact that the two concepts are so closely related that they are inseparable when we address ourselves to race problems in the United States. Social scientists are prone to say that objective physical differences between groups of people do not create race problems. It is only when these differences are recognized and are given social salience

---

[1] Pierre L. van den Berghe, *Race and Racism* (New York: John Wiley & Sons, Inc., 1967), p. 8.

that we have a race problem. By definition, racism is the practice of attributing positive or negative values to certain physical qualities that characterize a particular group. It seems clear that if physical characteristics made absolutely no difference in any way in social relations, there could be no racism. It is only because we *do* make distinctions in the way we deal with people who are members of identifed groups, based solely on physical qualities, that we have race problems.

This is, of course, what happens in the educational system in dealing with children of visible minorities. The visible minority child is handicapped in school precisely because many persons, including a sizable number of teachers, remain convinced that physical characteristics are "intrinsically related to moral, intellectual, and other non-physical attributes." It is as if racial identity were a summarizing variable from which all kinds of inferences could be drawn about a child's capacity to learn, potential achievement, future success in life, and so on. It is well documented that race is a powerful factor in determining the level of expectation that teachers set for children. Social status characteristics that can be inferred from the appearance of the child in the classroom prejudice the teacher's judgment about the capability of the child to achieve. It has also been documented that teachers expect less of lower-class children than they do of middle-class youngsters. This is the phenomenon of the self-fulfilling prophecy and is particularly relevant to the visible minority child because of the inclination to stereotype minorities, especially blacks, as of lower social class.

The practice of making invidious distinctions between persons on the basis of race is not limited to individuals who are basically evil, hateful, and malicious. Quite to the contrary, persons who make such judgments are frequently well-meaning, gentle, and caring people. Consequently, when they are confronted with the notion that they themselves may be engaging in racist behavior, their reaction is usually one of stunned disbelief and of personal umbrage. This lack of awareness results from racism's being given legitimacy and social approval. In other words, it is an institutionalized phenomenon.

Institutionalized racism consists of practices that have been *legitimized* by the society and that result in the *systematic discrimination* against members of *specific* groups. Practices that are legitimatized are accepted. Few question them. Even those against whom the discrimination is directed accept these practices when they are given legitimacy. It is important to note that institutionalized racism *systematically* discriminates. This means that it is not a random, idiosyncratic happening. Rather, it occurs with regularity and with predictable consistency. It is directed against certain specific groups because members of those groups have particular characteristics or qualities.

A few examples of institutionalized racism follows:

1. Imposing height requirements for certain jobs, such as those held by the police, fire fighters, bus drivers, and so forth. (This practice discriminates systematically against some Asian groups who tend to be physically short of stature.)

2. Literacy requirements for voting. (This discriminates against blacks and other ethnic minorities who are known to have lower literacy rates than the dominant group.)

3. High fees for filing for public office. (This practice discriminates against the low-income groups, many of whom are of ethnic minorities.)

4. Associating certain groups with specific positions. (This stereotyping discriminates against easily identifiable persons, such as ethnic minorities, because traditionally they have been in low-status occupations.)

5. Use of qualifying tests that require a high level of verbal behavior. (This discriminates against ethnic minorities.)

6. Segregated housing patterns. (This practice discriminates against individuals easily identified as members of certain groups, that is, visible minorities.)

7. Use of dual norms. (This discriminates against ethnic minorities because it implies inability to achieve as well as whites.)

8. Homogeneous grouping in classrooms. (This discriminates against ethnic minorities because it often results in their being in low-achieving groups.)

9. Automation, technology, labor-reducing practices. (These absorb jobs of low-skilled persons, thus of a high percentage of ethnic minorities.)

10. Specific racial quotas. (These quotas foreclose opportunities beyond the stated quota regardless of availability of qualified personnel from disallowed groups.)

11. Curriculum content unrelated to the life of certain groups.

(This discriminates against groups who are not represented in the subject matter of the school, usually ethnic minorities.)[2]

Racism, individual or institutionalized, always has to do with how the individual is treated by others as a result of his or her racial identity. Because the variables that are used to assign individuals to racial categories are so ambiguous, it is clear that the critical element is not what the person *is* in any objective sense but rather how he or she *is defined.* In integrated communities where people are not defined according to races, persons will be treated differently from the way they would be in other communities where they are so defined. Young children of many different races play and interact with each other and may even be aware of differences but attach no social value to them. Consequently, they do not treat each other any differently because of physical characteristics.

Professor James A. Banks reports interesting observations concerning color and race in Puerto Rico.[3] There, racial categories appear to be much more flexible than they are in the mainland United States. Many white individuals in Puerto Rico would be defined as black in the United States. Because racial identification there is influenced by physical, cultural, and social characteristics, an individual can, in a sense, *choose* his or her racial identity. It is not unusual for individuals of the same family to belong to different racial groups.

ETHNICITY

Race is often confused with ethnicity. The essential difference between the two concepts is that racial characteristics are genetically transmitted whereas ethnic qualities are culturally determined. This distinction, however, is not wholly adequate because of the overlap of racial and ethnic variables. For example, ethnic components and racial characteristics overlap greatly in the case of Asians, American Indians, Eskimos, and Arabs, but may not overlap at all in the case of Western

[2] John Jarolimek and Clifford D. Foster, *Teaching and Learning in the Elementary School* (New York: Macmillan Publishing Company, Inc., 1976), pp. 17–18.
[3] James A. Banks, "Multiethnic Education Across Cultures: United States, Mexico, Puerto Rico, France, and Great Britain," *Social Education* 42 (March 1978): 181.

Europeans. For instance, an individual might be identified as being ethnically Slavic and have no particular distinguishing physical features that would identify him as such. On the other hand, a person who is ethnically Japanese would also "look" Japanese. It would be entirely possible for a Slavic person to be mistaken for a Northern European, but it would be very unusual for a person who is ethnically Japanese to be taken for a European. In our society the relationship between ethnic, racial, social, and economic variables become extremely complex because we are a multiracial, multiethnic, and multisocioeconomic society.

The term *ethnicity* has been defined many times, and most authors who use the term provide their own definition. For example, Andrew Greeley, building on Max Weber's definition, speaks of ethnicity as people bound together by real or imagined common origin.[4] Rudolph Vecoli defines it as "group consciousness based on a sense of common origin."[5] A more extended definition is provided by Otto Feinstein:

> Ethnicity means peoplehood, a sense of commonality or community derived from networks of family relations which have over a number of generations been the carriers of common experiences. Ethnicity, in short, means the culture of people and is thus critical for values, attitudes, perceptions, needs, modes of expression, behavior and identity.[6]

Many authors use the term *peoplehood* in discussing and describing ethnicity. Some have used the expression *primordial ties* in speaking of the attachment of one to his or her ethnic heritage. The critical elements in ethnicity or ethnic identity are culturally based factors such as (1) language, (2) religion, (3) shared history, (4) nationality, (5) folklore, and (6) traditions, all of which are learned.

Individual Americans vary considerably in the extent to which they are influenced by their ethnic heritage and the extent to which they wish to identify with it. For example, some do not care to become involved with their ethnic heritage at all. They identify themselves as Americans and do not want to have anything to do with "old-country" ways. Others

[4] Andrew Greeley, *Why Can't They Be Like Us? America's White Ethnic Groups* (New York: E. P. Dutton & Co., Inc., 1975), p. 40.

[5] Rudolph J. Vecoli, "Ethnicity: A Neglected Dimension of American History," in *The State of American History*, ed. Herbert J. Bass (Chicago: Quadrangle Books, 1970), p. 70.

[6] Judith Herman, ed., *The Schools and Group Identity* (New York: Institute on Pluralism and Group Identity, 1974), p. 17.

identify themselves at least nominally with an ethnic group but do little else with it. Such a person may attend a Sons of Norway picnic once a year or go to a lutefisk dinner, tell a few Norwegian jokes in dialect, and forget about his or her Norse forebears for another year. Others go beyond that and work in fraternal associations on a regular basis. They meet with their "brothers and sisters" regularly, raise money for the support of their charities, work to organize charter trips to the homelands of their forebears, and so on. A step beyond this is the person who works actively in promoting ethnic language schools for his or her group's children, publicizes and subscribes to a foreign language newspaper, listens to radio programs in the language, and/or uses ethnic identity as a rallying ground to promote political issues, to pass legislation, or to influence foreign policy. Finally, there are some Americans who are totally immersed in the culture of their ethnic group, so much so that they may not even speak English as a second language. Perhaps one of the best examples of this last group is the Navaho people. On their huge reservation, which is a nation itself, many are far removed from the mainstream culture of white America. People who grow up there must of necessity learn to be bicultural if they are to live and work in the mainstream America.

Does one have to "feel ethnic" in order to have one's actions, ideas, and feelings influenced by one's ethnicity? Evidently not. That is, the effects of being brought up in a particular ethnic environment are so powerful and pervasive that it becomes an integral, and not necessarily a conscious, part of one's social, emotional, and intellectual orientations to life and living. For instance, there are documented ethnic differences in responses to pain, to joy, to affection, to sorrow, and so on. Some groups are more reserved, more stoic, less effusive, whereas others are more openly expressive, demonstrative, and intense. The ethnic environment in which one was reared will probably produce a particular lifelong mind set or mentality that is characteristic of that ethnic group.

When people develop and hold an exaggerated feeling of the importance of their own ethnic group, we say their behavior is *ethnocentric*. *Ethnocentrism* is the superior feeling people have about their own culture, with a corresponding attitude that others are *inferior*. In this time of increased ethnic awareness, there is a widespread belief—wholly incorrect—that although racism is bad, a little ethnocentrism can be a good thing in developing ethnic pride. The belief is that the results that flow from racism are basically evil but that those that flow from ethnocentrism can be positive. These beliefs and attitudes could hardly be farther from the truth. Persons who share these views are unmindful of the history of human relations or choose to ignore it. The fact is that some of the most vicious bloodletting in human history has come about not because of racial conflict but because of ethnic differences. Our own time has contributed numerous horrendous examples of the effects of ethnocentrism in the violent actions of various separatist movements. On the current world scene we see evidences of such ethnic conflicts in Northern Ireland, Cyprus, and the Middle East and, so far at least, evidence of a less violent one in English-French relations in eastern Canada.

THE DAWN OF THE NEW PLURALISM

There has been a strong resurgence of interest in ethnic heritage in recent years. This has been apparent from the interest shown in the tracing of family histories on a personal level, which has risen dramatically. But ethnic heritage studies have been encouraged in school programs, representing a complete reversal in attitude by the nation's educational establishment. John Carpenter, formerly of the U.S. Office of Education, writing about education and the new pluralism, makes the following observations:

> In 1909 an educator wrote that a major task of education in American cities was to "break up these immigrant groups or settlements, to assimilate and amalgamate these people as part of our American race, and to implant in their children, so far as can be done, the Anglo-Saxon conception of righteousness, law and order, and popular government . . . "
>
> Sixty years later the Congress of the United States passed the Ethnic Heritage Studies Act giving official "recognition to the heterogeneous composition of the nation and the fact that in a multiethnic society, a greater understanding of the contributions of one's own heritage and those of one's fellow citizens can contribute to a more harmonious, patriotic, and committed populace . . ."[7]

The author then asks, "What brought about this ideological switch?"

[7] John Carpenter, "Educating for a 'New Pluralism,' " The Schools and Group Identity, ed. Judith Herman (New York: Institute on Pluralism and Group Identity, 1974), p. 13.

It is easy to understand why the immigrant would maintain his or her ethnic identity; in any case, it could hardly be hidden. Living in a strange land, not knowing how to speak or understand the language, unfamiliar with customs, the immigrant could find security and a sense of belonging if he or she lived in an ethnic ghetto with others of "his [or her] people." In this sense, ethnic identity provided useful social, economic, and to some extent political functions. But children of these families went to American schools, learned the ways of living of the new land, and were presumably assimilated into the mainstream culture. Why, then, does ethnicity persist into the second, third, and fourth generations and even beyond? Not an easy question.

A variety of complex social forces coalesced in this country during the late 1950s and 1960s that gave rise to greatly increased militancy of minority groups, particularly blacks. Capable and articulate black leadership began calling attention to their three centuries of oppression in this country and to the social, educational, economic, and legal inequities that still prevailed. Although the movement began with nonviolent strategies, the feeling of frustration and anger could not be contained by the black leadership; and, in the social unrest that ensued, large sections of such cities as Los Angeles, Detroit, and Washington, D.C., were burned. Many cities experienced violence, although none as destructive as in these three. The demands to be heard could no longer be ignored, and the nation was faced with the frightening possibility of continued violent unrest approaching the dimensions of a civil war. The nation was in a frightened mood and was willing to make almost any concessions to contain the problem.

The Black Movement pressed hard for the achievement of social, economic, and legal goals, but additionally it advanced the concept of black identity. The notion that "black is beautiful" was promoted. Folk heroes of black ancestry were identified and popularized. Institutions were pressured into providing black studies programs. The lyrics and rhythms of popular music strongly reflected feelings of oppression. Designs characteristic of parent cultures became fashionable in fabrics and stationery. Afro hairstyles, along with other displays of Afro heritage, appeared and became popular not only among blacks but with white liberal intellectuals who identified with this cause. These thrusts by blacks to establish ethnic identity and respectability had a profound effect on the sensitivity of our society to ethnicity in general. Encouraged by the success of the blacks, other minority groups began to make themselves heard and to make their influence felt. After all, if black could be beautiful, so could red or brown or any other color, with the possible exception of white. Thus, in addition to "black power," there arose demands for "red power," "brown power," and so on. By the mid-1970s ethnic identity did not carry the stigma that it once did. In some instances, quite the reverse was true, as in the case of Native Americans—it had become "in" to be Indian.

Some believe that the renewal of interest in ethnic identity, especially among white ethnic groups, can be interpreted in part as a backlash effect to the concessions made to blacks and other visible minorities during the 1960s. Those people who immigrated to this country in huge numbers between 1870 and 1924 from eastern and southern Europe—Italians, Greeks, Poles, and other Slavs—prided themselves on becoming good citizens. They became gainfully employed, saved their money, educated their children, and served in the armed forces with distinction. It is almost literally true that they built industrial America with the sweat of their labor. They did everything they thought they were supposed to do to earn their place in this nation. Little wonder, therefore, that they resented being ridiculed as "hard hats." They especially resented the concessions made to blacks—benefits and privileges for which they themselves had to work. Their attitude is reflected in the often repeated question, "We pulled ourselves up by our bootstraps; why can't they?" An attitude of indignation expressed by the son of an immigrant Polish family is typical: "You don't have to tell me what discrimination is; I was called a 'dumb Polack' half my life."

As these white ethnic groups attempted to deal with the changing social conditions, they discovered that they could organize themselves around their ethnic identity. This has led some authors to suggest that there was not really a renewal of ethnic identity in recent years but that it had simply gone public. They would say that it had been there all of the time and that we failed to recognize it. Michael Novak makes this point in his book in speaking of the southern and eastern Europeans as "unmeltables."[8]

This view suggests that white ethnics have to some extent lived biculturally. Publicly they gave the appearance of being completely assimilated into the mainstream culture. In their private lives, however,

---

[8] Michael Novak, *The Rise of the Unmeltable Ethnics* (New York: Macmillan Publishing Company, Inc., 1971).

much of their ethnic heritage persisted. The practice of their ethnic customs was done without fanfare and without public notice; that is, they maintained fluency in their ethnic language, they attended their ethnic churches, and they married within their ethnic group. Their ethnic customs might come to public notice on such occasions as weddings, funerals, or special ethnic holidays such as St. Patrick's Day, Kolacky Days, or the Swedish Festival of Lights. The position suggests that these people were *acculturated* but not *assimilated* and that this has become evident in recent years because ethnic identity has been legitimatized.

Another explanation of the rise of interest in ethnicity may be that ethnic identity is profoundly pervasive in its influence on the individual. One researcher, Edward Gobetz Giles, has suggested that "ethnic identification is likely to persist for generations and perhaps, even if in attenuated or multiple form, forever."[9] This suggests that even after several generations one's ethnic heritage continues in its influence on one's behavior and mental outlook. Thus, if we want to understand the widespread interest in ethnicity, we must know something about the nature and extent of the sources of the ethnic groups. It is probably true that most Americans, even those who are well educated, do not comprehend the vastness or the social consequences of immigration to this country during the past two hundred years.

THE COMING OF THE "HUDDLED MASSES"

Beginning in the sixteenth and seventeenth centuries, for reasons that are not fully understood, people in Europe began increasing in number. Because of the nature of their economies and the level of technology at the time, the communities could not support this increase in human beings. As a result, a certain number from each generation was of necessity forced to leave the community and locate somewhere else. Thus, many years before the large migrations to the New World, people had been migrating and relocating throughout Europe. The migration to the New World was simply an extension of a process that had been going on for at least a couple of hundred years.

[9] Edward Gobetz Giles, *Slovenian Americans in Greater Cleveland, Ohio*, Kent State University, Department of Sociology and Anthropology (May 1973), p. 158.

The migration of people into the United States during the 100-year period from 1824 to 1924 represents the *largest movement of people in human history.* The exact figure is unknown, but it is estimated that over 36 million people were a part of that migration. Of these, 86.6 per cent were from Europe. It is not generally known that a sizable number, approximately 30 per cent, returned. These persons are referred to as "birds of passage," and some made several trips back and forth across the Atlantic. Often the immigrant (almost always male) wished to return to his homeland after he had accumulated a financial nest egg in America. But, alas, by the time he was able to return, he had been so acculturated to life in America that he was no longer comfortable living in the country of his birth. Often such persons returned to America.

During the heavy migration between 1896 and 1915, 60 per cent of the arrivals were from three countries—Austria, Italy, and Russia. Prior to 1899, records on nationality were not kept by the U.S. Immigration Service. Therefore, arrivals from Austria might have been Germans,

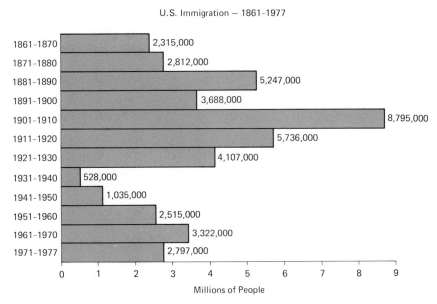

U.S. Immigration — 1861-1977

1861-1870	2,315,000
1871-1880	2,812,000
1881-1890	5,247,000
1891-1900	3,688,000
1901-1910	8,795,000
1911-1920	5,736,000
1921-1930	4,107,000
1931-1940	528,000
1941-1950	1,035,000
1951-1960	2,515,000
1961-1970	3,322,000
1971-1977	2,797,000

Millions of People

FIGURE 3. In the years between 1890 to 1929, would you say that the massive number of immigrants presented greater educational problems for the rural or urban areas? Is that still true today? How do you explain the sharp drop in immigration during the years 1930–1939? (Source: Table 120, *Statistical Abstracts of the United States, 1978,* U.S. Department of Commerce.)

Czechs, Slavs, Poles, Croatians, Moravians, Austrians, Hungarians, Slovenes, or other national groups residing within the Dual Monarchy of Austria-Hungary. In 1870 *half* the people living in Chicago were foreign born and 75 to 80 per cent of the city's population were of foreign stock—meaning that they or their parents were born outside the United States. As late as 1920, 40 per cent of the people living in this country were of foreign stock. Cities such as New York, Chicago, Pittsburgh, Milwaukee, Cleveland, Detroit, and St. Louis might have had fifty or more ethnic groups living in them.

The influx of people from abroad, mainly from southern and eastern Europe, gave rise to deep-seated feelings of resentment against the immigrant people. This eventually resulted in the restrictive Immigration Act of 1924. A few citations will help the reader appreciate the ill feeling toward the immigrant that prevailed at the time. Beginning in 1888, we see genuine concern and apprehension expressed by James Bryce in *The American Commonwealth:*

> Within the last decade new swarms of European immigrants have invaded America, drawn from their homes in the eastern part of Central Europe. There seems to be a danger that if they continue to come in large numbers they may retain their low standards of decency and comfort, and menace the continuence among the working class generally of that far higher standard which has hitherto prevailed in all but a few spots in the country.

On July 24, 1910, the Butte, Montana, *Evening News* published a full front-page story entitled "The Story of the Butte Bohunk." Notice that in the following excerpts from that story the group referred to is considered nonwhite:

> Butte, thrice cursed after its years of pride and prosperity, writhes under a malady which only the white light of publicity will help.
> . . . This story tells of the bohunks, three thousand strong, who are driving the white man slowly but surely out of the camp. Many never saw a bohunk; they only know that the breadwinner is out of a job and some mysterious form of foreigner has taken his job.
> . . . There are 3,000 bohunk miners in Butte today. Of these 2,175 are working and the balance are being supported by their brothers and are ready to slip into every job where a white man is laid off.
> . . . The bohunk miner is a low-grade foreigner who buys his job from

the foreman and pays him for keeping it; who lives in a cabin; who never adapts himself to American life anymore than does a Chinaman.

Then in the *Southern Labor Review* of October 24, 1928, just prior to the presidential election:

> Al Smith is against the present immigration laws. It took years of fighting to get this (1924) law passed. It excludes the dago, wop, polak, and other undesirable classes from any dangerous competition with American labor. For instance, under the present law, Italy is limited to 3845 immigrants per year. In 1923, the year before the unrestricted immigration law was passed, Italy sent us 265,000 undesirable Italians.

These excerpts are by no means atypical of public comment of the time in which they appeared. With the number of people involved, the ethnic element was, and to some extent still is, an important consideration in all decision-making concerning public policy. Most of our institutions—educational, social, political, religious—have been profoundly affected by the ethnic factor.

All of the evidence we have suggests that ethnic identity has strong staying power. In 1972 the *World Almanac* cites census data showing that out of a population of 200 million people, only 17,635,000 failed to report their ethnic identification. Over 91 per cent reported belonging to some ethnic group. Only 9.6 per cent reported belonging to the English ethnic group.

By rallying around an issue of common concern, groups having ethnic identity find a way to achieve political and social goals. There is no question that ethnic groups have been and continue to be powerful political forces. Politicians are very sensitive to the concerns of the Jewish block, the Catholic block, the black vote, the Slavic vote, and so on. Undoubtedly, President Ford's misstatement concerning the independence of Poland during the 1976 presidential campaign lost him votes. It is well known that Mr. Carter won the election because of the substantial support of black voters.

It is said that the country of Czechoslovakia was conceptualized and its constitution written in Pittsburgh. Then political pressure was brought to bear on President Wilson and Congress to make it become a reality. More recently, we have seen foreign policy decisions made because of pressure from ethnic constituents. The arms embargo against Turkey in 1975 was the direct result of pressure brought by Greek-Americans. David Danzig stated that "Roosevelt made the religio-ethnic group viable and relevant; Kennedy made it respectable."[10]

The recent resurgence of interest in ethnic heritage can also be explained in part in terms of a psychological need for identity. In the past, *to Americanize* meant "to Anglicize," that is, to be assimilated. "Leave your Old World ways behind you," was the appeal. "You never go back." In many ways this was more difficult for the immigrant's children and grandchildren than it was for the immigrant. Whereas the immigrant could be securely ensconced in the ethnic world of the ghetto neighborhood, the children had to contact the outer world through school attendance, serving in the armed forces, and seeking employment beyond the local neighborhood.

There can be little doubt that assimilation has been related directly to equality of opportunity. Ethnic groups that were easily assimilable were always the preferred immigrants. Opportunity meant that one had to discard one's ethnic ways and participate in the common culture. Consequently, the ethnic would often take drastic measures to hide his or her ethnicity. For instance, light-complected blacks might move to another part of the country and redefine themselves as white. This is called crossing the color line and applies to all persons of color, not only blacks. A Jew could become a Christian convert, preferably a Protestant. A Catholic might become a Protestant and a Mason, and many did for political and economic reasons.

Name changes were very common at the time of immigration or when the person became a naturalized citizen. In some instances, the immigration officers encouraged name changes because the immigrant's name was not sufficiently "American." The conversation might go something like this:

What is your name?

My name Milada Kadleckova.

That's not a good American name. You will be Mildred Walters.

---

[10] David Danzig, "The Social Framework of Ethnic Conflict in America" (New York: National Consultation on Ethnic America, n.d.), p. 14.

Or:

What is your name?

My name Vladamir Wisniewski.

How do you expect anyone in this country to pronounce a name like that? Let's call you Peter Howard.

Name changes provide a fascinating study of immigrant history. There are numerous cases of the same names being spelled in five or six different ways. The following is a documented case out of Montana; the reference is to the exact same individual: Dr. Dechman, Deckman, Dieckman, Dykeman, Dyckman, Dickman. In another case, the surname was Mulherin or Mulheron or Mulheren or Mullhern. In any case, the man had a creek named after him, and the name came out on the geological survey and forest service maps as Mal Heron—two words! Commonly, names were Anglicized by translating them into English language words, for example, Franco Capabianco to Frank White, Vaclav Cherney to James Black, Jan Kovar to John Smith, Angelo Campagnia to Angie Bell, and Jiri Rybar to George Fisher.

But when one changes his or her identity, it is always done at considerable risk. First there is the risk of being discovered. There is also the risk of marginality, not ever really being able to be one's true self. There is also the risk of losing one's identity altogether. Little wonder that third or fourth generation descendants of immigrants are today seeking to find out who they really are.

It is significant that the Alex Haley book *Roots* and the television program based on it were so enthusiastically accepted in our time. It articulates an unfulfilled need within us all to know who we are. Through ethnic identity we learn who we are, and this seems important to us psychologically. So today we see third and fourth generation Americans, now socially and financially secure, searching the little peasant villages and graveyards of eastern and southern Europe for traces of their forebears—their "roots." The yearning to know something about one's ancestry is very strong indeed. Robert Frost was probably right when he said, "Home is the place where, when you've got to go there, they've got to take you in." Ethnic identity is something like that.

101

THE ETHNIC LEGACY

How does one assess this social movement in America in terms of its implications for education? Clearly, there are both desirable and un-wholesome potentials in the present emphasis on pluralism. There can be no doubt that ethnic diversity contributes to the richness of cultural life in this country. We have been able to benefit from the contributions of *all* the world's cultures, and thus all of us can exercise a broader choice in the way we lead our lives. No other nation on earth can claim such diversity of origins. Lydio Tomasi put it well when he wrote:

> The United States got a good deal more out of immigration than just people. It acquired an "immigrant culture" brought over by the "huddled masses," no matter how tired and poor they were.[11]

An undue emphasis on diversity, however, without proper attention to participation in the common culture could create problems of enormous complexity for the country in terms of interethnic rivalry and strife. Diversity is not an easy condition with which to deal. Building multiple but not competing loyalties is possible but difficult. Most areas of the world where separatist movements succeeded have experienced much conflict. The notion of a multiplicity of ethnic groups living in their own little enclaves, speaking their own languages, educating their children in their own way is sheer fantasy. Even if such an arrangement were possible, most Americans would not choose to live that way. Today our mass media help to disseminate the popular culture and common values, making it very difficult for persons to isolate themselves from the mainstream culture. The fact is that even though the melting pot idea has fallen into disfavor in recent years, much has happened to break down ethnic barriers more thoroughly and form a more integrated society. Thomas Sowell speaks to this point:

> Attitude surveys showed major reversals of public opinion on race and ethnicity, and rising rates of intermarriage further substantiated these changes. More than 40 per cent of all Japanese-American men now marry women who are not Japanese-American, and more than half of all Irish-American, German-American, and Polish-American married men are mar-

[11] Lydio F. Tomasi, "The Ethnic Factor in the Future of Inequality" (New York: Center for Immigration Studies, 1973), p. 3.

ried to women outside their own respective ethnic groups. *Ironically, the once popular concept of America as a "melting pot" is now sweepingly dismissed by intellectuals at a time when it is closer to reality than ever before.*[12] [italics added]

How this society deals with its newly discovered pluralism will tell the story of whether this third century of our nation's growth will be characterized by mutual respect among diverse ethnic groups or whether the ethnic emphasis will simply nurture the seeds of dissension, conflict, and the striving for the achievement of self-interest goals. This challenge was articulated by President Carter in his acceptance of the nomination as his party's standard bearer in the 1976 election:

> We can have an America that encourages and takes pride in our ethnic diversity, our religious diversity, our cultural diversity, knowing that out of this pluralistic heritage has come the strength and vitality and creativity that has made America great and will keep us great.

SEX ROLES AND SEXISM

The terms *sex roles* and *sexism* have become popular in recent years because they are closely associated with the national movement to gain civil rights and equality of treatment for women. This movement has received much attention in the popular press as a result of the proposed Equal Rights Amendment (ERA), promoted largely, but not exclusively, by women's groups. Sex-related issues also have come to the attention of the public because of the openness with which sexual preferences are now being expressed—homosexuality, lesbianism, transvestism, bisexuality, and other variants. We are concerned here with sexism only in terms of a practice that results in the making of invidious distinctions between and among human beings solely on the basis of their gender, which, in turn, affects the kind of education they receive or the kind of treatment accorded them in school. Like racism, sexism can be overt or covert, benign or malicious, individual or institutional.

It is important to make a distinction between *sex* and *gender*. Sex has to do with the organic, biological, or physiological identity of a

---

[12] Thomas Sowell, "Ethnicity in a Changing America," *Daedalus* 107 (Winter 1978): 213.

human being, which in all cases would obviously be either male or female. Biological sex differences can be attributed to genetics, that is, chromosome differences, hormonal secretion, and anatomical structure. Gender, on the other hand, is a social and cultural concept relating to the way a society differentiates between males and females on the basis of the roles they play, the behavior that is expected of each, and the attributes ascribed to what might be called an "ideal type." What is masculine and what is feminine are gender differences defined by a society. Moreover, such definitions undergo revision from time to time as has been happening in the United States in recent years. The important point to make here is that the sex roles that are assigned to individual human beings are less of a biological imperative than that of a product of socialization, cultural conditioning, and learning.

Even the most cursory analysis of social policies makes it abundantly apparent that males and females have not shared equally in the benefits that flow from those basic values articulated in our great documents of freedom—equality, liberty, social justice. The case is too well documented to need repetition here. Women in this country did not even have the right to vote in national elections until August 1920, when the Nineteenth Amendment became the law of the land. But even that did not end discrimination against women in business, in the professions, in political affairs, in marriage contracts, and in education. Those who are concerned about this deficit in social justice point to the need to revise early socialization and education experiences of children if sexist attitudes and behaviors are to be reduced.

There have been numerous studies that document the claim that greater social value is assigned to male sex-role stereotypes with a corresponding devaluation of traits considered positive for females.[13] These attitudes are institutionalized to the extent that females themselves internalize devalued images of themselves as compared with males. Young children learn adult sex-role stereotypes of the culture and project those to themselves as self-concepts. As a result, not only boys but girls as well internalize more positive, valued, confident, and competent images of male sex roles than of female sex roles. Critics claim that textbooks, counseling procedures, grouping policies, and other school practices

---

[13] Kathryn Phillips Scott, "Elementary Pupils' Perceptions of Reading and Social Studies Materials: Does the Sex of the Main Character Make a Difference?" (Ph.D. diss., University of Washington, 1977), Chapter 2.

104

often teach or reinforce biased attitudes and behaviors, thereby contributing to the problem rather than to its solution.

Discrimination on the basis of sex in public education is illegal. Individuals are protected from such discrimination by the equal protection clause of the Fourteenth Amendment (Section 1 ". . . nor deny to any person . . . equal protection of the laws"); by Titles VI and VII of the Civil Rights Act of 1964, which expressly forbid discrimination on the basis of sex; by state laws and state constitutions; and in education specifically by Title IX of the Education Amendments, a law passed by Congress in 1972. Title IX prohibits sex discrimination in educational programs receiving federal financial assistance, which, in effect, means all public schools, colleges, and universities in the land. The intent of the law is clearly stated in its opening statement:

> No person in the United States shall on the basis of sex be excluded from participation in, be denied the benefits of, or be subjected to discrimination under any education program or activity receiving Federal financial assistance . . .

This law, Title IX, was first introduced in Congress in 1971 as an amendment to the Civil Rights Act of 1964. After congressional deliberation, it emerged as Title IX of the Education Amendments of 1972 and was signed into law on June 23 of that year. It was implemented by the Department of Health, Education, and Welfare* in June 1975. Title IX is similar to Title VI of the Civil Rights Act of 1964, except that Title IX applies only to education, is limited to sex discrimination, and includes employment.

The most widely publicized provisions of Title IX are those having to do with athletics. As originally set forth, guidelines called for such factors as these:

- whether the sports selected reflect the interests and abilities of both sexes.
- provision of supplies and equipment.
- game and practice schedules.

---

* Historical reference is made here and in several other places in this text, to the Department of Health, Education, and Welfare. Since the new Department of Education was activated in the spring of 1980, the old Department of HEW has ceased to exist and many of its programs and activities are now under the purview of the new department.

- travel and per diem allowance.
- coaching and academic tutoring opportunities and the assignment and pay of coaches and tutors.
- medical and training services.
- housing and dining facilities and services.
- publicity.

Institutions were required to provide equal opportunities in each of the categories listed, but equal expenditures in each category were not required.

Unfortunately, the guidelines under which Title IX is administered are sufficiently ambiguous to have invited several court challenges as to their constitutionality. Challenges to various provisions of Title IX have succeeded in federal district courts in Colorado, Wisconsin, Ohio, Pennsylvania, Tennessee, and Michigan. The power of this law is additionally weakened by its having to rely exclusively for enforcement on the Office of Civil Rights of the Department of Education. An individual citizen cannot file a private suit under Title IX. Some have suggested that the enforcement of Title IX should be given to the Justice Department. Revision and clarification are needed if Title IX is to be a potent weapon in the war on sex discrimination in public schools.

Title IX did not concern itself with sex bias and sex-role stereotyping in textbooks and other instructional materials, and many were disappointed that it did not address itself to these important issues. In the early 1970s a number of studies were conducted examining the treatment of women in textbooks. Undoubtedly, the study most frequently cited is the one conducted by Women on Words and Images (WOW) in 1972.[14] This extensive study surveyed 134 elementary school readers from fourteen different publishers and found a wide discrepancy in the representation of males and females in the 2,760 stories examined. Findings were typical of surveys of this type conducted at that time: The ratio of boy-centered stories to girl-centered stories was five to two. Male adult main characters outnumbered female adults by a three-to-one margin. Only three stories presented mothers working outside the home. Valued traits such as ingenuity, creativity, bravery, perseverance, achievement, adventurousness, curiosity, sportmanship, autonomy, and self-respect were assigned to boy characters rather than girls on a four to one ratio. The study found

[14] Women on Words and Images, *Dick and Jane as Victims: Sex Stereotyping in Children's Readers* (Princeton, N.J.: Women on Words and Images, 1972).

sixty-seven stories in which one sex demeaned the other; in sixty-five of these it was the girl who was ridiculed or demeaned. The neglect of girls and women in children's books was a frequent finding in studies conducted in the early 1970s.

At the high school level, the situation was similar. In 1971, Janice Trecker reported a study of women in United States history books used in high schools.[15] She reported finding little information on the roles of women during the colonial and pioneer periods, times when women had to have played vital and demanding roles if their families were to survive. She found minimal coverage—less than a full page—on suffrage and women's rights. She indicated that

> Texts omit many women of importance, while simultaneously minimizing the legal, social, and cultural disabilities which they faced. The authors tend to depict women in a passive role and to stress that their lives are determined by economic and political trends. Women are rarely shown fighting for anything; their rights have been "given" to them.[16]

Has the situation improved in the decade since many of the surveys of textbooks and instructional materials were conducted? We do not have a data-based response to that question. However, with the awareness building that has taken place, with the demand for greater equity by women, with judicial and legislative intervention, with the sensitization of publishers to sexism and sex-role stereotyping, we can assume that more equitable and balanced presentations appear today than was the case a decade ago. Careful scanning of reading and social studies textbooks would suggest that this is the case.

In a study of teacher education textbooks reported in 1979, Myra Sadker and David M. Sadker report finding widespread sex bias in the most popular teacher education textbooks.[17] These researchers report that of all twenty-four teacher education texts analyzed,

- Twenty-three give less than 1 per cent of space to the issue of sexism.

---

[15] Janice Trecker, "Women in U.S. History High School Textbooks," *Social Education* (March 1971): 249–260, 338.

[16] Ibid., p. 251.

[17] Myra P. Sadker and David M. Sadker, *Beyond Pictures and Pronouns: Sexism in Teacher Education Textbooks* (Washington, D.C.: U.S. Department of Health, Education, and Welfare, n.d., released in 1979).

- One-third do not mention the issue of sexism at all. Most of the texts guilty of this oversight are in math and science—the areas where girls are likely to have achievement difficulties.
- Not a single text provides future teachers with curricular resources and instructional strategies to counteract sexism in the classroom and its harmful impact on children.[18]

Culture, tradition, prejudice, and overt discrimination conspire to foreclose and restrict educational opportunities for women. Society in general and education in particular have paid a high price for its persistence in sexist attitudes. The evidence seems clear that women themselves—at least until recent years—have adapted to these social biases with the consequent underutilization of the resources and talents of women who make up 51 per cent of the population of this country. Quite apart from the issues of social justice and humanitarianism, the educational and occupational barriers that confront women exact a heavy penalty in terms of the potential productive contributions to society by women.

STUDY AND DISCUSSION

1. List as many examples of discrimination as you can think of in any form in all walks of life. Is discrimination ever justified? How do you define discrimination? Does discrimination create minority groups?
2. Discuss in some detail the difference between racism and ethnocentrism, and indicate the implications of each for public education.
3. Provide examples of institutional racism that prevail in schools and colleges. How can the school combat institutional racism?
4. What school practices tend to perpetuate sex-role stereotyping? How does sex-role stereotyping contribute to the development of attitudes that may be prejudicial to one or the other of the sexes?
5. Describe how social policies are being affected by changing relations between racial and ethnic groups.

[18] Ibid., p. 2.

6. Some think that advanced education always creates elitism. Do you share that view? Explain. If the assertion is valid, what implications are there in this for ethnic minority groups?
7. To what extent are the problems of racism and those of sexism the same? How are they different? Why are women referred to as "the 51 per cent minority"?
8. Provide examples to illustrate that the concept of race is relevant to education only because it has social consequences.
9. It has been said that cities with vivid ethnic legacies such as New York, Cleveland, Chicago, and Milwaukee have as many as fifty or more ethnic groups. What are the most active of these groups? Would you define all of them as minority groups? Why or why not?
10. What social and cultural forces contributed to the shift in attitude toward ethnic groups as described in the excerpt from Dr. John Carpenter early in this chapter?

SELECTED BIBLIOGRAPHY

Banks, James A. *Teaching Strategies for Ethnic Studies*. 2d ed. Boston: Allyn & Bacon, Inc., 1979.

Epps, Edgar G., ed. *Cultural Pluralism*. Berkeley, California: McCutchan Publishing Corporation, 1974.

Frazier, Nancy, and Myra Sadker. *Sexism in School and Society*. New York: Harper and Row, Publishers, Inc., 1973.

Grambs, Jean Dresden, ed. *Teaching About Women in the Social Studies: Concepts, Methods, and Materials*. Bulletin no. 48. Washington, D.C.: National Council for the Social Studies, 1976.

Greeley, Andrew M. *Why Can't They Be Like Us? America's White Ethnic Groups*. New York: E. P. Dutton & Co., Inc., 1975.

Green, Robert L. *The Urban Challenge: Poverty and Race*. Chicago: Follett Publishing Co., Inc., 1977.

Havighurst, Robert J., and Daniel U. Levine. *Society and Education*. 5th ed. Part 4: "The Educational System in the Wider Society." Boston: Allyn & Bacon, Inc., 1979.

Jarolimek, John. "Born Again Ethnics: Pluralism in Modern America." *Social Education* 43 (March 1979): 204–209.

Maccoby, Eleanor Emmons, and Carol Nagy Jacklin. *The Psychology of Sex Differences*. Stanford, California: Stanford University Press, 1974.

Novak, Michael. *The Rise of the Unmeltable Ethnics*. New York: Macmillan Publishing Co., Inc., 1971.

POTTKER, JANICE, and ANDREW FISHEL, eds. *Sex Bias in the Schools: The Research Evidence* (a volume of readings). Rutherford, New York: Fairleigh Dickinson University Press, 1977.

SCIMECCA, JOSEPH A. *Education and Society*, Part III. New York: Holt, Rinehart and Winston, Inc., 1980.

STACY, JUDITH, SUSAN BEREAUD, and JOAN DANIELS. *And Jill Came Tumbling After: Sexism in American Education*. New York: Dell Publishing Co., Inc., 1974.

STOCK, PHYLLIS. *Better Than Rubies*. New York: G. P. Putnam's Sons, 1978.

U.S. DEPARTMENT OF HEALTH, EDUCATION, AND WELFARE. The National Project on Women in Education. *Taking Sexism out of Education*. Washington, D.C.: U.S. Government Printing Office, 1978.

chapter 5

Schools and the World of Work

Society depends on a constant, reliable stream of competently trained adults to fill the various work roles needed to sustain social life. These socially defined work roles are what we call "jobs." It has always been true that a society cannot exist without work because work is clearly linked to survival in the most literal sense. What is often not clear—especially in Western societies—is the vital connection between the *individual* and work. The kind of work one performs, that activity that is defined as one's job, and how it is perceived by the one doing it and by others, have profound social, economic, and psychological effects on the individual:

> Today, as in the past, our relationship to work activity is a fundamental determinant of the way we live. Our relation to work has determined and influenced our status, the kind of food available to us, our ability to buy goods, our use of time and leisure, the nature of our family and sexual relations, the state of our mental health, and an endless host of other conditions. To put it succinctly, the importance of work is and has been most pervasive; it determines what we produce, what we consume, how we live, and what type of society we create and perpetuate.[1]

[1] Fred Best, ed., *The Future of Work* (Englewood Cliffs, N.J.: Prentice-Hall, Inc., 1973), p. 1.

111

What concerns us in this chapter is the interactive relationship between and among the individual, the world of work, the larger society, and the schools.

STATUS DIFFERENCES IN EDUCATION

Historically, schooling concerned itself with academic matters rather than with practical affairs of the workaday world. The way one learned a trade, a craft, or a profession was through the apprenticeship route. In the Middle Ages craft guilds developed a system of training new craftsmen and protecting their members. A young recruit was taken on as an apprentice. After a period of two to seven years, if he knew his trade well enough, he could hire out as a journeyman. When he became skillful enough to be on his own, he qualified as a master craftsman. It is interesting and significant that the terminology of the craft guilds of the Middle Ages is used in trade unions even today.

Young people who were learning to be carpenters, cabinetmakers, bakers, printers, blacksmiths, weavers, and brewers under the apprenticeship system obviously did not have time to go to school. Nor did the children of peasants have the time or the financial resources to be able to attend school. Traditionally, the children who attended school beyond the first few years were children of well-to-do families. These families constituted the elite of the society. They were the ones who had wealth and power and, consequently, were influential in government and policy decisions. They could spend their time studying the conventional liberal arts because it was not necessary for them to learn a craft or a trade. Indeed, the life-style associated with the upper strata of society required the kinds of knowledge and skills that a curriculum in the liberal arts could provide—largely intellectual, highly verbal, heavily loaded with the arts, humanities, and philosophy.

It is not difficult to understand, therefore, why traditional academic education has carried higher prestige value than has vocational education. For hundreds and hundreds of years in Western civilization the persons who were in positions of power, who commanded respect, who were leaders in society, who were affluent, who set the standards in tastes, fashions, manners, and morals were products of an academic education. They concerned themselves with intellectual affairs. They were not persons who worked for a living in the traditional sense, and most certainly they were not persons who worked with their hands. Those who were tradesmen and craftsmen or farmers or who provided personal service to others have never been considered a part of society's elite in Western culture. The status distinction between the affairs of the head and those of the hand have a very long history.

By the time of the founding of the Republic, a few prominent persons were beginning to question this traditional separation of education and work. After all, the men and women who came to the New World, carved their homes and communities out of the wilderness, and formed a new nation worked with their hands. Physical labor was nothing new to the colonists and early settlers. There was no room for serious intellectual pursuits in the environment of the frontier, where one waged a constant battle with the surroundings simply to survive. These conditions also were instrumental in generating ideas about equality. A man who tested his strength daily against the elements had little patience with traditional social class distinctions. No less a figure than Benjamin Franklin proposed the establishment of an academy in Philadelphia that would teach and practice things that were practical and useful. His ideas presaged trends in vocational education of the latter nineteenth and early twentieth centuries.

THE RISE OF VOCATIONALISM IN EDUCATION

A number of social forces began to converge in the middle of the nineteenth century that changed the traditional relationship between schools and the world of work. The United States was rapidly developing an industrial economy, and the country was not producing workers with skills needed for those jobs. Moreover, the schools were not including experiences in the curriculum that would help young people develop the knowledge and skills needed for the factory system. During this period immigration began to increase significantly, with many of the immigrants settling in the large cities of the North and the East. Within the country, rural youth in large numbers were migrating to the urban areas. Still another factor contributing to educational change in the decades following the Civil War was the need to provide viable educational experiences for recently emancipated black children and youth. This was assumed to include learning fundamental citizenship skills along with skills needed for productive labor. In the case of the blacks, it was taken for granted that physical or manual training would be the central component of work skills.

Thus, in the period following the Civil War, we see increasing interest in practical education, focusing on knowledge and skills needed for the work world. Manual training, introduced about 1880 and popularized by John Dewey and the Progressive Movement in the early part of this century, spread rapidly throughout the country. Also, early in this century, American business became alarmed about the growing industrial potential of Germany. Fearing the threat of competition presented by German industrial development, the American business community promoted the development of trade and vocational schools. By 1920 the curriculum of most schools in the country included some work in the practical, manual arts.

It is significant to note that major goal statements for American education have called for the inculcation of habits, attitudes, knowledge, and skills associated with productive labor. The NEA Commission on the Reorganization of Secondary Education in 1918 listed "vocation" as one of the Seven Cardinal Principles of Education. Twenty years later, in 1938, the Educational Policies Commission made "economic efficiency" one of its four broad goals of education. In recent years, a number of educational and political leaders of national prominence have spoken out forcefully on the need for education to concern itself with the career goals of students. One of the most articulate and enthusiastic promoters of vocational education in recent years has been Dr. Sidney P. Marland, Jr. As U.S. Commissioner of Education, he first introduced the concept of "career education" in 1971 in an address at the annual meeting of the National Association of Secondary School Principals in Houston:

> I suggest we dispose of the term *vocational education*, and adopt the term *career education*. Every young person in school belongs in that category at some point, whether engaged in preparation to be a surgeon, a brick layer, a mother or a secretary.

> All education is career education, or should be. And all our efforts as educators must be bent on preparing students either to become properly, usefully employed immediately upon graduation from high school or to go to further formal education. Anything else is dangerous nonsense. I propose that a universal goal of American education, starting now, be this: that

114

every young person completing our school program at grade 12 be ready to enter either higher education or useful and rewarding employment.

Of those students currently in high school, only three out of ten will go on to academic college-level work. One-third of those will drop out before getting a baccalaureate degree. That means that eight out of ten present high school students should be getting occupational training of some sort. But only about two of those eight students are, in fact, getting such training. Consequently, half our high school students, a total of approximately 1,500,000 a year, are being offered what amounts to irrelevant, general education pap![2]

Several significant pieces of federal legislation encouraged the growth of practical trade and vocational education. The Morrill Act of 1862, discussed in Chapter 2, supported the development of vocational and agricultural education at the college level. The provisions of this legislation were expanded in the Second Morrill Act of 1890, which provided additional funding to land grant colleges that offered instruction in what was called the "industries of life." Agricultural and vocational education were encouraged by the Hatch Act of 1877, which established agricultural experimental stations. Congress passed the Smith-Lever Act in 1914, which established the agricultural extension program and authorized the Commission on National Aid to Vocational Education. Many of the recommendations of the commission were incorporated in the Smith-Hughes Act of 1917. This act provided financial assistance to schools *below* the college level that provided job training for youth over the age of fourteen. It is generally recognized that the Smith-Hughes Act clearly committed the federal government to the support of vocational education. Because this act sharply delineated vocational from general education, it exacerbated the long-standing conflict between those who championed traditional academic education and those who supported general education. The George-Reed Act of 1929 and the George-Ellzey Act of 1935 expanded provisions of Smith-Hughes; and the George-Deen Act of 1937 funded programs in retailing, wholesaling, storing, transporting, and similar distributive services. The George-Barden Act of 1946 further expanded benefits to vocational education initiated under earlier legislation.

In more recent years the most significant pieces of legislation dealing with vocational education were the Vocational Education Act of 1963 and the Revised Vocational Education Act of 1968. The 1963 act greatly

[2] Sidney P. Marland, Jr., *Career Education Now*, NASSP Bulletin, vol. 55, no. 355 (May 1971), pp. 2–3.

broadened the occupational categories that were eligible for support. It also extended the population that could be served to (1) high school students, (2) dropouts or those who left school, (3) those who were employed but needed training or retraining, and (4) those who had special needs that could not be met by the regular vocational education program. Funds were also authorized for the construction of area vocational schools, a totally new provision for the support of vocational education. The Vocational Education Amendments of 1968 completely abolished traditional occupational categories and further extended services to groups not previously served, including handicapped persons and professionals.

THE REASONS PEOPLE WORK

Conventional wisdom tells us that people find work loathsome, a drudgery to be avoided whenever possible, an unfortunate penalty that is extracted as the price for becoming a mature, responsible adult. Perhaps everyone has had flights of fancy when one longs for that marvelous hobo land of the "Big Rock Candy Mountain" where one's needs are adequately cared for without engaging in Adam's curse: "By the sweat of your face shall you get bread to eat" (Genesis 3:19). But is this what people in this culture really want? Given a choice, would most adults prefer a life of inactivity and indolence to one that would subject them to the demands of hard work? Do people work only to satisfy their material needs of life, or is there something more to the phenomenon of work?

The meaning of work has been variously given to suit the philosophy and fancy of the writer. A popular view is that the "curse of work" concept prevailed among the civilizations of antiquity. A careful analysis of historical sources, however, suggests strongly that such was not the case. Although some authors cite sources that show that the early Greeks viewed work as demeaning and the Hebrews saw it as a curse, others argue that "both societies have traditions affirming work as basic to humanity and as a religious command. Likewise, both societies are aware of the difficulties and tribulations of work."[3]

[3] Francis Schussler Fiorenza, "Work and Critical Theology," in *A Matter of Dignity: Inquiries into the Humanization of Work*, ed. W. J. Heisler and John W. Houck (Notre Dame: University of Notre Dame Press, 1977), p. 31.

It seems reasonable to assume that in preliterate societies people worked in order to survive. Moreover, the levels of technology and agricultural development being what they were then, it is safe to say that doing work to meet the basic needs of life must have occupied most of the waking hours of those early people. It is doubtless true that the "golden rule of work" was applied long before it was articulated by St. Paul in his second letter to the Thessalonians (3:10): "anyone who would not work should not eat." Some sixteen centuries later, Captain John Smith locked the common storehouse of the Jamestown Colony and declared, "Only those who work shall eat." When it comes to a choice between not eating and working, history clearly shows that people will almost always choose to work!

The economic value of work is readily perceived, but why do people persist in working way beyond what is required to meet survival needs? Why do people continue to work when they have already met economic goals that would ensure comfortable retirement living for several lifetimes? The fact is that it is impossible to separate work from life. The excerpt at the beginning of this chapter illustrates this relationship vividly. In our society *everyone* (or at least *almost* everyone) works, has worked, or will work. Even the sons and daughters of this country's most wealthy and prestigious families work. In recent years, mandatory retirement laws are being revised in order to permit individuals to continue to work beyond age sixty-five. Harold Wilensky was doubtless correctly reflecting the attitudes of many Americans when he asserted that "employment remains a symbol of one's place among the living."[4]

Many basic American values, which emerged in the life-styles of the people of the colonial period, are related in one way or another to the work ethic. These attitudes and values regarding the work ethic trace their origins at least as far back as medieval European Catholicism and perhaps even earlier. Indeed, it is St. Benedict in the sixth century who coined the expression *Laborare est orare*—to work is to pray—as a way of motivating his idle monks to work. Centuries later this sanctification of labor was promoted by the Protestant religious leaders Martin Luther, John Wesley, John Calvin, and others. Transported to the English colonies of the New World, the concept of work as a religious imperative came to be known as the "Protestant Ethic." The relationship between

---

[4] Harold L. Wilensky, "Varieties of Work Experience," in *Man in a World at Work*, ed. Harry Borow (Boston: Houghton Mifflin Company, 1964), p. 148.

the work ethic and the growth of competitive capitalism is discussed in the seminal work of Max Weber under the title *The Protestant Ethic and the Spirit of Capitalism.*[5]

The Puritans in colonial America fully exploited the religious basis of the work ethic. It was through work that one gained status among the elect. Idleness was considered sinful and could lead only to evil. One was to approach one's work with diligence and as a duty. The products of one's work were to be invested in some productive enterprise and were not to be flaunted. Sloth, idleness, and the flaunting of wealth were considered displeasing in the eyes of the Lord. Diligence, frugality, and dedication to work, on the other hand, were seen as valued traits. Many of these same attitudes and values were reinforced in the American mentality once again in the nineteenth century in the *McGuffy Readers.* These basic reading books reached a circulation of 100 million by 1900, and their moralizing undoubtedly had great impact on American thought regarding work, use of time, use of money, and similar values. Even today such descriptors as loafer, slacker, lazy lout, good-for-nothing, idler, shirker are considered highly pejorative. No one would hire a person who is described as one of those!

Another tradition of the work ethic also was incorporated in the American value structure, that being derived from the guild system of Western Europe. It differed in significant ways from the religious conception of work, yet the two were compatible. This second concept of work has to do with the notion of craftsmanship. One did not have to despise what one did; one could enjoy doing it. There can be intrinsic value found in one's work. One can take pride in the product of one's labors. An artist or a craftsman can be so well pleased with his or her work that he or she is willing to identify it by signature. There is obviously a very close linkage between the worker and the product under this arrangement. Today this can be observed in items that are "custom built," in paintings and other works of art, in clothing that is individually tailored.

In colonial America there were many such craftsmen, some of them known even today. Paul Revere, for example, was well known as a silversmith and would have been remembered even if he had not made his

---

[5] Max Weber, *The Protestant Ethic and the Spirit of Capitalism,* trans. Talcott Parsons (New York: Charles Scribner's Sons, 1958).

famous ride. The name Duncan Phyfe is still used to characterize a particular style of furniture and carries the name of the American craftsman of Scottish descent; it was the first furniture made in America distinctive enough to carry its maker's name. Eli Whitney was also such a craftsman even though his fame was achieved in developing the assembly-line concept and through the invention of the cottin gin. The names Colt, Winchester, and Remington are well known to anyone familiar with firearms and bear the names of their originators. This concept of work is symbolized in the Longfellow poem "The Village Blacksmith."

Historically, therefore, work has been an important part of the American experience from the very beginning. The two traditions out of which the American work ethic is derived have left their mark on the American mentality and on its culture. There are countless folk songs and ballads that speak of work—in the mines, in the cotton fields, on the lone prairie. Similarly, the theme of the boy or girl of humble beginnings, perhaps an immigrant, who through hard work and dedication has achieved fame and fortune, has been a favorite theme in American literature. Work as represented in art forms has been very popular from Currier and Ives to Thomas Hart Benton. The concept of a social debt that one incurs by reaping the benefits of society and having to repay it by doing work that is socially useful, although not overtly expressed, often seems to influence the behavior of Americans.

There is no single or simple answer to the question, "Why do people work?" Some work simply and only to meet the material needs and wants of life—not only food, clothing, and shelter, but new golf clubs, a second television set, a boat, a camper, ski equipment, a pickup truck, or a vast cornucopia of creature comforts. Others work out of a sense of social service. For whatever reason, they feel a need to devote their lives to the service of other human beings. Some work in order to provide for a secure retirement in their later years. Still others work because they find the intrinsic values of work to be satisfying. They simply enjoy working. For them work, like virtue, is its own reward. No doubt, others work simply out of habit, and some work to satisfy other kinds of psychological needs. Individual human beings can perform the same tasks in what they do as work, yet perceive what they are doing and why they are doing it in a totally different way, as is illustrated by the following story about three men who were breaking up rocks. When the first one was asked what he was doing, he replied, "Making little ones out of big ones"; the second

119

said, "Making a living"; and the third, "Building a cathedral."[6] Could each be providing an accurate response?

PSYCHOLOGICAL DIMENSIONS OF WORK

Many years ago the psychologist Gordon Allport developed the concept of "functional autonomy of motives."[7] This idea has to do with the fact that many of our motives for behaviors and habits, which originally had a functional purpose, have long since lost that purpose or it has been obscured, but we continue to engage in those behaviors and habits anyway. The boy whose family had to have a vegetable garden during the Great Depression in order to survive is now a senior vice-president of a large corporation, but he continues to grow vegetables each year on his suburban estate. A woman who was placed on a swimming program in her mid-twenties in order to overcome a physical disability swims regularly at age fifty even though her physical problem was corrected in a matter of a couple years. The activity has developed a "functional autonomy" from its original purpose, yet people continue to engage in those activities because they fulfill other physical, psychological, or social needs.

There are many applications of this concept to the approach we take to work. A young executive will labor many hours at his job in order to come forth with a first-rate performance, thereby gaining salary increases and promotions. Year after year he spends twelve, fourteen, or more hours at his job each day, six and often seven days a week. Finally, he has "made it." He is now a senior officer of the company, but he continues to work as hard and as long as he ever did. Even on Sunday he cannot relax. He has what psychologists call "Sunday neurosis," meaning that if he relaxes and rests even at times set aside by society for just such relaxation, he feels guilty. He has a compulsion to "use his time wisely," that is, in work-related ways. He is the type who works hard even at his hobby. Such a person is called a "workaholic," indicating that work has

---

[6] John Julian Ryan, "Humanistic Work: Its Philosophical and Cultural Implications," in *A Matter of Dignity: Inquiries into the Humanization of Work* (Notre Dame: University of Notre Dame Press, 1977), p. 11.

[7] Gordon Allport, *Personality: A Psychological Interpretation* (New York: Henry Holt and Co., Inc., 1937), pp. 190–206.

become an addiction with the individual. When human beings engage in such excessive and compulsive striving behavior through their work, they run the risk of endangering their mental and physical health. They also do so at great personal sacrifice. Their home, family, community life, and friends often take second place to their work. They have become successful because of the singleness of their purpose, thereby shutting out or setting aside everything that interferes with that purpose.

There can be no question that work gives purpose and meaning to the lives of many people. Of course, people work to meet the basic material needs of life. But in today's welfare-oriented society, working to meet basic needs is not the only reason, or even the most important reason, why people work hard at what they do. People seek and achieve self-fulfillment and self-actualization through their work. Through work people satisfy a full range of esteem needs such as self-respect, self-confidence, independence, prestige, and pride. Beyond a certain level, money incentives are not by themselves very powerful in getting people to do their best work. "What people think of their labor, they think of themselves . . ."[8] Evidently, work continues to be perceived as a measure of social importance.

It is unfortunately true that the nature of work and the conditions under which it is performed in the industrial economies of today often make it difficult for the worker to fulfill psychological needs through working. The natural reward of seeing a product emerge as the result of one's own efforts is often absent. In many instances there is no product at all because the work is done in the way of a service. Service to others can, of course, be rewarding, too, but the connection between what is done and the individual being served may be remote. For instance, a person may spend eight hours a day running soiled laundry through a washing machine and dryer in a nursing home for the aged. The close linkage between the results of work and the person doing it is frequently lost in today's world of work. In recent years efforts have been intensified to find ways to reestablish that linkage, thereby making work itself more meaningful, dignified, and humane. This would seem to be a critical necessity, considering the relationship between mental health and work:

> The only happy people I know are the ones who are working well at something they consider important. . . . this [is] universal truth for all my self-

[8] Carl B. Kaufmann, *Man Incorporate* (Garden City, New York: Doubleday & Company, Inc., 1967), p. 65.

actualizing subjects. They [are] metamotivated by meta-needs . . . expressed in their devotion to, dedication to, and identification with some great and important job. This was true for every single case . . .[9]

A great deal has been said and written about increased job dissatisfaction in recent years. This is a controversial issue, but if one is to believe the sizable number of studies done on this subject over the last twenty years, the percentage of the labor force reporting job satisfaction has remained relatively constant at about 80 per cent.[10] The alleged job dissatisfaction of "exploited" workers has been a popular theme of social reformers since the writings of Marx and Engels in the last century. But one survey after another suggests that in America, at least, these allegations have been exaggerated. The attitude of many Americans that their work should be something more than a job for which one earns money to pay bills is succinctly stated by Rosabeth Moss Kanter:

> Work, then, may still be important to Americans for self-respect and meaning in life—but not just any work, and not under just any conditions. For a sizable segment of the population, work is expected to provide more than merely material rewards, and the cost of material rewards themselves should not be too high. At the very least, work should be a source of pride, and it should contribute to the realization of cherished personal values.[11]

SCHOOLING AND ECONOMIC ATTAINMENTS

A problem that has been subjected to repeated investigations here and abroad over a period of many years has to do with the way increased schooling relates to an individual's increased earnings. At issue is not whether lifetime earnings are associated with the amount of schooling an individual receives. The positive relationship between amount of schooling and earnings is so well documented that its validity can hardly be challenged. If one asks the question, "Does advanced education pay?" on the face of it the answer would have to be a resounding "Yes!" as is illustrated by the data represented in Table 1 and Figure 4. On the basis of

---

[9] Abraham Maslow, "A Theory of Human Motivation: The Goals of Work," in *The Future of Work*, ed. Fred Best (Englewood Cliffs, N.J.: Prentice-Hall, Inc., 1973), p. 26.

[10] Rosabeth Moss Kanter, "Work in a New America," *Daedalus* (Winter 1978): 51.

[11] Ibid., p. 58.

EDUCATIONAL ATTAINMENT AND INCOME
Mean Earnings for 1977 in Dollars*

Educational Attainment	ALL RACES			BLACKS AND WHITES			
	Both sexes	Males	Females	White Males	Black Males	White Females	Black Females
Less than 8 yrs.	6,323	7,721	3,417	8,204	6,054	3,568	3,000
8 yrs. elementary school	7,512	9,356	4,219	9,548	7,365	4,334	3,612
1–3 yrs. high school	7,181	9,291	4,153	9,731	6,862	4,160	4,139
4 yrs. high school	9,012	12,092	5,624	12,377	9,332	5,604	5,837
1–3 yrs. college	9,607	12,393	5,856	12,637	10,023	5,774	6,576
4 yrs. college	14,207	18,187	7,923	18,521	12,978	7,550	9,604
5 yrs. college	19,077	22,786	10,848	23,093	16,385	10,655	12,896

TABLE 1. These data clearly show the economic value of increased education. The same source makes the following observation concerning these variables as applied to heads of households: "Family income and educational attainment of the householder have a strong positive relationship. In 1977, the median income for families maintained by householders with 8 or less years of schooling was $9,610. For families who were high school graduates, the median income was $17,110, compared to $23,410 for families with householders who had completed 4 years of college and $26,040 for families with householders who had completed 5 or more years of college." (p. 6) (SOURCE: U.S. Bureau of the Census, *Current Population Reports*, Series P–60, No. 118, "Money Income in 1977 of Families and Persons in the United States," U.S. Government Printing Office, Washington, D.C., 1979.)

such data, one would have to conclude that an education is one of the best economic investments one could make.

The education profession has not been unmindful of this relationship, nor has it been reluctant to use it as a way of promoting education. When increased funding is sought for schools, for example, the idea is often advanced that "education is not an expense; it is an investment in the nation's future." This is what is known as the "human capital" theory, which considers education to be an investment in the human resources of a nation. The quality and supply of such "human capital" is of inestimable importance to a highly industrialized society with an advanced economy. The return on that investment will not only result in a large pool of competently trained persons who will presumably produce needed goods and perform worthwhile humanitarian services but also in individuals whose incomes will be increased, thereby returning more to the cash flow of the economic system by paying increased income taxes, by consuming more goods and services, by saving more for prudent investment, and so on. When it comes to education, the idea that "more is better" has been promoted and often justified on the basis of the economic returns that increased education brings to the individual and to society.

The line of reasoning described in the foregoing paragraph leads logically to the use of education as a major weapon in the nation's efforts to reduce the debilitating effects of poverty. If people with little education have low incomes and people with much education have high incomes, why not provide everyone with a lot of education and thereby eliminate poverty? Education prepares people for jobs by helping them develop job-related skills. Therefore, why not get more people in schools for longer periods of time, teach them the skills they need, and put them to work? Once they are working, it is expected that they will become contributing members of society. Instead of being welfare recipients who depend on others to provide for them, they will take care of themselves. This simplistic approach to an exceedingly complex set of relationships has had great appeal to the public, to politicians, and even to professional educators.

The basic problem here is that events that are positively correlated in their variation are not necessarily causally related; that is, the one need not be the cause of the other's variation. To explain low income only in terms of amount of schooling is analogous to explaining reading disability by associating it with the wearing of eyeglasses. If it can be shown that most people who wear glasses read well, one solution to the growing reading problem would be to provide poor readers with eyeglasses. Of course, such a program would not eliminate reading disability any more than providing everyone with higher levels of education would eliminate poverty.

The most serious and scholarly challenge to the assumption of a direct causal relationship between higher income and increased education came from Christopher Jencks and his associates as a result of research dealing with the effects of schooling on equality.[12] There has been a great deal of controversy surrounding the findings and conclusions

[12] Christopher Jencks et al., *Inequality: A Reassessment of the Effect of Family and Schooling in America* (New York: Harper and Row, Publishers, Inc., 1972).

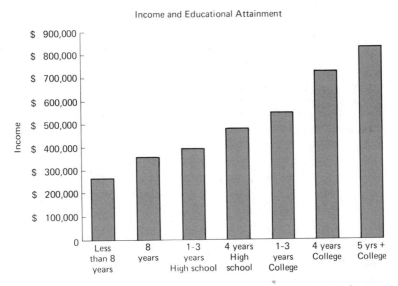

Income and Educational Attainment

FIGURE 4. Does education pay? How is that question answered in this graph that shows lifetime earnings of men from age 18 to death based on 1972 data? (SOURCE: U.S. Bureau of Census, *Current Population Reports*, Series P-60, No. 92, 1974.)

reported by Jencks. Additionally, there has been some criticism of the research procedures used. The analyses of Jencks and associates took into account those variables that are likely to extend an individual's stay in school and that, in turn, have a direct bearing on his or her income-generating potential—father's occupational status, father's IQ, educational attainment of the respondent, respondent's sixth grade test scores including IQ, and others.[13] Statistical procedures can be applied to the data to get estimates of the contribution of each of these variables to a dependent variable such as earned income. When these contributing associated variables are taken into account, the effect of "number years in school," taken by itself, is greatly diminished. Jencks and his colleagues were led to the conclusions that

> Rate-of-return estimates do tell us that efforts to keep everyone in school longer make little economic sense. The average rate of return for postsecondary education is quite low . . . Efforts to get everyone to finish

[13] Ibid., pp. 320–321.

125

high school and attend college must, therefore, be justified primarily on noneconomic grounds . . .[14]

Neither family background, cognitive skills, educational attainment, nor occupational status explains much of the variation in men's income. Indeed, when we compare men who are identical in all these respects, we find only 12 to 15 per cent less inequality than among random individuals.[15]

Income also depends on luck: chance acquaintances who steer you to one line of work rather than another . . .[16]

The Jencks book was published in 1972, just at a time when the nation was entering another cycle of reexamining its financial investment in education. For those who were looking for evidence to justify retrenchment of the support of education, especially at the federal level in programs for the poor and the minorities, the Jencks publication provided it. If education contributed so little to an individual's income-generating potential, it could hardly be regarded as a major weapon in the arsenal in the war on poverty! There can be little doubt that the Jencks publication and the controversy it generated relating to the economic value of education had considerable impact on the formation of educational policies in the early and middle 1970s.

Now after nearly a decade since the publication of *Inequality*, the findings and conclusions are being viewed with a great deal more skepticism than they were when they were first published. Professional economists view Jencks's estimate of the correlation between education and earnings as too low. Recent studies have provided additional insights into the relationships between schooling and attainments. One cannot seriously accept the proposition that the way to overcome poverty is to raise the educational level of the poor. Neither can one discount the importance of education as a *means* of attaining higher income advantages. The truth probably is found somewhere between the optimistic views of the War on Poverty advocates of the early sixties and the pessimistic views as reflected in *Inequality* in the early 1970s.

In a second book, published in 1979, Jencks and his associates report the results of an analysis of eleven major research studies focusing on determinants of individual economic success. In this book an attempt is

---

[14] Ibid., p. 224.
[15] Ibid., p. 226.
[16] Ibid., p. 227.

made to assess the impact of family background, cognitive skills, personality traits, years of schooling, and race on individual occupational status, earnings, and family income. They report that family background figures prominantly as a variable influencing economic outcomes and has the greatest relation to occupational status of any of the factors studied. The authors report a moderately strong relationship between adolescent non-cognitive traits and later economic success. They go on to say, "The best readily observable predictor of a young man's eventual status or earnings is the amount of schooling he has had."[17]

THE SOCIALIZING OF LEARNERS INTO THE WORLD OF WORK

Schools prepare young people for the work world in two general ways. First, they teach them specific job-related skills such as typing, filing, cooking, repairing cars, providing dental care, performing surgery, filling prescriptions, adjusting subluxated vertebra, and so on. Such occupation-specific skills usually come at advanced levels of schooling, perhaps as early as senior high school, but more likely at the postsecondary school level. Second, schools teach young people the attitudes, values, habits, and skills that are essential in securing and maintaining employment. These learnings begin early in the child's school experience and are taught and reinforced hundreds of times as the child moves from one grade to another. It is this second set of learnings that we will examine in this section.

Several authors have discussed the similarities of school life and the world of work.[18] It does not require great insight to see the parallel between the children as the "workers" and the teacher as the "boss" or "supervisor." This image is reinforced in many classrooms throughout the nation, especially at the elementary school level, because classrooms are

[17] Christopher Jencks and others. *Who Gets Ahead? The Determinants of Economic Success in America.* New York: Basic Books, 1979, p. 229.

[18] *See* Henry M. Levin, "Education Reform: Its Meaning?" in *The Limits of Educational Reform*, ed. Martin Carnoy and Henry M. Levin (New York: David McKay Company, Inc., 1976), pp. 23–51; Alex Inkeles, "The Socialization of Competence," *Harvard Educational Review* 36:3 (Summer 1966): 265–283; Clarence J. Karier, Paul Violas, and Joel Spring, *Roots of Crisis: American Education in the Twentieth Century* (Chicago: Rand-McNally & Company, 1973), Chapters 1 and 2.

127

managed precisely on that basis. Almost all jobs require employees to have an awareness of time. They are expected to be punctual in reporting to work and to continue to work diligently until the whistle blows. Schools also require this type of time consciousness, and tardiness has always been a sure way of earning demerits in school. Children are not supposed to waste time, for "time is money," according to traditional work ethic values. Children's report cards often had an item dealing with "wastes time" that the teacher could check if it applied. Similarly, schools require learners to do their best work. Sloppy, slipshod, and carelessly completed work is not acceptable in school anymore than it is in the world of work.

The development of attitudes, values, habits, and skills of the type discussed in the foregoing paragraph are part of the school's "hidden curriculum." They are rarely made explicit in curriculum documents, yet they are very much a part of what the school does and what it is expected to do. Employers are usually willing to teach the new hire the specific tasks demanded by the job, but they do not and will not be willing to put up with tardiness, insubordination, a lackadaisical attitude, or shoddiness of performance. The expectation is that the qualities that make for a responsible approach to one's job are developed elsewhere, usually in school. When employers secure recommendations from schools on prospective employees, they usually look for qualities of this type.

Another dimension of the hidden curriculum has to do with interpersonal relations. The individual is taught on the one hand to get along with others, to learn teamwork and cooperation skills, to build loyalty and be willing to commit oneself to a worthy cause and, at the same time, to develop attitudes of competitiveness that are needed in the work world. There is obviously some conflict in the values embraced both in school and in the business and work world—one cannot be cooperative and competitive at the same time. Much of what the school does in its extracurricular program, particularly in athletics at the secondary school level, is designed to achieve goals of this type. Some researchers have suggested that, because these programs have ordinarily excluded girls, women have been disadvantaged with regard to learning needed attitudes, values, skills, and habits that qualify them for executive and managerial roles in the business world.[19]

[19] Helen Diamond, "Patterns of Leadership," *Educational Horizons* 57 (Winter 1978–1979): 59–62.

In the area of academic learning, the most important contribution of the school to the training of young people for the work world is in the area of basic literacy skills. Perhaps this is why schools are so frequently criticized for not teaching basic skills adequately. Deficiencies in basic literacy become apparent to the employer immediately. If the applicant is required to file an application, spelling errors, handwriting, and grammatical mistakes are obvious. If the applicant is interviewed, careless enunciation, grammatical errors, and other deficiencies in verbal communication will easily be detected by the employer's personnel officer or interviewer. The same would hold true if the individual were applying to a post secondary college or vocational school. Many of these competencies have to do with communication, particularly written communication. The individual who cannot read well or who is limited in writing ability will be greatly handicapped in competing in the world of work.

THE TEACHING OF JOB SKILLS IN SCHOOLS

There has been a long-standing controversy among educators regarding the question of whether common schools, that is, elementary and secondary schools, should focus mainly on *general* education as discussed in the preceding section or should teach specific job-related skills. Sidney P. Marland, Jr. cited earlier in this chapter, clearly believes that schools should do more with vocational training, thereby preparing young people for careers in the work world. Others take a different point of view. They argue that occupations are constantly changing, that job requirements do not remain the same even for a decade, and that such school training programs would not be able to maintain currency. Moreover, they argue that most jobs do not require extensive specialized training and that the specific skills that are needed can best be learned on the job. Highly technical jobs, requiring extensive periods of training, would necessitate the trainee to attend a special school in any case. Therefore, advocates of general education believe that elementary and secondary schools should stress learnings that can be applied in many fields of work and defer specialized vocational preparation to the postsecondary level.

It is fair to say that since the early 1950s the point of view supporting general education has prevailed in this country. The ascendancy of

129

the comprehensive high school validated this philosophy. Specialized high schools, especially vocational high schools, have practically disappeared from the American educational scene. Today there are increased numbers of adult vocational schools, community and junior colleges, and proprietary schools, all at the postsecondary level, that train individuals for specific vocations. It is doubtful that this trend will be reversed in the foreseeable future although the relationship between the secondary school, the postsecondary institutions, and the world of work may undergo some realignment.

There is growing concern about the use of student time during the eleventh and twelfth grades of the senior high school. For those students anticipating long postsecondary training programs in the sciences, medicine, engineering, law, and other professions, the final year or two of conventional high school may seem to be a period of marking time. For this reason, in some urban areas high schools have developed cooperative programs with local colleges and universities that accommodate the need to challenge these students. So-called "honors" programs in high school also serve this purpose. For those students who will not be attending an academic postsecondary school, the final two years of high school may also seem to be a waste of time because of its liberal arts, general education orientation. Some schools have met the needs of these students by involving them in work experiences off the school campus for which they earn credits and money.

We are likely to see adjustments of the type described in the preceding paragraph being made with increasing frequency. The student in the junior and senior years in high school is able to move on and off the campus with relative ease. Many of them already hold part-time paying jobs. Somehow ways need to be found to relate that work experience to their school experience. Beyond that, most of what elementary and secondary schools do to prepare young people for the world of work is likely to continue to be general learnings that can be applied and transferred to many fields, along with assistance in making an intelligent choice of a vocation.

It is apparent that the efforts of reformers of the early 1970s to infuse the K–12 curriculum with a career education emphasis have not been successful. In the first place, the movement suffered from the lack of an acceptable definition of career education. Career education is often used interchangeably with occupational education and vocational education. That use of career education is not correct because an occupation or a vocation is not the same as a career. Moreover, much of the literature treats career education so broadly that it would include most of what is found in the school curriculum. The boundaries of career education are almost as extensive as those of citizenship education. Career education also suffered from too close an association with the Nixon administration's political philosophy, from a questionable set of assumptions about the social system, and from an unrealistic approach to curriculum revision. Any one of these limitations constituted a near fatal flaw and, in combination, ensured the early demise of career education as a curriculum movement.

In spite of the failings of the career education movement, it is clear that the K–12 curriculum has an obligation to acquaint students with the broad spectrum of occupations available to them and to assist them in the process of making a vocational choice. There are now over 30,000 different occupations from which to choose, yet most individuals consider only a half-dozen or so. The school must provide more information to students about the aptitudes and requirements needed to engage in various occupations. The school also has the responsibility to provide them with the necessary training to move them toward their vocational goals.

Through the years a great deal has been done to develop procedures and materials for disseminating vocational and occupational information to students. Many helpful suggestions have come out of the career education movement. The elementary school program can be designed to acquaint children with many aspects of the world of work. The social studies program is ideally suited for such an emphasis. Such awareness-building can lead to career exploration at the upper grade levels, which, in turn, leads to vocational guidance and eventually to a choice of an occupation. The choice of a vocation (or a "career") ought not to be made too early in the young person's life—the individual should be mature enough to be able to think through the consequences of the decision made. This is perhaps the strongest argument for keeping education *general* in its emphasis through the secondary school, thereby giving the student the widest possible choices in terms of postsecondary vocational paths.

THE FUTURE OF WORK AND THE SCHOOLS

Just how schools will relate to the world of work in the decade of the 1980s and beyond depends, of course, on what happens in the work world itself. On this subject we can only be speculative, although there appear to be trends and developments that provide us with clues as to its future. We have a strong tradition of work, as described here by Kaufmann, that is likely to continue to be a pervasive influence in the years ahead:

> Of the factors implicit in national growth, the one that deserves first attention is the American attitude. The country was born pro-work; and here, more than in any other major civilization, man's faith in his own perfectability became an instrument of economic improvement. Enterprise was reinforced by public sanction, on the implicit premise that it would work for the public good. Far from condemning the man of commerce or relegating him to an inferior status, society accepted and encouraged him. Technology, far from generating fear, was welcomed in America as a beneficent force, and made an ally in social and economic progress.[20]

Clearly Americans do respect work and those who engage in it. To have worked for what one has achieved has been a matter of some pride. It is a matter of public record that in this country even the most wealthy men *and* women engage in work. No one would want to be identified as being part of the "idle rich." There is no evidence that work has lost its attractiveness. Indeed, the evidence is to the contrary. Women, for example, have been entering the world of work at such a rapid rate that they now number nearly half of the work force of this nation. Rising affluence in the nation seems to have encouraged rather than discouraged individuals to work. Shorter work weeks and more time off have simply encouraged second job employment.

It is not always easy to distinguish between work and play or work and nonwork. For example, a high school choir director "works" five days a week during the school year for which he or she gets a paycheck each month. On Sundays he or she directs the church choir and conducts rehearsals of the group one night a week. For this the choir director receives no pay and admits that it is through this activity that he or she "gets his or her kicks." For the choir director, work and recreation are

---

[20] Kaufmann, op. cit., p. 96.

132

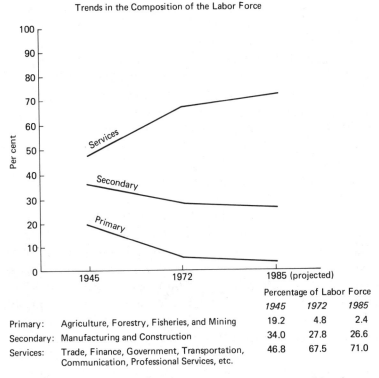

Trends in the Composition of the Labor Force

	Percentage of Labor Force		
	1945	*1972*	*1985*
Primary: Agriculture, Forestry, Fisheries, and Mining	19.2	4.8	2.4
Secondary: Manufacturing and Construction	34.0	27.8	26.6
Services: Trade, Finance, Government, Transportation, Communication, Professional Services, etc.	46.8	67.5	71.0

FIGURE 5. What implications for education are suggested by these data? (SOURCE: Herman Kahn et al., *The Next 200 Years: A Scenario for America and the World.* New York: William Morrow and Co. Inc., 1976. In *Social Policy*, November-December 1978.)

the same thing. Perhaps this is the meaning of a "busman's holiday." Perhaps, too, this is the ideal referred to by John Julian Ryan: "To work well, one must play at one's work; to play well, one must work at one's play."[21]

A number of changes have occurred—and many are presently underway—to make the conditions of work more pleasant. More is being done today than in the past to personalize work. Even in routine assembly-line production, ways are being found to help each worker identify with the finished product. Forming teams of workers to be responsible for a particular function or product seems to be an effective

[21] Ryan, op. cit., p. 18.

133

strategy in building esprit de corps and greater job satisfaction. Profit sharing also has had positive effects. There is a noticeable increase in various special benefits and entitlements that make work more attractive: trips to meetings; sabbatical leaves; educational benefits; moving expense reimbursement; medical, dental, retirement, and other fringe benefits; work schedule adjustments to individual needs; child care; and others.

In the news recently was the story of an airline's pilot who makes his home in San Francisco, commutes to New York City twice a month, and from there pilots an airliner to Hong Kong and back. Although it is *possible* today to have a job that takes one two-thirds of the way around the world twice a month, most jobs are not that dramatic and exciting. In spite of many improvements in jobs and in the work environment, many jobs are menial and stifling. This condition is likely to continue because the jobs are such that machines cannot be invented to do them. Fortunately, our economy has need for persons of many different interests, talents, and abilities. What pleases one person bores another. The great advantage that the individual has at this point in time is the luxury of *choice*. If one does not enjoy doing a particular job, he or she can, within limits, change to something else. It is not uncommon to see mid-life career shifts even among highly educated, narrowly specialized individuals.

The predictions of a few years ago that science and technology would in the near future eliminate the necessity of work were clearly exaggerated. For most persons in this country, work is likely to remain a necessity not so much to supply survival requirements but to satisfy social, psychological, and emotional needs associated with self-fulfillment. In this context, schools have a vital role to play in helping young people sort out what values relating to the world of work they are willing to embrace and for which they are willing to strive.

STUDY AND DISCUSSION

1. Provide examples of practices and customs that illustrate elitist attitudes toward individuals on the basis of institutions attended or education received.
2. In what ways are education and economic growth related? How does economic growth affect the type and length of education *individuals* receive?

3. Explain how the War on Poverty affected programs of the public schools. Why has education been perceived as such a powerful weapon in the war on poverty?

4. What are the advantages and disadvantages of having separate high schools, one being vocational and the other academic (pre-college)?

5. How do the goals and purposes of the community (or junior) college differ from those of the high school in the general area of vocational education?

6. Does a student have the right to expect the high school program to prepare him or her for a specific job? Defend your response.

7. Some critics of public vocational education have, at the same time, been staunch supporters of medical schools, law schools, and graduate schools in public universities and colleges. How do you explain this contradiction? How do you respond to the allegation that today's multipurpose university is simply a collection of vocational schools on a single campus?

8. Explain how the demand for increased education has affected the published requirements for jobs and vice-versa. Does one precede the other? If so, which one and why?

9. Study Table 1. Why do you suppose that completion of a level of education, that is, elementary school, high school, or college, results in such a marked increase in income? What reasonable explanation can you give for the higher income of black women over white women when each group has completed a high school or college education?

10. Some authors have been critical of the schools for socializing young learners for the world of work by instilling in them the attitudes, values, habits, and skills characteristic of the capitalistic business world. This, it is claimed, is little less than a scheme by the affluent elite to assure a sufficient number of docile, obedient, satisfied "worker elves" for the work force of the nation. What are your views on this subject?

SELECTED BIBLIOGRAPHY

Bailey, Stephen K. *The Purposes of Education.* Bloomington, Ind.: Phi Delta Kappa, 1976.

Berg, Ivar. *Education and Jobs: The Great Training Robbery.* New York: Praeger Publishers, Inc., 1970.

BEST, FRED, ed. *The Future of Work.* Englewood Cliffs, N.J.: Prentice-Hall, Inc., 1973.

BLAU, PETER M. and OTIS T. DUNCAN. *The American Occupational Structure.* New York: John Wiley and Sons, Inc., 1962.

BRAUDE, LEE. *Work and Workers: A Sociological Analysis.* New York: Praeger Publishers, Inc., 1975.

CARNOY, MARTIN, ed. *Schooling in a Corporate Society: The Political Economy of Education in America.* 2d ed. Part 1–B: "Equal Opportunity in the Labor Market." New York: David McKay Company, Inc., 1975.

HEISLER, W. J., and JOHN W. HOUCK, eds. *A Matter of Dignity: Inquiries into the Humanization of Work.* Notre Dame: University of Notre Dame Press, 1977.

KANTER, ROSABETH MOSS. "Work in a New America." *Daedalus* (Winter 1978): 47–78.

KARABEL, JEROME, and A. H. HALSEY, eds. *Power and Ideology in Education.* Part 3: "Education, 'Human Capital,' and the Labor Market." New York: Oxford University Press, 1977.

LEVITAN, SAR A., and WILLIAM B. JOHNSTON. *Work Is Here to Stay, Alas.* Salt Lake City, Utah: Olympus Publishing Company, 1973.

LUCAS, CHRISTOPHER J. *Challenges and Choice in Contemporary Education.* Part 4: "The New Vocationalism: Career Education." New York: Macmillan Publishing Company, Inc., 1976.

SPRING, JOEL. *The Sorting Machine.* New York: David McKay Company, Inc., 1976.

Work in America. Report of a Special Task Force to the Secretary of Health, Education, and Welfare. Cambridge, Mass.: MIT Press, 1973.

chapter 6

Equalizing Educational Opportunity

Achieving equitable educational opportunity for all America's children and youth presents society and education with one of its most profoundly complex challenges. In the past thirty years, a great deal has been done in this country to redress past social injustices and to open the doors of education to those groups who have traditionally not enjoyed the advantages that a good education can provide, namely, visible minorities, ethnic groups, and women. Through affirmative intervention, faith in America as a land of opportunity has been restored to some extent, and social mobility remains a realistic aspiration. On the other hand, the selection of individuals, for whatever purpose, on the basis of ascriptive status, that is, on the basis of group identity, is clearly contrary to the long-standing and firmly established principle that an individual should be judged on his or her own abilities, merits, and achievements. Moreover, any society needs to develop systems of selecting and placing individuals in a way that will ensure that the best-qualified individals are chosen for the various positions and statuses that need to be filled. Thus, the selecting and sorting of individuals is, and probably should remain, a competitive process.

Equalizing educational opportunity is a complicated process in any case but is made especially so in our society because of the fact that we are multisocioeconomic, multiracial, and multiethnic. Consequently, achieving educational equity becomes enmeshed in other volatile social problems such as racism, sexism, affirmative action, discrimination, reverse discrimination, and institutional racism. Legislative and judicial decisions relevant to any of these issues have consequences for educational opportunity. The reverse is also true. Accommodating the vocational aspirations of individuals and at the same time meeting the social needs of society in a nation as diverse as ours will probably never be achieved wholly to the satisfaction of everyone. It seems inevitable that there will always appear to be some measure of inequality to those least favored by the social system.

THE MEANING OF EQUALITY

We begin to learn about the principle of equality from those around us in our earliest childhood days. Young children are taught to be fair to others, to share, to be considerate—concepts clearly related to equality. In the elementary school we learn that the men who established this great nation endorsed the idea that "all men are created equal" and wrote this principle into that great document of freedom, the Declaration of Independence. This idea has since been reaffirmed countless numbers of times, most notably in Lincoln's Gettysburg Address, in which he proclaimed the nation as being "dedicated to the proposition that all men are created equal." In spite of all this rhetoric about equality, many persons would be hard put to provide a workable definition of it.

B. O. Smith and Donald E. Orlosky provide a useful analysis of this concept. For them, equality is a state of affairs in which

1. Any child is worth neither more nor less than any other child as an object of development.
2. The rules that apply to any child apply to all others alike.
3. Any child has just as good an opportunity to learn as any other child.

4. Any child acquires as much knowledge and skill as any other child.[1]

The authors refer to their first statement as "moral equality," to the second as "rules of equality," to the third as "equality of opportunity," and to the fourth as "substantive equality."

The equality principle, "all men are created equal," is understood to be an expression of a moral value. This is what Smith and Orlosky call "moral equality." If we accept moral equality as a value, and we must because our systems of law and justice as well as many ethical principles are based on it, then we must devise ways to deal with the consequences that flow from it. If, as an object of development, no child is worth either more or less than any other child, we must find ways to facilitate the development of all children. American education has tried through the years to achieve this by applying what Smith and Orlosky call "rules of equality" and "equality of opportunity." In recent years the notion of "substantive equality," meaning "equality of outcomes" and derived from socialistic social theory, has received attention as a means of achieving the principle of moral equality. These ideas need to be discussed in greater detail.

The traditional approaches to achieving educational opportunity are easy to describe. For the most part they deal with making education *available* and *accessible* to all in equal amounts. Coleman identifies four components that have been assumed to be a part of equality of educational opportunity:

1. Providing a *free* education up to a given level that constituted the principal entry point to the labor force.
2. Providing a *common curriculum* for all children, regardless of background.
3. Providing that children from diverse backgrounds attend the *same school*.
4. Providing equality within a given *locality*, since local taxes provided the source of support for schools.[2]

---

[1] B. Othanel Smith and Donald E. Orlosky, *Socialization and Schooling: The Basics of Reform* (Bloomington, Indiana: *Phi Delta Kappan*, 1975), pp. 78–79.

[2] James S. Coleman, "The Concept of Equality of Educational Opportunity," *Harvard Educational Review* 68 (Winter 1968): 9.

Coleman points out that these ideas developed out of the rural tradition in America. Quite obviously, equality of educational opportunity interpreted in this way places heavy responsibilities on the learners to avail themselves of that opportunity. The learner must be actively involved in the learning process. Therefore, it is fair to assume that the highly motivated and aggressive students are more likely to gain greater benefits from educational opportunity than those who do not have those qualities. That, however, is likely to be the case no matter what system of equalizing educational opportunity is used.

It is important to note that the traditional approaches to achieving educational opportunity stressed *sameness*. Educators and teachers like to say, "Our system treats everyone the same. I am color-blind when it comes to dealing with kids of different racial groups." If all children experience similarity of exposure to education and their achievement varies, as it always does, it can be assumed that these achievement differentials reside in variables associated with the *learner*. Some pupils work and study harder than others. In any case, the school, in this traditional view, cannot be held accountable for the lack of success of low-achieving pupils. The fault, rather, is with the pupil in not being more ambitious, more highly motivated, and more diligent in his or her studies or in Providence for not providing the child with more adequate intellectual equipment.

This view of educational opportunity has strongly influenced educational thought in this country. Even today teachers and professors are prone to blame students for their failure to learn, although the recent emphasis on accountability has tended to shift some of the responsibility to the teacher and the school. Nonetheless, the rhetoric of teachers suggests that we have a long way to go to achieve a sense of balance between teacher and learner responsibility for learning or failure to do so.

The idea of treating everyone alike is very attractive to many. It is consistent with our moral commitment to the notion that "all men are created equal," as discussed earlier. To treat some students differently from others runs contrary to our sense of fairness and justice. "Why should some children get special benefits, special privileges?" we ask ourselves. Be that as it may, when it comes to *education* and being able to take advantage of *educational opportunity*, to treat all learners alike simply ensures educational *inequality*. There is no way that children coming from a variety of home and community environments and with widely varying intellectual abilities will be able to benefit equally from identical exposures to educational experiences. Stressing *sameness* tends

140

to institutionalize inequality because some individuals and some groups are better able to take advantage of opportunities than are others. States may continue to provide "education" (that is, facilities, books, teachers, financial support) on the basis of allocating the same amount for each child for reasons of social policy or for political reasons. But when this happens, it should not be confused with providing equality in the opportunity to become educated.

There are, of course, a number of alternatives to the definition of equality as meaning "the same." Komisar and Coombs indicate that the concept of equality can also be defined as meaning doing what is "fitting" or "appropriate."[3] Applying the "fitting or appropriate" principle suggests that because of learner variables associated with environment— heredity, motivation, physical condition, psychological state, and others —learning requirements are different for different learners as individuals and even as groups. If these children are to learn effectively and efficiently, those learner variables have to be taken into account, and "fitting or appropriate" adjustments must be made. This is most apparent in the case of developing "least restrictive environments" for handicapped learners. One has little problem arguing that it is "fitting and/or appropriate" to have smaller class sizes, specially prepared teachers, special equipment, and so on, for the handicapped. The concept of individualization of instruction, which has been an accepted part of modern educational thought, if not practice, for at least fifty years, is the embodiment of the "equality as fitting or appropriate" principle.

Doing what is "fitting or appropriate," meaning individualizing learning, may mean that the methods of presentation are made fitting or suitable to the learner's style. For example, more time or less time may be allowed to complete tasks, thereby permitting the learner to proceed through the instructional sequence at his or her own pace. But the outcomes themselves may be adjusted in order to be more fitting to learner needs. The level of complexity of outcomes might be varied, the expected quality of completed tasks may vary from one learner to another, or other forms of expectations may be established in accordance with what is perceived to be learner needs.

The problem with defining equality of educational opportunity

---

[3] B. Paul Komisar and Jerrold R. Coombs, "The Concept of Equality in Education," *Studies in Philosophy and Education* 4:3 (Fall 1964), in C. Tesconi, Jr. and Emanuel Hurwitz, Jr., eds., *Education for Whom?* (New York: Dodd, Mead & Co., 1974), p. 68.

as discussed in the foregoing paragraphs is that it eventually leads to some form of segregated education. What the teacher or the school authorities may *believe* to be "fitting" may not be the case at all. In the name of doing what is fitting, students may be grouped or tracked in ways that are *convenient* for the conduct of instruction. Instead of facing up to the challenge of maintaining reasonable standards and teaching for them, school officials and teachers find it easier simply to pass children along year after year under the assumption that they are unable to learn the material anyway and that the appropriate thing to do is to promote them socially. What is being said here should not be construed as a case against the individualization of instruction. What is being stressed is that doing what *seems* to be fitting and appropriate for students can result in gross inequity. A most vivid recent example of such an actual case that came to national attention was the honor graduate from a Washington, D.C., high school who was denied admission to a local university because of inadequacy of scholarly performance. In California a nineteen-year-old graduated from high school, joined the air force, and a month later was sent home because he could not read. The same situation is doubtless repeated in one form or another hundreds of thousands of times throughout the country each year, the results of what well-meaning school officials and teachers thought to be "fitting and appropriate."

In order to avoid the pitfalls inherent in a "fitting and appropriate" approach and at the same time recognizing that treating everyone "the same" does not produce equality of educational opportunity, some educators have proposed that schools should concentrate on achieving *equality of outcomes.* This is what Smith and Orlosky refer to as "substantive equality," and, as they also indicate, it is a concept derived from the socialistic tradition. This approach to equality would allow the *methods* and *processes* of instruction to vary but would hold objectives and/or outcomes constant. Thus, some learners might be given more time to learn subject matter or skills that others could learn more quickly; some need instruction to be more tightly sequenced whereas others do not; some need more careful supervision whereas others are more self-directed; and so on. But all are expected to achieve the same objectives. According to this view, if optimum conditions of instruction prevail, there is no reason to assume that all learners cannot achieve the same outcomes.

The idea of equality of outcomes has received substantial support from the research of the highly respected psychologist Benjamin S. Bloom and has been reported in his widely cited book *Human Characteristics and School Learning*.[4] The book is based on Bloom's ten years of research on mastery learning. He does not deny individual differences, but he claims that these differences need not deter 95 per cent of all students from learning all that the school has to teach at or near the mastery level. Variations in student achievement are the result of each student's learning history and the quality of instruction received. Bloom's research represents a sophisticated, data-based analysis of the possibilities of achieving mastery learning. As such, it is an exception to most of what is said and written about achieving equality of outcomes.

The concept of equality of outcomes rests on several highly questionable and yet-to-be documented assumptions. For example, equality of outcomes assumes the following:

1. The learning environment is a major determinant of learning outcomes.

This assumption fails to take into account innate and immutable genetic differences in intellectual ability from one individual to the next.

2. All pupils are capable of achieving at the desired level.

This assumption applies, of course, if the "desired level" is set so low that the lowest achieving pupil can attain it, and this would probably not be socially acceptable as a minimum or "floor" level of achievement. The assumption might be valid for a narrow band of educational objectives such as literacy in language and mathematics; it would probably not be valid when applied to achievement tasks requiring high-level, abstract cognitive operations.

3. Education can compensate for differences in socioeconomic background.

The evidence would seem to be to the contrary, namely, that the school experience in itself cannot effectively make up for the deficiencies that are the product of poverty, racial isolation, discrimination, poor health, family instability, and other social inequities.

[4] Benjamin S. Bloom, *Human Characteristics and School Learning* (New York: McGraw-Hill Book Company, Inc., 1976).

4. All pupils will be motivated to learn.

It is, of course, true that inspired instruction can enhance the student's desire to learn and that the teacher has a responsibility to create interest where none exists. But even with the most enlightened instruction, some pupils will not be motivated to engage in school learning for any one of a great number of reasons.

SOCIAL POLICY OF EQUALITY OF EDUCATIONAL OPPORTUNITY

The social policy regarding educational opportunity that appears to be emerging in this country is one that contains elements of all three of the approaches discussed in the foregoing section. Indeed, we seem to have moved through three distinct periods in our educational history wherein each of the approaches seemed to be the dominant one. Until about 1920, our chief concern was to make education *available* to all. That goal in itself was a large order, considering that the country covered a vast area, with a large rural population and with a great many open spaces. We forget that without modern means of transportation, our present system could not operate as it does today. Thus, during the nineteenth and early twentieth centuries, we see the growth of elementary and secondary schools in every community of this vast land. School attendance was not only made convenient and accessible to all, but it was made compulsory.

But getting children to school is one thing; teaching them something meaningful once they are there is something else. As more children attended school, differences between and among them become more apparent. Moreover, the measurement and testing movement, which captured the attention of educators in the early part of the twentieth century, provided what was believed to be an objective and quantifiable assessment of learner differences. Thus, from about 1920 into the 1960s, a great deal of attention was being given to individual differences and individualizing instruction. It was in this period that we saw the rise of homogeneous grouping practices, tracking in high schools, individually guided programs, self-paced learning materials, and a great many other variations on the theme of individualizing teaching and learning. The following excerpt is typical of the orientation of sophisticated educators of that period:

> We have seen that the homogeneity of groups sufficient for uniform standards, materials, and procedures is probably unattainable. Certainly such groups cannot be achieved through general-ability grouping, judicious policies of promotion, or effective teaching. What then should be done? *Simply this: Accept the wide range of ability found in all classes as inevitable, accept it as something good, highly desirable, and necessary in this scheme of things. Then set about to find effective ways of meeting the individual needs of children in heterogeneous groups.* Modern educational thinking is quite largely devoted to this objective.[5] [italics in the original]

With the increased sensitivity to the special learning problems of minority and ethnic children that surfaced during the 1960s, the concept of equality of outcomes gained prominence. During this period, postsecondary institutions were under great pressure to enroll increased numbers of minority students. Consequently, admission requirements were relaxed enough to admit students who seemed to show reasonable potential for success but whose past school records were such that they would not be admissable. The idea was to relax admission requirements but to hold to the same exit requirements for all. Presumably, the students admitted under these arrangements would work at a slower pace, would have their work individualized, would be provided tutorial help as needed, and so on.

What actually happened, when adjustments of the type described in the foregoing paragraph were made, should have been easily predicted. Once admitted, the students were often cast adrift in the sea of academia with little attention being given to their special learning requirements. Little was done to individualize their programs, and even less was done to provide tutoring assistance. Students, therefore, failed their courses and dropped out of college or were simply given passing grades by instructors who did so out of a feeling of guilt for failing minority students. In many cases, instructors were intimidated by the minority student and thus gave such students passing grades rather than have themselves subjected to harassment and be branded "racist."

[5] Robert H. Beck, Walter W. Cook, and Nolan C. Kearney, *Curriculum in the Modern Elementary School* (Englewood Cliffs, N.J.: Prentice-Hall, Inc., 1953), pp. 46–47.

There can be no question that there was much abuse of these policies when they were first instituted. Gradually, however, the picture began to change. Public funds were made available for tutoring services and for improved counseling of these students. Additionally, improved selection and recruitment procedures were inaugurated that tended to choose students who had reasonable chances of succeeding. Also, instructors and institutions became more aware of the special problems of minorities and were more willing to individualize programs of study for them. With increased contact with minorities and a better understanding of their learning needs, instructors were less inclined to be intimidated and more able to deal with the objective reality of institutional accountability to students.

At the elementary and secondary school levels, the concept of equality of outcomes gained support from the national mood of a concern to go "back to the basics." Achievement tests based on national samples indicated declining test scores. Mastery learning, mentioned earlier, seemed to be a viable response to the concern over depressed pupil achievement. Egalitarian attitudes emerging from a growing socialistic ideology in education also put the spurs to school officials to work toward attaining equality of outcomes, even though most of them recognized that such a goal is realistically unattainable under the conditions and constraints that obtain in public education today.

COMPENSATORY EDUCATION

The concept of compensatory education grew out of the national concern for desegregation and integration. In the late 1940s and early 1950s, developments in human relations emphasized similarities rather than differences among people. The theme "people are more alike than they are different" was a popular one in promoting human relations at the national as well as the global level. This led to the practice of identifying the qualities that characterized the "ideal" type—qualities of the "ideal" American, the "ideal" citizen, student, homemaker, teacher, and so on. This practice simply underscored the fact that some Americans found it impossible to achieve "ideal" anything status because of certain obvious deficits. These "shortcomings" were interpreted as deficits because "people are more alike than different," and if they are not "more

146

alike," let us see what can be done to make them that way. Hence, compensatory education was based on a deficit theory of cultural development that emerged from the humanitarian concern over equality.

Compensatory education places great faith in education as a means of achieving social reform. In 1964, President Lyndon B. Johnson signed into law the Economic Opportunity Act. This was the first shot that was fired in what President Johnson called the "War on Poverty." Carnoy and Levin call attention to the role of education in this effort:

> if such a war was actually declared during this period, then education and training were its artillery.[6]

No doubt, Mr. Johnson's own training and experience as a teacher in Texas contributed to the prominent role that education was to play in the poverty programs of the 1960s. Clearly, equality became *the* principal pillar of social policy in the Johnson administration, and education was to play a central role in its implementation.

The rationale for compensatory education is based on the principle that appropriate intervention is justified on the basis of the presence of learner deficiencies and that such intervention will produce the desired results. Thus, preschool programs were designed to give pupils a "head start," thereby enabling disadvantaged pupils to enter first grade on an equal footing with their more advantaged classmates. Special training programs were developed to improve work skills of unemployed young adults. School busing was used to move ghetto children to more stimulating school environments in other neighborhoods. A policy of "affirmative action" was proclaimed by President Johnson himself:

> Imagine a hundred yard dash in which one of the two runners has his legs shackled together. He has progressed 10 yards, while the unshackled runner has gone 50 yards. At that point the judges decide that the race is unfair. How do they rectify the situation? Do they merely remove the shackles and allow the race to proceed? Then they could say that "equal opportunity" now prevailed. But one of the runners would still be forty yards ahead of the other. Would it not be the better part of justice to allow the previously shackled runner to make up the forty yard gap; or to start the race all over again? That would be *affirmative action* toward equality.[7] [italics added]

[6] Martin Carnoy and Henry M. Levin, *The Limits of Educational Reform* (New York: David McKay Company, Inc., 1976), p. 2.

[7] Executive Order 11246, September 1965, cited in Earl Raab, "Quotes By Any Other Name," *Commentary* (January 1972), p. 41.

From the standpoint of public policy, the expenditure of tax dollars for compensatory education is often justified on the basis of some combination of the following:

1. To prevent further isolation.

The poor and the disadvantaged, many of whom are visible minorities, are already isolated from the mainstream culture. Efforts to educate them in conventional ways have been singularly unsuccessful. Therefore, if the cycle of poverty, isolation, and alienation is to be broken, an additional effort—compensatory education—will be required.

2. As a moral issue that must receive attention in terms of simple justice.

> undeserved inequalities call for redress, and since the inequalities of birth and natural endowment are undeserved, these inequalities are to be somehow compensated for. Thus the principle holds that in order to treat all persons equally, to provide genuine equality of opportunity, society must give more attention to those with fewer native assets and to those born into the less favorable social position. The idea is to redress the bias of contingencies in the direction of equality. In pursuit of this principle greater resources might be spent on the education of the less rather than the more intelligent, at least over a certain time of life, say the earlier years of school.[8]

3. As a hedge against even greater expenditures later.

The beneficiaries of compensatory education present the greatest potential for social problems later in life—crime, drug use, unemployment, welfare, family instability, neglect of health, and so on. Because many of these persons are not able to take care of themselves, they become the responsibility of society. They are incarcerated or are on welfare or require some other type of custodial care. Many of these problems could be avoided, so the argument goes, if these persons had been educated properly as young children. Therefore, the additional money spent on compensatory programs is money well spent as a way of relieving human misery and as a way of avoiding even greater expenditures later. In this sense, compensatory education, like all education, is an investment in "human capital," on which dividends can be expected in later years.

[8] John Rawls, *A Theory of Justice* (Cambridge, Mass.: Harvard University Press, 1971), pp. 100–101.

148

4. As a search for talent.

It can be assumed that much talent lies fallow among the children of the nation's poor. Unless ways are devised to tap that talent, it will remain hidden, and the nation is the loser. Compensatory education is designed to uncover such talent. This is, of course, a responsibility that the nation's schools have. But in the case of the poor and disadvantaged, the conventional school program may be unable to tap their talents.

5. To promote the general welfare.

Compensatory education can be justified on the basis that the nation has a constitutional mandate to *promote* the welfare of its citizens. The phrase *to promote* suggests active involvement, which can be interpreted to mean affirmative action.

6. To provide equal protection as required by the Fourteenth Amendment: "nor deny any person . . . equal protection of the laws."

The argument here is that disadvantaged and poor children are not provided equal protection when they are placed in the regular school environment without some type of additional assistance. They are not able to take advantage of educational opportunities immediately in front of them because of prior debilitating conditions. This is analogous to a paraplegic who is seated across the room from a wheelchair. Even though it is *available* to him, he cannot take advantage of it without additional help.

7. As a redress of earlier wrongdoings.

This argument usually is applied to the treatment of minorities. In the past this society has treated visible minorities badly. It enslaved the blacks; it massacred the Indians and took their land; it mistreated the Chicanos and Mexican-Americans; it incarcerated the Japanese and discriminated against other Asians in employment, immigration, and so on. Now that the society has become sensitized to these earlier injustices, society has a responsibility to compensate for them. This position argues that society itself is partly responsible for putting the minority groups in the position in which they find themselves today and to that extent has a responsibility to help them improve their situation.

The concept of compensatory education seems so utterly sensible, and its rationale appears soundly based. In practice, however, there have been many doubts raised as to its efficacy. The programs that seemed to produce the best results were those that made tutoring and other special services available to highly motivated students at the postsecondary level. The Job Corps program, which provided residential training for unemployed school dropouts between the ages of sixteen and twenty-one who were in poverty, was very expensive and its results were disappointing. *The New York Times* reported on March 19, 1969, that a study of Job Corps by Congress showed that "Corps trainees did little better in the labor market than poor youth without such training." Similarly, the results of such programs as the Neighborhood Youth Corps, Upward Bound, Educational Talent Search, and Career Opportunity Program are very questionable in terms of the amount of money invested in them.

In the case of Head Start, a preschool compensatory program, we see the research of Professor Benjamin S. Bloom once again contributing significantly to educational policy. The publication of his book *Stability and Change in Human Characteristics* (1964)[9] coincided with the national concern over poverty and the education of the disadvantaged. In this book, Bloom summarized research dealing with the stability of intelligence and concluded that, in terms of intelligence measured at age seventeen, about 50 per cent of the development takes place between conception and age four, about 30 per cent between ages four and eight, and about 20 per cent between ages eight and seventeen.[10] Bloom was careful to point out that there is considerable evidence that intelligence may continue to develop into the adult years, but that citation is usually ignored when using the Bloom data in justifying the importance of preschool educational programs. Needless to say, the Bloom publication provided the advocates of preschool education powerful and convincing support for such programs.

The success of Head Start and its companion program, Follow Ihrough, is spotty.[11] What seems to come through most frequently is that these programs do not produce a reliable or lasting effect. Children in these programs usually show some initial advantage over their classmates who come from similar social environments but who have not had the Head Start experience. After two or three years in school, however, it is

[9] Benjamin S. Bloom, *Stability and Change in Human Characteristics* (New York: John Wiley and Sons, Inc., 1964).

[10] Ibid., p. 88.

[11] See "Perspectives on the Follow Through Evaluation," *Harvard Educational Review* 48:2 (May 1978): 125–192.

not possible to differentiate one group from the other on the basis of school achievement or social adjustment variables. The picture is far from complete, however, and some Head Start programs report a high degree of success with their pupils. In the Soviet Union, where preschool education is much more extensively developed than it is in the United States, the seeming failure to produce long-term effects also prevails. Again, as in the United States, initial advantage is apparent in the preschool establishment participants.

It is not possible to make an objective assessment of the concept of compensatory education as it was implemented under federal funding. Federal guidelines under which these programs operated not only spoke to their substantive aspects but also to the procedures to be followed in carrying them out. These programs were intended to achieve social goals quite different from their stated main purposes. In order to develop democratic participation and decision-making skills, executive boards governing these programs were required to have representatives of the constituencies served. Thus, poor people who lacked the ability to manage their own lives or their own financial resources suddenly found themselves in a position of making decisions concerning complex educational programs and the disbursal of thousands, perhaps even hundreds of thousands, of dollars. Staffs for these programs were often assembled quickly, and programs lacked any semblance of a theoretical base. The questionable expertise of persons in positions of responsibility for directing the programs and the extent to which they were political rather than educational make it impossible to assess fairly compensatory efforts as *educational* endeavors.

AFFIRMATIVE ACTION

With the introduction of the affirmative action principle, a whole new set of ethical and legal considerations surfaced in dealing with the equality of opportunity issue. Indeed, if we use Mr. Johnson's allegorical explanation as a guideline, some active measures are required to rectify the effects of past injustices or inequities. Under this policy it is not enough to provide open admission or easy access to education. What is required is intervention that will compensate for prior inequalities in the social environment.

It is ironic that what is required today by affirmative action guidelines was formerly specifically prohibited by law because such practices were considered discriminatory. Students could not be admitted to programs and individuals could not be hired on the basis of race, sex, religion, or national origin. Indeed, to ask questions relating to these matters was explicitly forbidden; even photographs of individuals had to be removed from personnel documents in the early 1960s. President Johnson introduced the principle of affirmative action as a way of further reducing possibilities for discrimination. As it has been implemented by federal guidelines since then, it has dealt less with reducing discrimination and more with representation. This is a significant shift in public policy, as is indicated by Daniel Bell:

> What is extraordinary about this change is that, without public debate, an entirely new principle of rights has been introduced into the polity. In the nature of the practice, *the principle has changed from discrimination to representation.* Women, blacks, and Chicanos are to be employed, as a matter of right, in proportion to their number, and the principle of professional qualification or individual achievement is subordinated to the new ascriptive principle of corporate identity.[12]

Actually, it was President John F. Kennedy who first called for "affirmative steps" in an executive order issued in 1961. In essence, it called on contractors involved in federal projects to recruit and promote minority workers. But it was not until the 1964 Civil Rights Act came into full force that affirmative action became a reality. Under Title VI, discrimination was prohibited in education, and, under Title VII, it was barred in employment. The original intent of the legislation was to provide for equality of opportunity, not for racial balance or preferential treatment, although federal courts were authorized under Title VII to "order such affirmative action as may be appropriate."

Under Title VI of the Civil Rights Act of 1964, the Office of Education in the Department of Health, Education and Welfare was empowered to refuse federal financial assistance to any institutions and school districts that were not in compliance with Title VI, that is, were not meeting the guidelines having to do with the requirement that no person because of race, color, or national origin could be excluded from or denied the benefits of any program receiving federal financial support.

[12] Daniel Bell, *The Coming of Post-Industrial Society* (New York: Basic Books, Inc., Publishers, 1973), p. 417.

For all practical purposes, this meant every public institution and school district in the country, because by 1965, when the law was actually implemented, most of them were receiving federal financial assistance in some form. The U.S. Office of Education was, therefore, in the very powerful position of (1) establishing the guidelines under which institutions and school districts would meet the requirements of Title VI, (2) overseeing and determining whether or not units were in compliance, and (3) releasing or withholding federal assistance on the basis of its own interpretation of whether or not a unit was in compliance. This procedure was a very heavy weapon held by the federal government in enforcing antidiscrimination legislation as well as eliminating segregation in schools. Under Title VI, if a parent filed a segregation complaint with the attorney general, that office could bring legal action against the offending school district to force compliance with desegregation regulations. In some instances that action constituted more of a threat than did the possibility of loss of federal funding.

Title VI gave the federal government unprecedented power in regulating the affairs of school districts and institutions of higher education all over the nation. A single bureaucrat in a regional office of the Department of Education is able to wield enormous power over the social policies of institutions within the region because the threat of withdrawal of federal funds is applied to the *entire institution*, not only to a single subunit that may not be in compliance. Thus an entire university could lose its federal funding because a single department happened not to be in compliance with Title VI guidelines. Although it remains true that the school district or institution does not have to accept federal assistance, most of them have grown accustomed to getting it, and many simply could not operate without it. Thus, the specter of federal control, so long a fear of those who championed local decision making in school affairs, has materialized in the present generation.

JUDICIAL INTERVENTION IN SCHOOL POLICY FORMATION

On May 17, 1954, in a precedent-setting case, the U.S. Supreme Court unanimously held that the segregation of black and white children in state public schools on the basis of race was a denial to black children

153

of equal protection of the laws guaranteed by the Fourteenth Amendment, thereby declaring such practices and the state laws requiring such practices unconstitutional. This case, known as *Brown* v. *the Board of Education of Topeka,* was followed by one judicial decision after another in federal and state courts for a period of twenty-five years, all having to do with the extension of equality of educational opportunity. A year following the original Brown decision (*Brown I*), a second Brown decision was issued (*Brown II*) by the Supreme Court, requiring lower federal courts to see that local school districts make a "prompt and reasonable start" in implementing the desegregation of schools and that the process proceed "with all deliberate speed."

The implementation of the Brown decisions was delayed by the ruling in a case known as *Briggs* v. *Elliott.* In this case a three-judge district court in South Carolina held that it

> is important that we point out exactly what the Supreme Court decided and what it has not decided in this [the *Brown*] case. It has not decided that the federal courts are to take over or regulate the public schools of the states. It has not decided that the states must mix persons of different races in the schools or must require them to attend schools or must deprive them of the right of choosing the schools they attend. What it has decided, and all that it has decided, is that a state may not deny to any person on account of race the right to attend any school that it maintains . . . The Constitution, in other words, does not require integration. It merely forbids discrimination.[13]

The final sentence in the excerpt differentiated between active integration and discrimination, and many of the judges made this distinction in the years following the Brown decision. This distinction was eventually discarded as the result of a footnote by Judge John Minor Wisdom to the effect that the principle "should be laid to rest. It is inconsistent with Brown and the later development of decisional and statutory law in the area of civil rights."[14]

In the decade that followed the Brown decision, numerous attempts were made to frustrate its implementation. A number of them came to national attention: Court-ordered desegregation of schools in Houston and Dallas, Texas; problems surrounding the matriculation of James H. Meredith at the University of Mississippi in 1962; the refusal of Governor

[13] *Briggs* v. *Elliott,* 132 F. Supplement (F.D.S.C. 1955), Three-Judge Court.
[14] *Singleton* v. *Jackson Municipal Separate School District,* 348 F. 2nd., 730 fn. 5, Fifth Circuit Court, 1965.

Orval Faubus to allow the desegregation of the Central High School in Little Rock, Arkansas, and the subsequent intervention by President Eisenhower and federal troops; the challenge to federal authorities at the doorway of the University of Alabama by Governor George Wallace in opposing the enrollment of two black students, James Hood and Vivian Malone; and numerous racial confrontations in Boston, Chicago, Birmingham, and other cities. Frank T. Read describes the situation in New Orleans as

> an encyclopedia of every tactic of resistance ever employed by all other states combined . . . (by the end of the decade the judges) . . . had invalidated a total of forty-four statutes enacted by the Louisiana legislature; had cited and convicted two state officials for contempt of court; and had issued injunctions forbidding the continued flouting of their orders against a state court, all state executives, and the entire membership of the Louisiana legislature.[15]

After 1964 the pace of desegregation of schools accelerated. In one community after another opposition to the requirements of desegregation was struck down in court or was dissipated voluntarily. The constitutional rights of all students to attend nonsegregated public schools were being implemented. What follows is a synopsis of a few of the most important landmark cases relating to equality of educational opportunity and related issues.

1. Singleton v. *Jackson Municipal Separate School District (Singleton I* and *II)*, Fifth Circuit Court, 1965 and 1966; Court of Appeals, 1970.

2. United States v. *Jefferson County Board of Education (Jefferson I* and *II)*, Fifth Circuit Court, 1966 and 1967.

The Singleton and Jefferson cases mark the end of foot-dragging, tokenism, and endless subterfuges to stall implementation of the Brown decisions. They established the use of HEW Office of Education guidelines under Title VI of the Civil Rights Act of 1964 as uniform legal standards in determining whether or not a local school district's desegregation plan was in compliance with federal requirements. The decisions in

---

[15] Frank T. Read, "School Integration Since *Brown*," *Law and Contemporary Problems* 39:1 (Winter 1975): 14–15.

these cases required affirmative action by school districts in ensuring desegregation of learning environments for all students, including desegregation of faculty and staff.

3. Green v. *County School Board*, U.S. Supreme Court, 1968.

The Green case resulted in a unanimous U.S. Supreme Court decision marking the end of judicially sanctioned "freedom of choice" methods of desegregation. Freedom of choice methods of desegregation were unacceptable because few black children or their parents were "courageous enough to break with tradition." Subsequent to the Green case, federal courts looked more carefully at the percentage in the mix of black and white students that would be achieved by a proposed desegregation plan. This ruling required school boards to prepare and present a realistic plan to integrate their public schools.

4. Alexander v. *Holmes County Board of Education*, U.S. Supreme Court, 1969.

The U.S. Supreme Court reversed a Fifth Circuit Court of Appeals order to delay the desegregation of schools and ordered immediate action. The order came during the school year, which meant that thousands of children had to change schools at midterm. The action signaled the beginning of massive integration of schools in the South.

5. Swann v. *Charlotte-Mecklenburg Board of Education*, U.S. Supreme Court, 1971.

In the complex Swann case, the U.S. Supreme Court called for desegregation of faculty, staff, transportation, extracurricular activities, and facilities. It allowed limited use of mathematical ratios in determining the number of white and black children permitted in racially desegregated schools. It authorized the revision of attendance zones to achieve a racially balanced school population, along with "pairing 'clustering,' or 'grouping' of schools with attendance assignments made deliberately to accomplish the transfer of Negro students out of formerly segregated Negro schools and the transfer of white students to formerly all-Negro schools." The Court specifically approved the use of school busing as a means of achieving racially integrated schools.

6. Milliken v. *Bradley*, U.S. Supreme Court, 1974.

In a five-to-four decision, the U.S. Supreme Court reversed a lower

156

court decision that would have required fifty-three suburban Detroit school districts in three counties to join with Detroit in a school desegregation plan. The Court decision indicated that an interdistrict, metropolitan effort was not justified in meeting the requirements of desegregated schools.

7. *Lau* v. *Nichols*, U.S. Supreme Court, 1974.

The ruling by the U.S. Supreme Court in *Lau* v. *Nichols* reversed that of the district court of appeals and obligated public schools to provide assistance for non-English-speaking students to acquire a meaningful education. No specific remedy was prescribed by the Court, thereby leaving that decision to the expertise at the local level. The decision gave strong impetus to programs in English as a second language (ESL) and to bilingual-bicultural education.

8. *Serrano* v. *Priest*, California State Supreme Court, 1971 and 1977.

The Serrano case was a California State Supreme Court precedent-setting case that struck down the state's system of financing public education on the basis of discriminating against pupils residing in school districts with low-valued property. It represented a giant step in removing the financial support of schools from a dependence on local and nonuniform property taxes. The case was argued on the basis of rights guaranteed by the California State Constitution because the U.S. Constitution does not obligate the states to finance public schools on the basis of equality of property values (see number 9 for the Rodriguez case).

9. *San Antonio Independent School District* v. *Rodriguez*, U.S. Supreme Court, 1973.

The Rodriguez case was perceived by many as a stunning setback in achieving equality in the funding of the nation's public elementary and secondary schools. The U.S. Supreme Court, in a close five-to-four decision, found that the equal protection clause of the Fourteenth Amendment *did not* apply to inequities based on wealth between school districts as these related to state school financing programs. The majority opinion stated, "It has simply never been within the constitutional prerogative of this Court to nullify statewide measures for financing public services merely because the burdens or benefits thereof fall unevenly depending upon the relative wealth of the political subdivisions in which citizens

157

live." The Court ruled that these issues were to be resolved at the state level. Following the Rodriguez decision, the Serrano case *was* resolved by the California State Supreme Court (see number 8 for the Serrano case).

10. *Hobson* v. *Hansen*, District Court of the District of Columbia, 1971.

The Court held that gross differences in resources provided to schools attended by affluent white students and those provided in schools attended mainly by poor and minority students in Washington, D.C., did, indeed, constitute a denial of equal protection of the laws. This was the first case to test the legality of intradistrict disparities in resources. The Court also held that the homogeneous grouping of students into "tracks" that resulted in placements based on status or race was unacceptable: "With respect to the track system, the track system simply must be abolished."

11. *Pennsylvania Association for Retarded Children* (PARC) v. *Commonwealth of Pennsylvania*, Consent decree U.S. District Court for the Eastern District of Pennsylvania, 1972.

In the PARC case the Court required that children with mental handicaps had an equivalent right to a free education as did nonhandicapped children. It held also that, where possible, placement in a regular class was to be preferable to placement in a special class for the handicapped in the public schools.

12. *Mills* v. *Board of Education*, U.S. District Court of the District of Columbia, 1972.

In the Mills case a federal court extended the right to an education to *all* handicapped children, not only to those who are mentally retarded. This case, along with PARC (see number 11), resulted in thirty-six similar right-to-education cases in twenty-seven states and led to the enactment of federal legislation for the handicapped, specifically PL94–142, the Education for All Handicapped Act of 1975.

13. *Keyes* v. *School District No. 1*, U.S. Supreme Court, 1973.

The Keyes case was based on facts brought out in a trial court that found School District No. 1, Denver, Colorado, to be practicing intentional segregation of schools in the Park Hill area of northeastern Denver. The Supreme Court concluded that where intentional segregation is practiced in a "meaningful or significant segment of a school system," it is presumed that the entire system is segregated by intent. The case was remanded to the district court, which required that an acceptable desegregation plan be implemented systemwide by the Denver Public Schools. This case had the effect of blurring the constitutional distinction between de jure and de facto segregation. The Court noted that each produced the same effect. The outcome of this case served notice on school districts that desegregation vis-à-vis Brown was not confined to the South alone but would henceforth be an issue in the cities of the North and West as well.

14. Regents of the University of California v. *Allan Bakke*, U.S. Supreme Court, 1978.

The highly publicized Bakke case dealt with the issue popularly referred to as "reverse discrimination," in which a white student (Allan Bakke) was denied admission to medical school at the University of California, Davis, although less well-qualified students *were* admitted because the school had reserved spaces for minority applicants. The Court held five to four that the practice of establishing "quotas"—the reserving of a specific number of places for minorities in a public university class—is not constitutionally acceptable. It also found five to four that race *may* be considered as *one* factor in a university's admission policy, providing it is done in the context of a broad range of admission criteria. Affirmative action admission policies are sanctioned, but rigid numerical quotas are not allowed. Mr. Justice Lewis Powell, in the majority opinion wrote: "The guarantee of equal protection cannot mean one thing when applied to one individual and something else when applied to a person of another color. If both are not accorded the same protection, then it is not equal."

15. Columbus Board of Education v. *Pennick*, U.S. Supreme Court, 1979. *Dayton Board of Education* v. *Brinkman*, U.S. Supreme Court, 1979.

The Columbus and Dayton cases applied findings of the Court in *Keyes* v. *School District No. 1* (see number 13). This means that if a judge finds intentional segregation in a substantial portion of the school district, a presumption is created that other segregation in the district did not occur by chance. In such findings, it is the responsibility of the school officials to prove that segregation in other schools within the system was

159

not caused by "intentionally segregative actions." If such proof cannot be provided, districtwide busing is a permissible remedy. By a seven-to-two margin in the Columbus case and a five-to-four margin in the Dayton case, the High Court upheld racial desegregation plans requiring the busing of schoolchildren in the two cities. The decision reaffirmed the power of the federal courts to outlaw school segregation in the North and West, just as had been done earlier in the South.

AFTERWORD

The state can make a valiant effort to provide equally for all its children with respect to educational opportunity. Indeed, it is constitutionally obligated to do so if it provides any educational opportunity for anyone. It seems clear, however, that there are feasibility limits that foreshorten what even the best educational system can provide. In spite of the substantial gains that have been made in reducing inequities in educational opportunities—through legislation, through judicial intervention, through special programs and financial aid, through revised school policies, and many other means—in spite of all of these efforts, it remains true even today that one's parents' education and income, one's place of birth, and one's race and ethnic identity have a great deal to do with the quality and amount of education one receives.

There remain millions of children who today are not getting an adequate education because of a variety of social, economic, racial, or other environmental circumstances they are unable to control, circumstances that continue to spell inequality of educational opportunity . . .

> They are the victims—the victims of racial discrimination and class prejudice, poor schools, unfit housing, inadequate health care, malnutrition, unemployment and poverty. They are the victims of virtually every institution in our society—of which our public education system is among the most important—institutions that are insensitive and unresponsive to the needs of racial minorities and disadvantaged groups. The fact is that many of the school systems in this Nation that are confronted with children from families whose racial or cultural heritage or spoken language are different from those of most white middle-class American children are somehow institutionally unable to respond to their needs . . .[16]

[16] United States Senate Select Committee on Equal Educational Opportunity, *Report*, 92nd Congress, 2nd Session, December 31, 1972, p. 13.

Median Number of School Years Completed by Persons 25 Years Old or Older

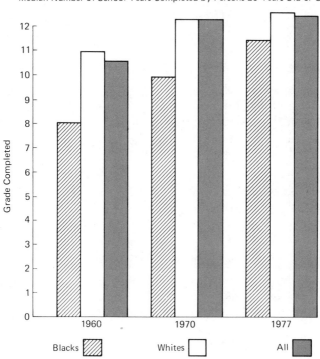

FIGURE 6. Notice the median for blacks in 1977 exceeds the 1960 median for whites and for all groups combined. What factors contributed to the increase in median years completed by blacks during that seventeen-year interval? (SOURCE: Table 226, *Statistical Abstracts of the United States*, 1978. U.S. Department of Commerce, Bureau of the Census.)

STUDY AND DISCUSSION

1. What social forces get in the way of providing equality of educational opportunity for all students?
2. Discuss social trends and conditions that encouraged legislative and judicial actions favoring distributive justice since 1950. What are your thoughts concerning Daniel Bell's observation that our social policy regarding affirmative action shifted from discrimination to representation without public debate?

161

3. Explain how the desire for justice and equality has affected the role of the school. Are the states obligated by the U.S. Constitution to provide free public education? What is the basis for your response?

4. Identify curriculum, instruction, and administrative practices that encourage the sorting and selecting of learners for future statuses. Do you believe it is appropriate for the public schools to engage in such "allocation functions," that is, the allocation of human resources, by steering individuals in certain directions vocationally?

5. Provide specific examples of school practices that indicate attempts of teachers and school officials to do what is "fitting and appropriate" in meeting needs of students.

6. What are your views on the policy of vesting enforcement power in a single federal agency as is the case of the implementation of the antidiscrimination provision of Title VI? Is there an alternative? Should such matters fall under the jurisdiction of the Justice Department?

7. What is the difference between a school's being "integrated" as opposed to one's being "desegregated"? Which condition is easier to achieve? Why?

8. What is the difference between de jure and de facto segregation? Which type would be the most complicated to deal with from a legal point of view? Why? How have the courts been able to resolve the legal issues in order to act in cases that are brought as a result of de facto segregation?

9. How might a school be legally desegregated and yet, without intending to do so, provide instruction on a racially segregated basis? Explain how and why such a set of circumstances could develop.

10. Some have interpreted the Supreme Court's admonition to desegregate "with all deliberate speed" in the Brown II decision as a contradiction. What do you suppose the Court intended when it used this particular choice of words?

SELECTED BIBLIOGRAPHY

BLACKSTONE, WILLIAM T., and ROBERT D. HESLEP, eds. *Social Justice and Preferential Treatment*. Athens, Georgia: University of Georgia Press, 1977. (A volume of readings.)

BLOOM, BENJAMIN S. *Human Characteristics and School Learning*. New York: McGraw-Hill Book Company, Inc., 1976.

BOUDAN, RAYMOND. *Education, Opportunity and Social Inequality*. New York: John Wiley and Sons, 1974.

COLEMAN, JAMES S. *Equality of Educational Opportunity*. Washington, D.C.: U.S. Government Printing Office, 1966.

GLAZER, NATHAN. *Affirmative Discrimination: Ethnic Inequality and Public Policy*. New York: Harper and Row, Publishers, Inc., 1976.

HOROWITZ, DONALD L. *The Courts and Social Policy*. Washington, D.C.: The Brookings Institution, 1977.

JENCKS, CHRISTOPHER, ET AL. *Inequality: A Reassessment of the Effect of Family and Schooling in America*. New York: Harper and Row, Publishers, Inc., 1972.

JENCKS, CHRISTOPHER, ET AL. *Who Gets Ahead? The Determinants of Economic Success in America*. New York: Basic Books, 1979.

KIRP, DAVID L. "Law, Politics, and Equal Educational Opportunity: The Limits of Judicial Involvement." *Harvard Educational Review* (May 1977): 117–137.

MORRIS, ARVAL A. *The Constitution and American Education*. St. Paul, Minnesota: West Publishing Company, 1974.

MOSTELLER, FREDERICK, and DANIEL PATRICK MOYNIHAN, eds. *On Equality of Educational Opportunity*. New York: Random House, Inc., 1972. (A volume of readings.)

PERSELL, CAROLINE HODGES. *Education and Inequality: A Theoretical and Empirical Synthesis*. New York: The Free Press (Macmillan), 1977.

READ, FRANK T. "School Integration Since *Brown*." *Law and Contemporary Problems* 39:1 (Winter 1975): 9–49.

SIEBER, SAM D., and DAVID E. WILDER, eds. *The School in Society*, Part 2: "Socialization and Learning." New York: The Free Press (Macmillan), 1973.

chapter 7

Social Status, Wealth, and Prestige as Dimensions of Power

In this and several succeeding chapters, we direct our attention to the concept of "power" as it relates to school decision making, along with such related concepts as social stratification, status, role, social class, social mobility, and culture of poverty. We are, of course, discussing power in a social context, that is, the ability to regulate or direct the behavior of others in accordance with our own desires. Max Weber spoke of power as "the probability that one actor within a social relationship will be in a position to carry out his own will despite resistance.[1] We speak of power as the capacity and/or the authority to make and implement fundamental decisions regarding school policies. Authority is power that has been legitimatized. Such social power, when one has it, can be exercised with or without the consent of those who are affected by it.

It is important to emphasize that our concern is with "fundamental decisions regarding school policies." This excludes the vast number of decisions made in schools each day that may be important to the day-to-

[1] Max Weber, *The Theory of Social and Economic Organization* (New York: The Free Press, 1957), p. 152.

day operation but deal with more or less trivial matters such as what color to paint the classroom walls, whether or not there should be playground equipment provided, how to manage the dismissal schedule, and similar issues of little significance in the total educational scheme of things. Instead, we examine the exercise of power and decision making in three areas that shape basic school policy: (1) *personnel*—the hiring, firing, and assignment of individuals to particular statuses in the educational system; (2) *curriculum matters*—deciding what is taught, how it is taught, what materials are to be used, and what standards are to be maintained; and (3) *funding*—securing and expending funds and deciding who and what programs get what amounts of money. Whatever group or groups influence decisions in these three areas wield great power over school policies and programs.

STATUS AND ROLE

The term *status* has a number of meanings and connotations when used in everyday parlance that confuse its specialized meaning when used as a sociological concept. For our purposes, *status* is defined as a social position that carries with it defined rights, duties, responsibilities, and limitations of rights. Occupational positions are examples of statuses: lawyer, truck driver, president, physician, banker, mechanic, cook, mayor, teacher, and so on. Other examples of statuses include father, mother, child, uncle, son, taxpayer, Catholic, pupil, citizen, parent, soldier, Democrat, and female. It is obvious that most individuals occupy several social positions, or statuses, simultaneously. One could be a mother, a teacher, a citizen, a Catholic, a female, and a Democrat all at the same time.

Status, in the strictest sense, does not mean differential social ranking on some criteria of preference. But because statuses tend to arrange themselves in a hierarchy, "the term itself *has*—since Roman times—had the additional meaning of rank."[2] Status carries with it certain rights, privileges, and rewards; and, therefore, there are often certain symbols that are associated with statuses—white coats, judicial or ceremonial robes, titles, perquisites, pins, athletic letters, uniforms, certain types of

[2] Everett Cherrington Hughes, "Dilemmas and Contradictions of Status," *Sociological Theory: A Book of Readings*, ed. Lewis A. Coser and Bernard Rosenberg (New York: Macmillan Publishing Co., Inc., 1964), p. 375.

homes, cars, and, of course, many, many more. These conspicuous symbols of status additionally reinforce the notion of social rank with social position or status.

Whereas status refers to a position within a social pattern, the concept "role" is used to define the particular behavior of the person occupying the status. The role behavior of a physician (a status position) provides a good illustration because it is so well established. When we go to a clinic to see our physician, we expect to see someone who is well groomed, dressed in a white coat, with a stethoscope either dangling from his neck or tucked visibly in his pocket, and moving about with a confident air of authority. Because this status is usually occupied by a male, our stereotype of the role behavior associated with it is that of a male, rather than a female. Furthermore, we would be surprised if our physician came out dressed like an auto mechanic. The reverse would also be true. The way individuals dress and act is, of course, functionally related to the statuses they occupy. We come to expect certain behavior in persons who occupy a particular status, and this is referred to, not surprisingly, as *role expectation*.

The expectation that individuals will function in the roles associated with various social positions is very strong. We are always caught up short when we are in situations where this is not happening. For example, we have certain behavior expectations of persons who occupy the status of teacher. Their role behavior makes it possible for us to relate to them appropriately. Occasionally, one finds a teacher who tries to establish a peer relationship with his or her students. This rarely works well because of the role confusion that results in the minds of pupils and parents. They do not expect the teacher to act like a *student;* they expect the teacher to stay in the *role* associated with the position (status) *teacher.* Clearly, in our day-to-day social relationships, we rely heavily on individuals to carry out their duties and responsibilities in the positions they occupy in role behavior that is commonly understood to be associated with those positions.

SOCIAL STRATIFICATION

Social stratification is the phenomenon of social differentiation that ranks individuals as higher or lower on the basis of some standard or criteria of preference. When such social differentiation becomes institu-

167

tionalized, the result is a social class system. In spite of the fact that there are societies in the world today that claim to be classless, a close examination of them reveals that such a claim is not valid. All societies have some form of stratification simply because people are rewarded differentially for various status positions. The class system may be less apparent in some societies than in others, but some form of social differentiation that ranks individuals on the basis of the statuses they occupy is found everywhere.

Although most students of human societies agree that stratification is a universal characteristic of human groups, they do not agree on why it occurs. Two theories are offered as explanations, both of which are based on the reality that resources perceived to be valuable are unequally distributed. The *functional* theory suggests that stratification is one means that a society uses to maintain social order. It is functional in the sense that it serves a purpose; it is socially useful. *Conflict* theory, on the other hand, suggests that stratification is a strategy used by the elites of a society as a way of keeping themselves in a position of privilege; that is, stratification is forced or imposed by elites on other members of society as a way of keeping them in their place. Conflict enters the picture because those who are in positions of privilege are not willing to relinquish such benefits easily or willingly; those who are in subservient positions are not willing to be content without sharing more completely in society's benefits. The result is dissension and, in the Marxist tradition, class struggle, a situation perceived as a quite normal state of things in society from the point of view of the conflict theorists. Neither of these theories is by itself a wholly adequate explanation of stratification, but each does provide us with important perspectives on this phenomenon.

The functional theory of stratification implies that societies offer different rewards deliberately in order to encourage individuals to enter certain social positions, or statuses. In this sense, stratification is useful in that it motivates individuals to be attracted to different positions that need to be filled. In general, social positions that require large investments of time, energy, and money will carry larger rewards than those that do not make such demands on the individual. There are, of course, many exceptions to this generalization. Nonetheless, in modern, industrial societies such as ours, occupations that command the greatest rewards in terms of wealth, prestige, and power are those that demand advanced, intellectual education.

Functional theory relies heavily on the viability of the concept of "achieved status." Achieved status means that the individual, through his or her own efforts, is able to secure a status or position that carries favorable social ranking. For example, he or she may work diligently at a job and, as a result, win one promotion after another. Or the individual may be motivated to enroll in an arduous course of study in order to enter a prestigious occupation. In an open society, presumably, there are many avenues of opportunity available to individuals who wish to enhance their social ranking.

Achieved status may be contrasted with *ascribed status.* Ascribed status means that the individual, through his or her own efforts, *cannot* secure a status or position that carries a favorable social ranking. Most societies, for example, do not ascribe the same status to children that they do to adults. Although we have made great strides in recent years in achieving equality among the various racial groups and between the sexes, there is still evidence of status ascription on the basis of race and sex. Also, persons who live in a culture of poverty characterized by extreme poverty, hopelessness, and despair may find themselves in a situation in which it is nearly impossible to do much to improve their social ranking.

Social stratification undoubtedly began to take shape when some individuals were able to accumulate more of the valued possessions than others. Having these desired commodities gave their holder power to control the lives of others, and this, in turn, accorded them a measure of prestige and esteem. Thus, the unequal distribution of the resources of wealth, power, and prestige associated with acquisitive social systems is the basis of social stratification. The disparities in wealth that are the basis of stratification are accentuated in societies linked to the industrial economies of the Western World because modern technology provides an enormous capacity to provide a surplus of needed goods. Historically, valued resources have been transmitted from a parent to children through inheritance as legal heirs, and, of course, this practice continues today.

If society provides free and open education to all the children of all the people, it obviously does a great deal to make it possible for all to compete for available social positions. Millions of Americans have used the school as a vehicle to enhance their social rank. At the same time, we cannot ignore the great advantages that inhere in being born into a family that is able to enjoy special privileges and the great disadvantages associated with being born into a family suffering special deprivation. Because of the genetic and environmental differences that stem from family background, often additionally confounded by negatively stereo-typed racial and ethnic characteristics, the ideal of giving everyone equal access to valued statuses is impossible to achieve. Although there are many important individual exceptions, to a large extent people are born into different social strata, and they stay there.

SOCIAL CLASS

The scientific study of society has shown that social stratification takes the form of layers, so to speak, each with its own set of values and behavior characteristics. These layers are what are referred to as *social classes* and are usually spoken of as some variation of high, middle, or low on the basis of privilege or lack of it. A social class may be defined as an aggregate of people in society who perceive themselves or whom others perceive as having some similarity in values as evidenced by education, occupation, income, and/or family history.

The beginning of the systematic study of the social class structure of American communities is usually associated with the Middletown study of the Lynds in the 1920s.[3] In the decades that followed, several em-pirical studies were conducted that documented the existence of a social class system and its relationship to education. Much of the literature in the sociology of education has been greatly influenced by the seminal research of W. Lloyd Warner and his associates and contemporaries:[4]

Warner used an interview technique called "evaluated participa-tion," in which informants were asked to identify and rank local social

[3] Robert S. Lynd and Helen M. Lynd, *Middletown: A Study in American Culture* (New York: Harcourt Brace, 1929).

[4] Yankee City Series (Newburyport, Massachusetts): W. L. Warner and P. S. Lunt, *The Social Life of a Modern Community* (1941) and *The Status System of a Modern Commu-nity* (1942); W. L. Warner and L. Strole, *The Social Systems of American Ethnic Groups* (1945); W. L. Warner and J. O. Low, *The Social System of a Modern Factory* (1947), all published by Yale University Press. Jonesville Series (Morris, Illinois, also referred to as "Elm-town," "Hometown," and "Prairie City"): W. L. Warner and associates, *Democracy in Jones-ville* (New York: Harper & Brothers, 1949); W. L. Warner, Marchia Meeker, and Kenneth Eels, *Social Class in America* (Chicago: Science Research Associates, Inc., 1949): A. B. Hol-lingshead, *Elmtown's Youth* (New York: John Wiley and Sons, 1949); Allison Davis, Burleigh B. Gardner, and Mary R. Gardner, *Deep South* (Chicago: University of Chicago Press, 1941); W. Lloyd Warner, Robert J. Havighurst, and Martin B. Loeb, *Who Shall Be Educated?* (New York: Harper & Brothers, 1944); Richard Centers, *The Psychology of Social Classes* (Princeton, New Jersey: Princeton University Press, 1949).

classes and to place persons from the community into those ranks. Thus, each informant placed persons to be ranked above, equal to, or below himself or herself. This procedure provided the empirical basis for determining how many classes existed in a community. The research led Warner and his associates to conclude that there were six clearly identifiable social classes in America: (1) upper-upper, (2) lower-upper, (3) upper-middle, (4) lower-middle, (5) upper-lower, (6) lower-lower. Warner and his associates found that there was a high correlation between class placement obtained by evaluated participation and four factors: (1) occupation, (2) source of income (inherited wealth, salary, wages, welfare payments), (3) house type, and (4) dwelling area.

Although the work of Warner has been widely cited, it has not been without its critics.[5] Some believe that it is out-of-date; that it does not apply to large, complex urban areas; that it does not adequately differentiate the relative importance of the factors of wealth, power, and prestige in determining social class; and that it fails to distinguish between class and status. Nonetheless, this pioneer research has provided us with a valuable set of concepts and procedures that has extended our understanding of social class structure.

The social class structure of a community quite clearly relates to its size. In small communities, that is, up to a population of about 5,000, there are usually three distinct social classes. The upper class in such communities consists of the educated and/or affluent families who live in the preferred part of town and make up most of its professional persons and business personnel. This group pretty much sets the social and cultural aspirations for the community and is very influential in community and school governance. The second level or middle class is larger in number, is less-well educated, and is less affluent but financially self-sufficient. The lower class in the small community is characterized by low income, little education, and erratic employment at jobs needing unskilled labor. This last group has very little influence in community and school decision making and their children, as a group, do poorly in school. The barriers between the three classes are fairly penetrable; indeed, there may be a great deal of interaction among them in the work world and in the marketplace. In school, friendship patterns may develop among children of

[5] Ruth Rosner Kornhauser, "The Warner Approach to Social Stratification" in *Class, Status, and Power: A Reader in Social Stratification* (New York: The Free Press, 1953), pp. 224–255; Milton Gordon, *Social Class in American Sociology* (New York: McGraw-Hill Book Company, Inc., 1963), pp. 85–123; 210–233.

different social classes at the early levels. Gradually, however, as the effects of cultural conditioning because of home background become more apparent, social interactions tend to follow similarity of social class backgrounds.

Havighurst and Levine believe that five levels of social class stratification can be identified in cities that vary in size from 5,000 to 500,000: (1) upper class, 1 to 3 per cent; (2) upper middle, 7 to 12 per cent; (3) lower middle, 20 to 35 per cent; (4) upper working, 20 to 45 per cent; and (5) lower working, 10 to 20 per cent.

Havighurst and Levine use the term *working* rather than *lower class* because they believe it to be less pejorative.[6] It is obvious that this classification closely resembles that of Warner. What seems to be omitted in the Havighurst and Levine taxonomy is that group in the culture of poverty at the very bottom of the social structure.

In the case of very large conglomerates of people such as our largest cities and metropolitan regions, the social class structure becomes much more diverse than it is in smaller communities. Additionally, it becomes more difficult to gather social class data through the use of interview procedures such as evaluated social participation. Individuals cannot possibly know enough about the city to be able to identify persons who are members of various clubs, churches, social cliques, and other formal and informal associations. Consequently, researchers depend on variables such as education, occupation, and income that are correlated with social class to determine social class membership of individuals. The evidence suggests that in large cities and metropolitan regions there will be many variations of the five or six basic social classes as identified by Havighurst and Levine, and by Warner, representing a much more diversified social class structure. For example, in their study of Kansas City, Coleman and Neugarten were able to distinguish *thirteen* levels of social class.[7] Undoubtedly, that many or more could be found in all large cities and metropolitan regions.

The social class composition of a community depends to some extent on the social and economic geography of it. For example, smaller cities where large institutions of higher education are located, such as Madison, Wisconsin; Pullman, Washington; and Lincoln, Nebraska, will have a

---

[6] Robert J. Havighurst and Daniel U. Levine, *Society and Education*, 5th ed. (Boston: Allyn & Bacon Books, Inc., 1979), pp. 18–22.

[7] Richard P. Coleman and Bernice L. Neugarten, *Social Status in the City* (San Francisco: Jossey-Bass, 1971).

social class distribution skewed toward the upper-middle range. The same applies to cities that are industrial or financial centers, as, for example, Tulsa, Oklahoma. Such places are apt to have a higher than average number of college-trained intellectuals, which is reflected in occupation and income, which, in turn, relates to social class.

Although the Warner sixfold classification cannot be regarded as a completely accurate description of social class structure in America, it does provide us with a frame of reference for the study of the social class phenomenon in specific American communities. For example, Warner and Lunt report the relative size of social classes in the United States as follows:[8]

Upper-upper class	1.4%
Lower-upper class	1.6%
Upper-middle class	10.2%
Lower-middle class	28.1%
Upper-lower class	32.6%
Lower-lower class	25.2%

These percentages are based on data collected in the early forties and are probably not correct if applied to today's population. Numerous social and economic changes have occurred in the past forty years that have influenced the social class structure. Nevertheless, it is still true that the upper classes represent a far smaller percentage of the total population than do other social classes. It is still true that the bulk of the population clusters about the lower-middle and upper-lower class range. It is still true that vast income differences separate the upper from the lower classes. It is still true that differences between the social class groups can be observed based on value and life-style variables. Some of these differences are summarized in Table 2.

Generalizations concerning values and life-styles of persons in various social class groups can be misleading. This is particularly true of the lower-lower social class, in which there appears to be a wide range of behavior that characterizes persons in this group. For example, included in this group are families who have a low level of education, who are economically marginal, but who are regularly employed and do have a

[8] W. Lloyd Warner and Paul S. Lunt, *The Status Systems of a Modern Community* (New Haven: Yale University Press, 1942).

Visual Representation of the Relative Size of Social Classes
Based on Data from Studies By Warner and his Associates

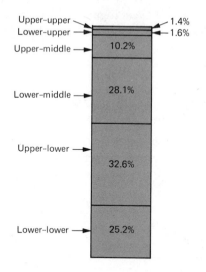

Upper-upper — 1.4%
Lower-upper — 1.6%
Upper-middle — 10.2%
Lower-middle — 28.1%
Upper-lower — 32.6%
Lower-lower — 25.2%

FIGURE 7. How do you believe these percentages compare with the social class composition of the community in which you live? Suggest criteria that could be used to define the following four social classes: (1) upper; (2) middle; (3) working; (4) lower. What would you estimate the per cent of the total population to be, based on these four social classes?

stable family life. Children from such a family might receive strong encouragement and support in their school work from their parents. This family's social class placement is largely a result of the low income, low education, and low work skills of the parents. Contrast this with another family also classified as lower-lower social class that have been members of a culture of poverty[9] for several generations. In this latter case we have a multiproblem family in which there are no economic or personal security, no regular income, and many children (each of whom may have a different father) and which presents a general picture of instability. Clearly, there are great variations in the values and life-styles of persons in lower classes, and teachers are cautioned against stereotyping children and their achievement expectations solely on the basis of social class identity.

Numerous research studies spanning the past half century have documented clear value differences among the social classes. These are, of

[9] The concept "culture of poverty" is developed in the writing of Oscar Lewis and means almost total separation of a poverty-stricken group from the remainder of society. Most importantly, such separation includes a separation from the values of the larger society. Thus, persons in a culture of poverty never become fully assimilated. See the Introduction to Oscar Lewis, *La Vida* (New York: Random House, Inc., 1965). Other authors question whether there actually is such a phenomenon as a culture of poverty and would at best refer to it as a subculture.

174

course, implied in the column labeled "Life-style" in Table 2. More explicitly, the following value differences among social classes are of particular importance to teachers because of their direct influence on pupil learning:

1. *Time orientation.* Lower-class children tend to be more present-oriented than are middle-class children. Middle-class children are taught to think in terms of the future. They learn to "save for a rainy day," to plan for high school or college, and to think of themselves in their future statuses. They develop an intellectual orientation that makes present hardships and sacrifices bearable because there are long-term payoffs associated with them that make them worthwhile. Middle- or upper-class children hear such references as "*when* you go to college . . .," not "*if* you go to college . . .," The lower-class child is not socialized into that type of time orientation.

2. *Person orientation.* The value patterns of middle-class persons tend often to make them task-oriented and things-oriented rather than person-oriented. An executive is supposed to be able to fire his or her best friend for not doing an adequate job and sleep soundly that night. Objectivity and impersonality are qualities that are prized in order to make decisions. "Just give me the facts, Ma'm." Lower-class children, perhaps for reasons of survival, tend to develop stronger personal ties. It "isn't what you know, it is who you know that counts." Among some lower-class ethnic groups one gets a job by depending on a friend or a relative to "put in a good word" for him or her. It is significant that, in the underworld, affiliated power groups are referred to as "families."

3. *Self-concept.* In our society, as is true of most societies of the world, feelings about oneself develop as a result of success experiences in competitive goal seeking. Middle-class children, known to do well in school, have many opportunities to build a backlog of success experiences. Moreover, their parents are part of the decision-making group of the community. Quite the reverse is the case of lower-class children. They live in poverty while others around them live in affluence. Their parents are not significant decision makers in the community. In school these

175

children often do poorly. It would have to be expected that these children develop poor images of themselves. When this is combined with what we know about the relationship between self-concept and school achievement, the implications for the teacher are obvious.

4. *Physical aggressiveness.* For many children of lower-class background, physical aggressiveness is a natural adaptive mechanism. It may be needed to survive. If there is never enough of anything to go around, whether it be food, clothing, money, or other rewards, one has to fight to get one's share. Consequently, the one who is the best or most clever fighter has the most prized things. It follows, therefore, that physical aggressiveness would be perceived as a valued trait among lower social class persons.

Middle- and upper-class children are taught to keep their physical aggressiveness in tow. "Nice boys and girls do not fight for what they want." These children are taught to be polite, not to strike back, not to take advantage of a less fortunate adversary *in the physical sense.* Evidently this characteristic does not apply to intellectual aggressiveness, which is prized among middle- and upper-class groups. A child who might resist striking another might give the child an unmerciful tongue-lashing without thinking too much about it. Regrettably, some teachers who come out of middle-class value orientations engage in such intellectual aggressiveness themselves. Physical aggressiveness is fed by frustrations caused by an inability to do what one aspires to do. Considering the conditions under which most lower social class children live, especially in the large cities, it is little wonder that they become physically aggressive. It could hardly be otherwise.

SOCIAL MOBILITY

Social mobility refers to the movement of persons upwards or downwards in the social structure. Lower middle-class parents, for instance, who want their children to get good educations in order to become doctors, lawyers, scientists, or business executives are expressing an aspiration for the upward social mobility of their children. This is a very com-

SOCIAL CLASS	OCCUPATION	EDUCATION	INCOME	LIFE-STYLE
Upper-upper	Occupations tied to family corporate and/or industrial enterprise. High level government posts: ambassadorships, presidential advisers, special commissions and boards.	Exclusive private education, best private "prep" schools. Private tutors and governesses. Often some education in Europe. Most prestigious colleges and universities.	"Old money" family wealth. Corporate and industrial income. Independently wealthy.	Long and distinguished family background. Travel socially with the international elite. Sensitive to familial history and "good" name. Try to avoid publicity, especially of the gossip column type.
Lower-upper	Corporate wealth; industrial ownership. High-level managerial and executive posts: bank presidents, board chairmen; insurance and financial executives; Topflight athletes, movie and TV stars; entertainers.	Seek out the "best" schools, usually private; therefore, select many of the same schools as upper-uppers. Concerned about learning appropriate protocols.	"New money," i.e., newly acquired fortunes. Income level typically very high.	Much conspicuous consumption. "Jet set" behavior. Try to emulate behavior of upper-upper class. Concerned about belonging to the "right" groups, to socialize with the "right" people.
Upper-middle	High status professionals: physicians, lawyers, judges, university presidents. High level corporation executives. Airline pilots. College professors.	Solid, well-regarded private or public institutions. Specialized college training, often postgraduate. Strong preference for first or second level colleges or universities, public or private.	Considerably better than average, but for the most part is "earned" income.	Suburbanites who commute to central city. Very influential in local community politics. Constitute the "local elite". Intellectual orientation to life.
Lower-middle	Small businessmen and entrepreneurs. Lower level professionals, teachers, clergy, nurses. Skilled craftsmen, salesmen, clerical workers.	Public schools K-12. State colleges or universities. Advanced trade or vocational schools offering specialized curriculum. Education highly regarded.	Earned income adequate but not excessive.	So-called "typical" American so often stereotyped in fiction. Concerned about maintaining traditional family and community values. Constitute the core of local social, religious, and public service group membership.
Upper-lower	Unskilled workers: domestics, custodians, day laborers, street maintenance workers, assembly line workers. Low-income self-employed: small farmers, trappers, hunters, corner grocery operators.	Usually no more than public or parochial high school.	Marginal; subsistence level; barely adequate for necessities of life.	On the margin of poverty: few "extras" available; "poor but honest" characterization often applied.
Lower-lower	Often not regularly employed. Unskilled workers. Seasonal farm workers. Often work outside the law.	Children do poorly in school; often drop out psychologically long before they leave school physically. Family values often not in accord with those of the school.	Inadequate. Much financial insecurity. Often need public assistance and welfare.	Great variation, but mainly great economic need, poverty stricken, multiproblem life-style.

mon practice, especially among lower middle-class families. Needless to say, this results in severe internal family conflicts when children do not share these parental aspirations or embrace the values that gave rise to them.

Education can be used as a powerful means of enhancing one's social class position, and millions of Americans have used education for that purpose. This is so because through education one is able to gain that knowledge and those skills that make it possible to gain entry into prestigious occupations. This does not mean that education causes upward social mobility. It is rather a means or a vehicle of achieving it. This circumstance has very important implications for the relationship of education to social class structure. For example, those pupils who typically do not do well in school, that is, children from lower-class groups, quite clearly cannot make use of education for social mobility to the extent that children from middle-class families are able to do. In other words, there are prior socializing conditions in the home life of the child that affect whether or not the education establishment will be useful as a vehicle for social mobility.

A number of factors have a direct effect on the social mobility of people. Among the most important in recent years have been the legal and political changes that have taken place that forbid racial and sex discrimination in the world of work. The growing population of the nation, along with the increased need for persons with advanced levels of education in scientific and technical fields, has also enhanced upward social mobility. Downward social mobility occurs much less frequently than upward mobility and is usually the result of personal problems such as alcoholism, personal bankruptcy, mental health problems, or other personal disasters. In the case of women, there is some downward mobility as a result of marriage and/or divorce.

The extent to which an individual or a group can be upwardly socially mobile depends in some measure on how thoroughly the person or group has been assimilated by the host group. An important distinction needs to be made between acculturation and assimilation in this regard. When one is acculturated, it simply means that the person has learned the behaviors of the host group. This does not mean or even imply acceptance by that group. If, however, the individual becomes thoroughly integrated and accepted by the host group so that there are no barriers whatever to prevent the individual from doing what he or she chooses to do, we have what Milton Gordon refers to as "structural assimilation."[10] The effects of the absence of structural assimilation would be felt at the upper end of the social class continuum, where special requirements beyond income, occupation, and education are needed for entry into the elite. It is at this point that ethnic, religious, or racial restrictions to social mobility are applied, even though cultural assimilation, or acculturation, has taken place.

It would seem that the role of the school in this process is more effective in promoting cultural assimilation, or acculturation, and less effective in promoting structural assimilation. Many boundaries to structural assimilation have been destroyed in recent years through legislation, court decisions, and liberal social movements. No doubt education has also contributed to increased structural assimilation. But ethnics and minorities still have problems in upward social mobility. This country has yet to elect a black person or a woman of *any* ethnic or racial background as its president.

NEW FORMS OF IDEOLOGICAL AND CLASS CONFLICT

Over the past two decades, social processes have been taking place that have had the effect of changing some of the traditional conflicts between social classes in America. Everett Ladd, Jr., in a series of interesting and instructive articles for *Public Opinion* cites data taken from national surveys that demonstrate that the main class conflict today is between the upper middle class and the lower middle class.[11] He concludes that education is the *key* factor in defining today's class divisions. This concept requires greater elaboration.

At the time of the New Deal and the growth of traditional liberalism in this country, upper middle-class groups, largely college educated, were, as a group, closely associated with business and professional occupations. Moreover, on personal and social issues they tended to be conservative in their value orientation. Persons in these groups tended to

[10] Milton Gordon, "Assimilation in America: Theory and Reality," in *Challenges to Education*, ed. Emanuel Hurwitz, Jr., and Charles A. Tesconi (New York: Dodd, Mead & Company, Inc., 1972), p. 370.

[11] Everett Ladd, Jr., "The New Lines Are Drawn: Class and Ideology in America," *Public Opinion* 1:3 (July–August 1978): 48–53.

resist public spending on social welfare programs. Meanwhile, those in the lower class, which might be called the "working" class, were in strong support of social changes and worked for their implementation through trade unionism. The lines on most social issues such as social security, workmen's compensation, welfare programs, medicare, and so on were clearly drawn between the business and professional, college-educated upper middle class and the blue-collar workers who were educated at the high school and elementary school levels only.

In the past two decades there has been an unprecedented growth in affluence, and although all groups have benefited by it, the working class has gained the most, relatively speaking. They have moved out of the traditional position of "have-nots" and have secured for themselves a generous claim to the nation's affluence.

In the case of the upper middle-class group, significant shifts have also taken place. First of all, the group has expanded in number beyond even the most optimistic predictions. All sorts of business, technological, scientific, economic, and professional occupations have mushroomed, all of which require advanced levels of education. This is the group that Ladd refers to as the "intelligensia" because their backgrounds and voca-tions associate them with the application of trained intelligence and may include as many as 40 million Americans. It is this group that has shed its conservative mantle; it no longer embraces the traditional values of the business world; it has a value system associated with intellectual and humanitarian ideals.

These changes that relate to education and the marketplace have resulted in profound changes in value commitments on the part of these two groups. The working class—now solidly a part of the lower middle class—is no longer championing the cause of social reform and humani-tarian concern to the extent that it once did, even though its members still identify with trade unionism. The data indicate that the less-well educated group today takes a significantly more conservative position than does the more highly educated group on such values as working diligently, saving money, striving for success, being in debt, seeking economic security, and sacrificing for one's children. This represents almost a reversal of positions of these groups when compared with the period of the New Deal. The same findings obtain when one examines the views of these Americans on such social issues as homosexuality, premarital sexual experiences, adultery, miscegenation, abortion, wom-en's rights, immigration, and others.

These shifts in value commitments have important implications for American education. If education is the key factor that separates the new liberalism from the new conservatism, the relevance and importance of life-style differences among social classes that are simply the result of income differentials will need to be reevaluated. We can expect even more in the way of open conflict between the "eggheads" on the one hand and the "hard hats" on the other than we have had in the past. Because of the liberal leanings of the intellectuals, they will continue to be suspect for their so-called leftist associations. This could have serious political consequences for the nation should the long period of affluence come to an abrupt end.

SOCIAL STRATIFICATION AND COMMUNITY POWER STRUCTURES

Social power has been a much studied social phenomenon, but, because of its complexity, a great deal remains to be known about the perplexing combination of factors that give power to some groups and deny it to others. There can be no question that social power relates in some direct way to social stratification. When reference is made to "the powerless" in the literature of sociology and education, for example, the groups referred to are those occupying the lower stratum of the social class structure—the poor, the undereducated, the so-called "underclass." In recent years there has been a growing awareness of the presence of social power in most social relationships. Indeed, social power has become an essential element in any strategy that is used to achieve social, political, and economic goals.

Three interacting variables seem to contribute to the power of a group. The first of these is the *number* of individuals involved. Although there are many exceptions to this general rule, larger groups will tend to be more powerful than smaller groups. For instance, if a lobbyist for a special interest group (a union, an ethnic group, a teachers' association, and so forth) can say to the politicians, "I speak for the 100,000 members of our organization," such a group is likely to be more influential than if the lobbyist could claim to speak for only 5,000. This is why groups that are ascending in power try hard to garner as many constituent members as possible. The National Education Association provides such an example, as it boasts a membership of "nearly 2,000,000."

181

Numbers alone, however, do not give a group strength. It must also be organized in a way that will allow it to exercise power. The strength of numbers derives from the fact that all are willing to act in concert—they will vote as a block to defeat an uncooperative politician, they are willing to boycott a product or a place of business, they will "withhold services" (strike), and so on. If an aggregate of people is so poorly organized that it cannot discipline its membership into acting as a body, it is relatively impotent as a base of social power. As a minimum, the social organization of a power group has to be such that it can (1) force membership of those who identify with its cause in a *direct* way, (2) take action that binds the entire membership, and (3) exercise sanctions against individual members who do not or will not conform to the policies and mandates of the group. Strong trade unions provide a good example of tight, well-disciplined social organization. The phenomenon of "wildcat" (unauthorized) strikes represents a breakdown of the discipline of the union to control its members and always weakens the parent union's case at the bargaining table. The NEA for many years was a large but relatively powerless group because it lacked the social organization needed to harness its potential strength. This limitation has been corrected in recent years, as is discussed in Chapter 11.

A third dimension of social power has to do with the *resources*— money—a group has available to it. A small group that is tightly organized and is well-heeled can exercise enormous power. If a group has enough money, it can pay to bring its point of view to the attention of the public through the media. It can finance the political campaigns of politicians sympathetic to its views. It can engage a headquarters staff and maintain a public relations office to get its views presented to the public in a favorable light.

For purposes of example, we might compare the power in a local community of two groups: the PTA and the local Business and Professional Association. The PTA may have a large membership, especially of parents of elementary school pupils. Ordinarily, however, it is very loosely organized and has no mechanism for requiring membership or for disciplining its members. In terms of resources it has some small amount of money collected in the way of membership dues and what is earned in annual fund-raising activities such as a "Penny Carnival." Although it may claim to speak for parents on issues having to do with schools, its voice is weak and often muted by more powerful groups in the community. The local Business and Professional Association, on the other hand, is usually much smaller in its membership than is the PTA but is much more tightly organized and structured. It meets regularly, and members are expected to attend. Moreover, it has generous resources available to it as an organization and by virtue of individual members. Because of its resources, the Business and Professional Association probably controls the local newspaper, indirectly at least, because of the paper's reliance on local advertising. The association can count on its views on issues receiving favorable treatment in the local press. Local school officials, including members of the school board, compromise their position of independence by participating in the activities of the Business and Professional Association or by being members of it. In terms of actual power to influence decisions relating to schools, the local Business and Professional Association is clearly much more influential than is the PTA. Of course, often the PTA and the local Business and Professional Association are in accord on issues; the example cited should not be construed to mean that there is a necessary conflict of interest between these two community power groups.

Two theories have been advanced to explain the phenomenon of social power. One is known as the "power elite" theory;[12] the other, the "pluralistic power" theory.[13] There are, obviously, variants of these patterns of control over the educational system that could be observed in many communities. The control of education and decision making in the schools is closely tied to the political system of the local community. In studying school decision making, therefore, one must know a great deal about the power structure governing the community at large.

The power elite theory has been conceptualized as a pyramid of power tied to the social class structure of the community. The upper class is, of course, at the apex of the pyramid and is the embodiment of power. It rules the community and does so in its own self-interest. The strength of the power elite is pervasive to the extent that it controls the political, economic, and civic activities of the community. New businesses

---

[12] See C. Wright Mills, *The Power Elite* (New York: Oxford University Press, 1956); Floyd Hunter, *Community Power Structure* (Chapel Hill, N.C.: University of North Carolina Press, 1953); G. William Domhoff, *Who Rules America?* (Englewood Cliffs, N.J.: Prentice-Hall, Inc., 1967); G. William Domhoff, *Who Really Rules?* (New Brunswick, N.J.: Transaction Books, Inc., 1978).

[13] See Robert A. Dahl, *Who Governs? Democracy and Power in an American City* (New Haven: Yale University Press, 1961); Nelson W. Polsby, *Community Power and Political Theory* (New Haven: Yale University Press, 1963); Raymond E. Wolfinger, *The Politics of Progress* (Englewood Cliffs, N.J.: Prentice-Hall, Inc., 1974).

cannot enter the community without its explicit approval. Persons who are in nominal positions of leadership are in such positions because the power elite approves of their occupying those statuses. In return, these civic leaders are expected to govern the community in accordance with the desires of the clique holding power. The power elite may, and usually does, exercise its strength covertly and subtly. Nonetheless, it may control the economic activity of the community, the jobs that key people in the community hold, and the availability of financial resources for business activity. Local power elites may form part of an interlocking network that extends nationwide.

In every community there are a few individuals who may be regarded as "opinion shapers"; that is, they are highly respected citizens to whom the rest of the community looks for guidance and direction. If those individuals take a stand on an issue, they are likely to carry with them a substantial portion of the community. Such opinion shapers are not necessarily a part of the power elite, although they could be. In any case, the power elite will use whatever leverage it has to gain the support of these influential and trusted citizens. They may be persuaded to run for public office or be placed in other positions of high visibility. It is not suggested here that such relationships are in any way clandestine or sub rosa. Far from it. In many communities such relationships are considered entirely legitimate and are perceived simply as good for the community.

The pluralistic power theory takes an altogether different view of the phenomenon of community power. Instead of a single, monolithic power structure, pluralistic power theory suggests that there are many power bases in a community—many small pyramids of power, so to speak, instead of one big one. These centers of power are numerous, and individuals may, and often do, hold membership in more than one. For example, a specific individual may be a member of his or her church's parish council, be on the board of directors of a local banking firm, and be an officer of the neighborhood protection and preservation association. This overlapping membership in various power clusters brings the individual in contact with others who are similarly attached to other power centers. Because they each seek goals that the other can help them achieve, they engage in trade-offs that are of mutual benefit—mutual "back scratching," in other words. Problems arise, of course, when one individual is a part of two power groups that seek conflicting goals. Such dilemmas seem to characterize modern life and must be resolved by individual value clarification.

Pluralistic power theory suggests that in community life today individuals are a part of so many different groups, each of which has some power, each of which is able to influence an unknown number of other decision makers, that an explanation of power in terms of a single power elite based on social class is unrealistic. To know how decisions are made and where real power lies back of those decisions is so complex that it would require intensive and detailed study of many individuals and, in fact, may never be known precisely.

To dichotomize community power as being based on a power elite theory or a pluralistic theory is misleading because, in reality, the distinctions are not ordinarily that sharp. Studies of community power show quite clearly that in most communities there is some amount of pluralism and some diffusion of power. Studies also confirm that those individuals who are the "influentials," those we have referred to as "opinion shapers," are consistently and strongly of middle-class background. On the other hand, there also is evidence that influentials themselves, representing various constituents, form coalitions or interlocking networks—perhaps loosely structured but nevertheless real—that relate to the economic, political, social, and legal affairs of the community.[14]

Community power structures have been studied from a variety of perspectives, and what one finds depends to some extent on the approach used to study community power.[15] The three approaches most frequently used have been identified as the *positional, reputational,* and *issues* approaches. The positional approach examines the community in terms of who the people are who occupy positions of leadership and whom they represent. This provides information about the legal and nominal leadership of a community. It assumes, of course, that those in nominal positions of leadership are actually the ones who exercise power. It does not tell anything about whether or not the person's leadership is perceived as legitimate, nor does it tell us anything about the "power behind the throne."

In using reputational approaches to the study of community power, one assumes that power resides in a relatively small group of "influentials." This could be a power elite, as previously discussed, or simply highly regarded opinion shapers in the community. These persons might

[14] Domhoff, *Who Really Rules?* (op. cit.)

[15] Arnold M. Rose, *The Power Structure* (New York: Oxford University Press, 1967), pp. 255–280.

have a charismatic quality about them that causes their fellow citizens to turn to them for leadership. Such individuals would be very powerful in shaping public opinion regarding school financial support, curriculum development, personnel matters, and other school-related issues.

The third approach to the study of community power has to do with the examination of specific issues and tracing the involvement of specific individuals in the resolution of those issues. The best-known study of this type is the one done of New Haven, Connecticut, by Robert A. Dahl and his associates.[16] This approach assumes that real power resides in those individuals who were able to be successful in having decisions made in their favor or were successful in blocking action on an issue they did not favor. Presumably, such individuals would be different for different issues. Much depends on the strength and influence of individuals in transactions and interactions with other influentials. This approach would reject the idea that there is a single power elite that is influential in deciding all issues of substance. It is oriented, rather, to a pluralistic concept of community power.

No matter what method is used to study community power structure, one cannot get away from the fact that community power *is* related to social class structure. Community power is vested in persons from the middle and upper social classes. These are the individuals who have a better-than-average education themselves and who live in reasonably affluent environments. They are the ones who set standards of excellence in achievement and who are most influential in determining the nature of the curriculum in the public schools at the local level. They determine the level of school funding and strongly influence the selection of local school leadership. Lower social classes, including substantial numbers of visible minorities, namely, blacks, Latinos, and Indians and, to a lesser extent, Asians, do not play a significant role in the power structure of integrated American communities on the mainland.

DECISION–MAKING MODELS

Millions of Americans over forty years of age were sent off to school in their childhood with the admonition, "If you get a lickin' in school, you will get another one when you get home." It is safe to say that the

---

[16] Dahl, *Who Governs?* (op. cit.).

threat was rarely carried out, but this homely example of nostalgia illustrates an attitude of support that that generation was willing to give to the schools. Most children did not really believe they would get a "lickin' " at school *or* at home, but they understood that the parent was saying, "We agree with what your teacher and school are doing, so you had better mind your p's and q's there." Outwardly, at least, there was consensus between the school and home that the child was expected to behave appropriately in school and that the home had confidence in the school authorities' judgment in enforcing codes of conduct.

The concept of consensus has been the traditional cornerstone of decision making in public life generally and particularly in the public schools.[17] Writing for the 1974 Yearbook of the Association for Supervision and Curriculum Development, Dan W. Dodson says straightaway in his opening sentence,

> The basic issue confronting American education is that, today, it serves a society characterized by dissension and conflict, and its organization is still for a society in which there was a high degree of consensus.[18]

There may not be as much dissension and conflict apparent today as when the passage was written, but that does not detract from the validity of Dodson's observation. Pluralism in America is a fact of life, not only racial and ethnic pluralism, but also in terms of every special interest group imaginable. Jon Margolis, writing for the *Chicago Tribune* in July 1979, observes,

> Along with the new "balkanized" mood has come an increasing shrillness in public life, marked by a disinclination to compromise and an easy resort to confrontation.[19]

Let us examine some of the characteristics of a consensus model of decision making.

In a consensus model of decision making, there is the assumption that there can be agreement among all parties as to the goals and pur-

---

[17] Robert A. Dahl, *Pluralist Democracy in the United States: Conflict and Consent* (Chicago: Rand-McNally & Company, 1967).

[18] Dan W. Dodson, "Authority, Power, and Education" *Education For An Open Society*, 1974 Yearbook, (Chapter 7), ed. Delmo Della-Dora and James E. House (Washington, D.C.: Association for Supervision and Curriculum Development, 1972), p. 99.

[19] Jon Margolis, "One Nation but 'indivisible'?" *Chicago Tribune*, July 1979.

poses sought and that there will be support for the procedures used in achieving those goals. Individuals affected by decisions may not have been directly involved in making them; indeed, they usually were not. There was a level of trust accorded those in charge of things, a belief that whatever they would do would be done in the best interest of all involved. Dodson refers to this in terms of the "consent of the governed."[20] Individuals associated with the operation are expected to "work within the system." The "system" typically is organized along the lines of a line and a staff hierarchical administrative structure not unlike that of a corporation or the military. The rhetoric associated with "the system" often makes reference to *loyalty*, which is a prized value. In speaking of "the system," apologists are inclined to use athletic analogies, with especial reference to football: "he or she is a good team member"; "he rarely drops the ball"; "we can made an end run"; "by doing it this way we can get extra yardage"; "we ran out of downs." Or, using tennis: "the ball is in his court"; or baseball: "he hit one out of the park"; and so on. It is often stressed that it is the "American way" to "play the game according to the rules."

Schools that operate under a consensus model of decision making establish many trade-offs that work to the mutual benefit of the parties involved. The principal is supposed to "back his or her teachers"—meaning he or she supports them in conflicts with pupils and parents no matter who is at fault. In return for this kind of support, the system expects loyalty from the teachers. There is no place under this arrangement for "telling tales out of school" or for challenging the authority of those in charge. Those who question decisions or challenge the authority of those "in charge" are perceived as troublemakers and "boat rockers." Matters can be discussed in their formative stages, and individuals or groups can provide "input," but, once a decision is made, the expectation is that everyone will support it. A solid front on decisions arrived at through consensus—that is the "American way." Conflict is to be avoided because agreement is reached through consensus even though the situation has to be manipulated to gain such consensus. "It sometimes takes a lot of arm twisting to get consensus," one school official was heard to say!

Middle- and upper-class Americans may experience some uneasiness with the consensus model of decision making, but they have developed their social and communication skills well enough to deal with it. Be-

---

[20] Dodson, op. cit., p. 100.

sides, many have a value system that supports such decision-making policies. They might even agree that the minorities who question certain school practices and policies are "nothing but a damn bunch of trouble-makers." They are likely to think of education as a privilege that is really wasted on many who will never be ambitious enough to take advantage of the opportunities available to them. They—the middle- and upper-class parents—are likely to show deference to the teachers who are truly intellectuals and who have earned honors and advanced degrees. Conversely, they would be less willing to support teachers whose scholarly credibility was found wanting. Until recent years, even those who were disenfranchised by consensus type decision-making procedures conceded their legitimacy. A clear example of institutionalized discrimination.

All of the procedures associated with consensual decision making and the assumptions on which they are based underwent serious challenge during the decade of the 1960s. A variety of social and political conditions—a struggle for equity and civil rights by minorities, the involvement of the nation in an unpopular war, the increasing strength of the military, the popularity of participatory democracy, the spread of socialistic ideology, the rise in power of third world people—these conditions and others spurred the powerless and the disenfranchised—including many minorities—to *demand* to be heard and to be involved in decision making. They said, "To hell with doing things within the system! You listen to us or we will throw you out, Mr. School Official (or Dean or President), and trash your office, close the building, or burn it." Institutional leaders and authority figures were not accorded respect and legitimacy simply because they were in nominal positions of leadership and authority. No school official could any longer assume that a decision would go unchallenged. Teachers were "hassled" by disruptive and unruly students and were powerless to do much about it. Thus, instead of supporting a teacher's judgment and decision by the "a lickin' at home if you get one at school" attitude, parents were more likely to say, "If you lay a hand on my kid, I will see you in court."

It is in the period of the mid-1960s that we see the rise of the *conflict* or *confrontation* model of decision making. Individuals intimidate school officials and teachers. Groups confront each other in a power struggle. The rhetoric is abusive, often vulgar, profane. Decisions are not resolved by attempting to arrive at consensus but by generating conflict and resolving that conflict. Schools and school officials lost legitimacy and credibility and may not have regained it totally to this day. During

189

the period of a high level of conflict, school governance was so seriously threatened, especially at the college level, that there was some question as to whether or not schools and other educational institutions could be governed at all. If any lesson was learned from the experiences of that period, it should be that constant conflict is destructive and counter-productive. It destroys institutions and the individuals associated with them.

Out of this period of conflict and confrontation in decision making has come what some call "shared power" or collaborative decision-making strategies that restore some degree of consensus. Consensual decision making is more acceptable today than it was two decades ago because it involves directly representatives of constituents who are affected by the decisions. In making major decisions about education today, we fully expect that the business and professional community will be represented as will be parents, students, teachers, administrators, and other patrons, along with the superintendent and the board of education. This type of involvement is presumed to take place in accordance with some degree of parity, meaning that all voices share equally in the decision-making process. The parity principle cannot be fully functioning, of course, because certain specific individuals and groups are held legally responsible for decisions. There is, however, a greater sensitivity today to *procedures* that must be followed in gaining consensual support than there was earlier.

Conflict and confrontation strategies may have a purpose in calling attention to problems when all other efforts fail. They are also useful in intimidating school authorities and thereby forcing them to take action. But conflict and confrontation have little to offer in terms of addressing long-term solutions to problems. If a militant group is frustrated in its efforts to make itself heard and eventually burns down the school building, then what happens? Does that act in itself alleviate the inequity? Hardly so. It may even strengthen prejudices and make a long-term solution even more difficult to attain.

In order to achieve long-term solutions to complex problems that involve social injustice, the best hope seems to be collaborative efforts among constituents who are willing to work together cooperatively in achieving goals of common concern. If special interest groups insist on setting their own agenda, if they insist on having their way on every issue, no collaborative system of decision making will work. Decision making under such circumstances boils down to an exercise in raw power and legal recourse. There remains no substitute for trust and goodwill among people who are earnest in their desire to resolve problems in terms of the best interests of everyone. With those conditions absent, there can be little hope for democratic decision-making processes.

STUDY AND DISCUSSION

1. Select a community with which you are familiar. What is there about that community that would suggest the presence of a social class structure? Can you think of individuals in that community who elevated their social class standing? How was that achieved?

2. Teachers are drawn from the middle ranges of the social class system and, therefore, embrace those values characteristic of the middle class. Moreover, it is well known that many successful teachers conduct their classrooms in accordance with middle-class values. Provide specific examples of how this set of conditions can, and often does, work to the disadvantage *or* advantage of certain children.

3. Mr. Charles M. Spinner, a high school teacher in Parma, Ohio, involved his students in fascinating studies of the social-class structure of a community by making a study of local cemeteries. What is there about a cemetery that would give one clues as to the social-class structure of the community?

4. Is there a difference between describing role behavior and developing a stereotype? Explain. Is there any merit in stereotyping the behavior of individuals who occupy certain statuses? Why or why not?

5. What effect do you think each of the following may have on the social-class structure: (1) decline in the size of middle- and upper-class families, (2) removal of race and sex barriers to hiring, (3) decrease in the number of inherited positions, (4) increase in "knowledge industries", and (5) affirmative action and other legal and political restrictions to job and education opportunities?

6. Provide examples of, and exceptions to, the functionalists' idea that those social statuses (that is, positions) that are most highly rewarded by society will attract the most capable persons to them. What factors other than ability get people into the positions they occupy?

7. Identify an organization you know to have social power and another one that you are certain does not have such power. Analyze and compare these two organizations in terms of (1) the number of individual members, (2) their social organization, and (3) the resources each has available. Can these three variables be used to explain the strength of the one and the weakness of the other?

8. What distinction can you make between "authority" and "power"? Does a person in authority necessarily have power? Does a person in power necessarily have authority? Explain your views on these matters.

9. Is the concept of *parity* more important to advisory groups or to executive (that is, decison-making or policy-forming) groups? Why?

10. Name four social developments and/or trends that have promoted and encouraged the involvement of constituent groups in collaborative decision making in resolving school issues. Explain how and why these developments have had an impact on the schools of the nation.

SELECTED BIBLIOGRAPHY

BEEGHLEY, LEONARD. *Social Stratification in America*. Santa Monica, California: Goodyear Publishing Company, Inc., 1978.

DELLA-DORA, DELMO, and JAMES E. HOUSE, eds. *Education for an Open Society*. 1974 Yearbook. Part 3: "The Use of Power in an Open Society." Washington, D.C.: Association for Supervision and Curriculum Development, 1974.

DOMHOFF, G. WILLIAM. *Who Really Rules?* New Brunswick, New Jersey: Transaction Books, 1978.

———. *Who Rules America?* Englewood Cliffs, New Jersey: Prentice-Hall, Inc., 1967.

DUBERMAN, LUCILLE. *Social Inequality: Class and Caste in America*. Philadelphia: J. B. Lippincott Company, Inc., 1978.

KARABEL, JEROME, and A. H. HALSEY, eds. *Power and Ideology in Education*.

Part 2: "Education and Social Selection." New York: Oxford University Press, 1977.

KIMBROUGH, RALPH B. *Political Power and Educational Decision Making.* Chicago: Rand-McNally & Company, 1964.

MILLER, HARRY L. *Social Foundations of Education: An Urban Focus*, 3d ed. Part 1. New York: Holt, Rinehart and Winston, Inc., 1978.

MILLS, C. WRIGHT. *The Power Elite.* New York: Oxford University Press, 1956.

POLSBY, NELSON W. *Community Power and Political Theory.* New Haven: Yale University Press, 1963.

PRICHARD, KEITH W., and THOMAS H. BUXTON. *Concepts and Theories in Sociology of Education.* Lincoln, Nebraska: Professional Educators Publications, Inc., 1973.

SARASAN, SEYMOUR B. *The Culture of the School and the Problem of Change.* Boston: Allyn & Bacon Books, Inc., 1971.

TUMIN, MELVIN M. *Social Stratification: The Forms and Functions of Inequality.* Englewood Cliffs, New Jersey: Prentice-Hall, Inc., 1967.

WEBER, MAX. *The Protestant Ethic and the Spirit of Capitalism.* New York: Charles Scribner's Sons, 1958.

chapter 8

Social, Cultural, and Ethnic Variables and Their Influence on Schooling

The concepts relating to stratification and social class discussed in the previous chapter have been well documented by research studies spanning the past fifty or more years. There are areas of disagreement among scholars on some specific issues, but the reality of social class structure is generally accepted as valid. What is less clear is the effect that stratification and social class identity have on the individual's life chances, education, and schooling. For instance, what difference does it make in the kind of school experience an individual gets if he or she is the product of one or another of the various social classes? Does membership in one social class rather than another provide the individual with predictable advantages or disadvantages? The reader may protest that this is obviously the case, that such relationships are self-evident. Perhaps so; but the issue is not that simple when social class background is combined with other relevant variables such as intelligence or otherwise defined intellectual ability, achievement history, motivation, aspiration, and so on. In this chapter, we will examine these relationships in some detail.

SOCIAL CLASS INFLUENCES: MERITOCRATIC AND REVISIONIST POSITIONS

Let us begin by noting two diametrically opposed views on how social class membership relates to the life chances of an individual:

> We conclude that education is the chief means by which the lower class individual . . . may improve his [*sic*] social position. In our achievement-oriented society, although ascribed characteristics of individuals (such as social class) still make a difference in one's chances for success, the school provides an important mechanism that allows high ability and motivation to find its own level in the occupational structure of society.[1]

A quite different view is articulated by Bowles and Gintis:

> We have suggested that education should be viewed as reproducing inequality by legitimating the allocation of individuals to economic positions on the basis of ostensibly objective merit. Moreover, the basis for assessing merit—competitive academic performance—is only weakly associated with personal attributes indicative of individual success in economic life. Thus the legitimation process in education assumes a largely symbolic form. [p. 123]

> The perpetuation of the class structure requires that the hierarchical division of labor be reproduced in the consciousness of its participants. The educational system is one of the several reproduction mechanisms through which dominant elites seek to achieve this objective. The educational system reproduces the capitalist social division of labor, in part, through a correspondence between its own internal social relationships and those of the workplace. [p. 147]

> The educational system, basically, neither adds to nor subtracts from the degree of inequality and repression originating in the economic sphere. Rather, it reproduces and legitimates a pre-existing pattern in the process of training and stratifying the work force. [p. 265][2]

Of course, these excerpts, taken alone, oversimplify the complex philosophical positions they are cited to represent. Nonetheless, from these brief citations, the reader is able to understand that the relationship

---

[1] David A. Goslin, *The School in Contemporary Society* (Glenview, Illinois: Scott, Foresman & Co., 1965), pp. 125–126.

[2] Samuel Bowles and Herbert Gintis, *Schooling in Capitalist America* (New York: Basic Books, Inc., Publishers, 1976), pp. 123, 147, 265.

196

between social class status and schooling is not as simple as it may appear at first blush.

The first excerpt describes a position that has come to be called "meritocratic." This view holds that the reward system of society—jobs, promotions, salary increases, higher education—favors those individuals who are most competent. If a meritocratic system is working properly, such factors as social class, racial or ethnic background, political affiliation, and income have nothing to do with one's attainment of desired goals. Presumably the goal-seeking is competitive, and the most functionally capable and ambitious individuals win.

But the identification of an individual with his or her family's social class cannot be overlooked, even in a meritocratic system, because of the profound effect it has on the individual. The question that follows, therefore, is, "Are the forces associated with one's social class background so pervasive that they are able to discount the effects of an individual's scholastic aptitude and ambition?" The meritocratic position on this question, though not denying the importance of these factors, would suggest that they are not so powerful as to exclude the individual from competing with others in our achievement-oriented society:

> Proponents of the meritocratic thesis are convinced by the results of their empirical research that scholastic ability, educational ambition, and academic achievement are at least as important as social class, if not more so, in the schooling process. Most of the proponents of this thesis are acutely aware of the presence of social-class bias in schooling; few, however, have argued that the roots of that bias are a permanent fixture of an exploitative capitalist system. Almost all the proponents of this thesis advocate programs and policies that would either reduce or eliminate social-class bias in the schools.[3]

Clearly, proponents of the meritocratic thesis do not believe that social class identification is the *major* determinant of how far an individual will go in school or what his or her future status will be.

The second excerpt at the beginning of this chapter is what might be defined as a "revisionist" position. It is neo-Marxist, socialistic in its orientation. The authors of the excerpt, Bowles and Gintis, are perhaps the most widely cited proponents of this view and certainly among the

---

[3] Richard A. Rehberg and Evelyn R. Rosenthal, *Class and Merit in the American High School* (New York: Longman Inc., 1978), p. 249.

most articulate, although there are many others whose writings support this position.[4] The revisionists argue that the capitalist society is exploitative, and, therefore, schools reflect that exploitative characteristic. In this sense, this position is similar to the power elite theory of decision making; that is, the elites, who are a part of the ruling class, control society and the schools, and they see to it that both serve their best interests. Schools do this, according to the revisionists' view, by reproducing the existing social class structure. Thus, the notion of the allocation of rewards on the basis of merit is a calculated but believable misrepresentation of reality. In actual fact, the schools are designed to maintain the present class structure, and this means that they perpetuate existing inequalities. These inequalities are indigenous to the social class structure, which, in turn, is an essential component of the capitalist society.

Because the fundamental purpose of schools, according to this thesis, is to reproduce the existing unequal social relations of production, social class origin becomes a major factor in differential reward distribution—amount and quality of schooling, career selection, grades, and curricular placement. According to Bowles, "the available data suggest that the number of years of schooling attained by a child depends upon the social-class standing of his father at least as much in the recent period as it did fifty years ago."[5] This view would seem to be contradicted by the research of others, including Raymond Boudon, who reports that "all western societies have been characterized since the end of World War II both by a steady decrease in inequality of educational opportunity and by an almost complete stability of inequality of social opportunity."[6] In

[4] Martin Carnoy, *Education as Cultural Imperialism* (New York: David McKay Company, Inc., 1974); Martin Carnoy, ed., *Schooling in a Corporate State*, 2d ed. (New York: David McKay Company, Inc., 1975); Martin Carnoy and Henry M. Levin, *The Limits of Educational Reform* (New York: David McKay Company, Inc., 1976); Michael B. Katz, *Class, Bureaucracy, and Schools* (New York: Praeger Books, 1971); Christopher Jencks, et al., *Inequality: A Reassessment of the Effect of Family and Schooling in America* (New York: Basic Books, Inc., Publishers, 1972); Clarence J. Karier, Paul Violas, and Joel Spring, *Roots of Crisis: American Education in the Twentieth Century* (Chicago: Rand-McNally College Publishing Company, 1973); Joel Spring, *The Sorting Machine* (New York: David McKay Company, Inc., 1976); John Rawls, *A Theory of Justice* (Cambridge, Massachusetts: Harvard University Press, 1971).

[5] Samuel Bowles, "Unequal Education and the Social Division of Labor," in *Schooling in a Corporate Society*, 2d ed., Martin Carnoy (New York: David McKay Company, Inc., 1975), p. 54.

[6] Raymond Boudon, *Education, Opportunity, and Social Inequality: Changing Prospects in Western Society* (New York: John Wiley and Sons, 1974), Preface.

other words, in spite of increased opportunities for education, social class structures have remained about the same throughout the Western world.

Although the revisionists' position has been a popular one in recent years and has been exceedingly well articulated by its proponents, there is a fair amount of empirically derived evidence that leads one to raise questions as to its validity. For example, Rehberg and Rosenthal surveyed several thousand New York students at four different points in time, beginning in ninth grade in 1967, followed by tenth grade in 1968 and twelfth grade in 1970, and at the postsecondary school level in 1970 and 1971.[7] Some of the findings reported are these:

1. At the ninth grade level, location in a college preparatory program was determined more by merit than by social class membership, but ambition to enter college was determined more by social class than by merit.
2. In the tenth grade, location in an academic program depended more on ability than on social class.
3. The encouragement of students by counselors to continue education beyond high school was found to be influenced by scholastic ability to a far greater degree than by social class.
4. Academic achievement in grades nine through eleven reflected much more of the student's scholastic ability and educational ambition than it did social class origin.
5. The most influential factor in the decision to join the labor force or go into college was scholastic ability.
6. This study found almost no evidence to support the idea that the most important variable in predicting how far a person will go in school is social class.
7. Merit emerged as a determinant of greater consequence than social class of the individual's progress through school and of his or her ultimate schooling attainment.

Rehberg and Rosenthal conclude:

> Within our sample of several thousand students, then, it was individual merit more than family social class that influenced progress from grade nine to grade twelve and subsequent entry into college or the labor market.

[7] Richard A. Rehberg and Evelyn R. Rosenthal, *Class and Merit in the American High School* (New York: Longman Inc., 1978).

> We were able to find little empirical support for the propositions advanced
> by advocates of the revisionist thesis regarding social class and schooling in
> the United States.[8]

This is an astounding conclusion and implies that it is the *individual* himself or herself who is responsible for his or her success or failure in the educational enterprise after all. Not a popular view with those who would want to shift that responsibility to family background, community environment, or the schools.

SOCIAL CLASS INFLUENCES: THE FAMILY

Educational literature frequently makes reference to "family background" as a summarizing variable that impacts on school achievement, IQ, level of aspiration, and other learner outcomes associated with the school experience. This practice has become so common as to create stereotyped expectations associated with family background, social class identity, and family structure. For example, when a teacher speaks of a child coming from a "good home," this is usually interpreted to mean that the child is the product of a two-parent, middle-class, white family of adequate economic means who are loving and supportive of the child. By implication, variations in this stereotype mean that the home is less "good." This generalization is, of course, often incorrect. A child can be the product of a middle-class family and have a psychologically and emotionally devastating family experience. A child from a working-class (lower-class) family might have a family background that provides strong psychological and emotional support. A child from a one-parent family can be and often is secure, stable, well adjusted, and a high achiever. The number of children coming from one-parent families is so high today that it can no longer be considered in any sense unusual. The teaching profession would be well served by dropping the use of the expression "broken home" because of its pejorative and inaccurate connotations.

The human family is a small *kinship system*, which means that it helps us identify who is related to whom by blood or by marriage. The smallest family unit is the conjugal family and includes only the husband and wife. If children are added to this basic unit, it is called a *nuclear family*. If, within the same household, there reside other relatives besides

---

[8] Ibid., p. 254.

the father, mother, and children, we have an *extended family*. Extended families usually include parents, children, grandparents, aunts, uncles, cousins, and possibly great-grandparents. In modern, urban-oriented societies, and especially in the United States, the nuclear family is the dominant arrangement. In the traditional societies of the world, some form of the extended family is the more common pattern.

The family is what sociologists refer to as a "primary group," and it is the most significant instrument of socialization in the lives of most persons. It is a "primary group" because there is a great deal of face-to-face, direct contact among members and because much of the individual's life is spent in such a group. It is from the family that the individual learns some of the most important things he or she needs to know in life. The family teaches the individual the traditions, folkways, and mores of society—to speak a language, to develop a value system, and to form a conscience. How the individual views himself or herself and the world is largely conditioned by family life.

There is convincing research support for the idea that social class influence of the family is felt early in life. Kagan reports several studies conducted in recent years that document the early—as early as the first birthday—and persistent influence of family social class identity.[9] He reports studies indicating that "by 20 and 29 months of age, the class of the child's family had become a major predictor of attentiveness, vocalization, and smiling."[10] In another study, over 27,000 children were followed from birth to age four in an investigation of variables associated with the mother and her effect on the intelligence test scores of four-year-olds. Kagan reports that "the major predictor of the child's IQ at age 4 was the mother's social class."[11]

One of the most educationally relevant differences associated with family social class identity is in the area of language development and use. These differences have been consistently confirmed by studies that extend over a period of forty or more years. The differences on whatever measures are taken uniformly favor the middle social class children over those from lower or working-class families. The middle-class child typically has learned both restricted and elaborated linguistic modes and is able to adjust to the appropriate mode as the social setting varies. The lower-class child has his or her communication limited to the restricted

[9] Jerome Kagan, "The Child in the Family," *Daedalus* (Spring 1977): 33–56.
[10] Ibid., p. 48.
[11] Ibid., p. 49.

linguistic mode. Middle-class children have more extensive vocabularies, produce more mature sentence structures, and are more precise in their articulation and pronunciation than are lower-class children. These differences seem to be associated with early family upbringing in which mothers encourage cognitive development by talking to their young children, providing explanations, encouraging freedom of exploration, and avoiding unnecessary intrusions into the activities of the child. The middle-class child's socialization provides more freedom, more self-involvement, more of an attitude of being able to control one's destiny. The environments of lower-class families are less conducive to this type of cognitive development, especially in language development.

These differences are related directly to the child's performance in school. The sequence of achievement disability proceeds somewhat as follows: The child comes to school with limited linguistic facility and with restricted firsthand experience out of which concepts can be intellectualized. These deficiencies become immediately apparent when the child is confronted with the task of learning to read, usually in the first grade. Most reading specialists agree that reading is a complex intellectual process that relates to linguistic facility and experience background. Thus, the language-impoverished child is likely to encounter problems learning to read. This difficulty, in turn, handicaps the child in learning to construct ideas in written form. Because reading and writing are basic tools in learning other subjects in the school curriculum, the child who does not have them well developed can be expected to fall farther and farther behind in his or her school achievement. In other words, the learning deficits whose origins can be traced to early home environment accumulate as the child proceeds through school. Eventually, of course, the child can no longer cope with the intellectual components of the school curriculum and drops out psychologically. Kagan, cited earlier, summarizes the relationship between a child's social class identity and several significant outcome variables as follows:

> One of the firmest facts in psychology, a discipline with few replicable pieces of knowledge, is the positive relation between a child's social class and a variety of indexes of cognitive functioning, including IQ or achievement-test scores, grades in school, richness of vocabulary and memory, and inferential ability.[12]

[12] Ibid., p. 49.

202

The French sociologist Raymond Boudon has developed an instructive theoretical scheme to account for differences in educational attainment of members of different social classes.[13] Boudon would expect children from poor cultural backgrounds to have lower achievement scores than those from culturally rich environments. Such relationships are so firmly established that they may be referred to as the *primary effects of stratification.* But what about two children, one from a lower-class background and the other from an upper middle-class family, who have identical (and high) scores on an achievement examination? How would one predict their educational futures? Let us say, for example, that they are both high school senior boys and that they are about to make a choice of going either to a trade school or to a conventional four-year liberal arts college. What factors influence the decision of each of these students?

Boudon suggests that the decision of each student is influenced by (1) costs, (2) benefits, and (3) utility. The social costs to the upper-class child selecting a trade school are so great in terms of social demotion, loss of friends (who would be attending four-year colleges), and damaged family pride that the cards are stacked against his making such a choice. The lower-class child can make the trade school choice with the prospect of its leading him to *higher* social status. Such a choice may be more meaningful to his family than a liberal arts curriculum, where he would not learn a trade. What is perceived as having greater utility is related to family social class. Moreover, at least some of his friends are likely to make the same choice, in which case he is not socially isolated. Thus, in terms of costs, benefits, and utility, it is clear that, owing to the social milieu in which each of these students lives, the trade school choice is reinforced for the lower-class student and not for the upper middle-class one.

A reverse set of conditions obtains when the two students consider the liberal arts college choice. The costs in this choice for the lower-class student are loss of friends, alienation from his family, high financial outlays, and lack of the development of obvious work skills. There is no question that the anticipated costs of the liberal arts college choice are many times greater than they are for the upper middle-class student. Thus, social circumstances increase the *probability* that lower-class children will select trade and vocational schools and that middle and upper-

---

[13] Boudon, op. cit., pp. 29–31.

class students will select academically oriented colleges and universities. Boudon concludes that students not only differ in achievement with respect to the primary effects of stratification but differ in these secondary effects of social class identity as well.

THE DEFICIT THEORY VS. CULTURAL DIFFERENCES THEORY OF DEVELOPMENT

In chapter 6, which deals with equality of educational opportunity, the concept of compensatory education was discussed. That concept is also relevant to the present discussion. As was noted in the foregoing section, the primary effects of stratification have been well documented. In terms of lower social class youngsters, the usual way of dealing with these primary effects has been to handle them as *deficits*. All programs designed to enhance the school success of the disadvantaged child are by definition based on a deficit theory of development. Something is missing in the child's developmental pattern that is impeding his or her school achievement. Compensatory education is intended to shore up those deficiencies.

The issue here is not that there are differences between children as a result of stratification but, rather, the nature of those differences; that is, some would argue that such differences should be interpreted as cultural or subcultural variations. Although they may be handicapping in the sense of a child's schoolwork, to label them as deficits contributes to the problem rather than to its solution. Instead of initiating programs to eliminate the child's deficiencies and deprivations, school programs, it is claimed, should build on strengths the child has developed through the years, no matter what his or her social class background has been. Rather than attempt to refashion the child in a standardized image, the school should accept the child for what he or she is and use the skills this person already has to further extend his or her education. For instance, the child may not speak the school's language or dialect, but he or she uses *some* language. The child may not be motivated to learn the tasks assigned in school but may be very clever in dealing with the contingencies of survival on the streets of the ghetto. Frank Riessman has been a spokesman for this point of view:

Most approaches concerned with educating the disadvantaged child either overlook the positives entirely, or merely mention in passing that there are positive features in the culture of low socioeconomic groups, that middle-class groups might learn from, but they do not spell out what these strengths are, and they build educational programs almost exclusively around the weaknesses or deficits.[14]

Later in the same article Riessman lists some of what he perceives to be positive dimensions of lower-class culture and the life-styles of disadvantaged people:

cooperativeness and mutual aid that mark the extended family; the avoidance of the strain accompanying competitiveness and individualism; the equalitarianism, in informality and humor; the freedom from self-blame and parental overprotection; the children's enjoyment of each other's company and lessened sibling rivalry; the security found in the extended family and a traditional outlook; the enjoyment of music, games, sports, and cards; the ability to express anger; the freedom from being word-bound; an externally oriented rather than a temporal perspective; an expressive orientation in contrast to an instrumental one; content-centered not a form-centered mental style; a problem-centered rather than an abstract-centered approach; and finally, the use of physical and visual style in learning.[15]

There is some considerable doubt about the validity of this line of reasoning. Many would question the assertion that "the ability to express anger, the freedom from being word-bound, and freedom from self-blame" could be interpreted as strengths in our culture. Havighurst is sharply critical of this approach as is apparent in the following excerpt:

there is substantial doubt that the socially disadvantaged children in our big cities have *any* positive qualities of potential value in urban society in which they are systematically better than the children of families who participate fully in the mass culture. The writer does not know any comparative study which shows American lower-lower class children to be superior in any positive respect to American upper working-class or middle-class children.[16]

[14] Frank Riessman, "The Overlooked Positives of Disadvantaged Groups," in *The Disadvantaged Child: Issues and Innovations*, ed. Joe L. Frost and Glenn R. Hawkes (Boston: Houghton Mifflin Company, 1966), p. 51.

[15] Ibid., p. 56.

[16] Robert J. Havighurst, "Who Are the Socially Disadvantaged?" in *Readings for Social Studies in Elementary Education*, 2d ed., ed. John Jarolimek and Huber M. Walsh (New York: Macmillan Publishing Company, Inc., 1969), p. 235.

We are dealing here with this central question: Are poor, socially disadvantaged, and educationally handicapped people that way because they are somehow less capable to begin with, or are they less capable because they are poor, socially disadvantaged, and educationally handicapped? This question cannot be answered on the basis of life histories of individual people because there are too many exceptions to any generalization formed on the basis of group data. Indeed, we are really not able to answer it at all. Education in this country has been conducted on the assumption that the latter relationship is the most accurate; that is, it is assumed that the effects of disadvantaged circumstances recycle and become causes of the problem. Consequently, we have undertaken remedial measures that are intended to break the cycle. Compensatory programs for the poor, the socially disadvantaged, and the educationally handicapped have been planned and implemented to serve that purpose.

As was noted in Chapter 6, such compensatory programs have enjoyed only limited success. Critics would say the effects are predictable and that these programs can never be effective because they are based on an erroneous assumption, that is, that environmental factors are primarily responsible for an individual's intellectual development. Apologists would respond by saying that the intervention efforts to date have been so miniscule that they could not possibly be expected to produce the desired effects; that is, one does not overcome the effects of years of deprivation, discrimination, malnutrition, intellectual numbness, and poverty in a few easy lessons. The issue, although clouded and unresolved, is discussed in the next section.

WELLSPRINGS OF INTELLECTUAL COMPETENCE

The controversy introduced in the foregoing section invites our attention to the relative importance of genetic endowment as contrasted with the environment within which one is reared to one's intellectual competence. This issue is often referred to in the literature of education, psychology, and sociology as the "nature-nurture controversy." An awareness that one's parentage, as well as one's surroundings, contribute to the development of a human being is doubtless of ancient origin, a claim that can be documented by reference to conventional wisdom, Biblical passages, fables, folklore, and other such sources:

HEREDITY
"Like father, like son."
"He's a chip off the old block."
"What is born of a hen will scratch."
"The fruit don't [*sic*] fall too far from the tree."

ENVIRONMENT
"Train a boy in the way he should go; even when he is old, he will not swerve [depart] from it." (Proverbs 22:6)
"As the twig is bent, so grows the tree."
"Life consists not in holding good cards, but in playing those you hold well." [Josh Billings]
"He was born with a silver spoon in his mouth."

These quotations, some of which in one form or another go back hundreds of years, provide a good example of the character of the nature-nurture controversy. Each one contains a pearl of wisdom that we are able to validate through personal knowledge. Everyone of us knows someone who is a "chip off the old block"; of course, we recognize the advantage of being "born with a silver spoon" in one's mouth! There are truths in these sayings on both sides of the issue. Few authorities or researchers are willing to discount totally either heredity *or* environment as crucial variables in the development of human beings. The central question, however, is, "How *much* does each one count?"

This controversy has persisted for over six decades. Shortly after the turn of the century, psychologists in this country and in Western Europe began experimenting with ways to differentiate among human beings in terms of their ability to perform certain intellectual operations. A forerunner of the measurement of intelligence today is generally conceded to be the French psychologist Alfred Binet. He, along with his collaborator, Theodore Simon, was commissioned by the minister of education in Paris to develop mental tests to be used to identify mentally deficient children in the schools of Paris. It does not suit our purpose here to provide a history of the development of intelligence tests. Suffice it to say that the field of psychology and especially the interest in the measurement of human traits were both growing at a rapid rate during the first half of this century and contributed much to the development of mental measurement instruments. Out of this work came the concept of the IQ—intelligence quotient—defined as the ratio between a "mental age," a score based on the individual's performance on a set of standardized intellectual tasks, and the person's actual or chronological age. The best-known individually administered intelligence test is the *Stanford-Binet Intelligence Scale*, and it is the one most frequently used in validating other individual or group intelligence tests.

Over the past several decades there have been endless debates over the meaning of intelligence, what it "really" is, and whether or not it can be measured. Indeed, not all specialists agree on a definition of it, to say nothing of measuring it! Discussions continue around such issues as whether intelligence is a unitary concept (that is, consists mainly of a general intelligence factor) or pluralistic (that is, consists of many "intelligences") or is represented best by some combination of these. In order to extricate themselves from this tangled definitional web, some researchers have simply defined intelligence operationally as consisting of whatever it is that an intelligence test measures. But as can be seen from the following two excerpts, there can be considerable disagreement as to what is actually measured by intelligence tests:

> We conclude that IQ tests measure important intellectual qualities in children and adults; that these qualities are very important both in education and in professions and jobs requiring abilities for abstract thinking and problem solving; and that while such tests cannot be culture free, they can be culture fair to varying degrees.[17]

And a different view:

> Are IQ tests biased against working people and especially blacks? Our answer is unequivocal. They are. This is not so only because the language is "white" and items are middle class oriented. IQ tests are an obstacle to the educational advancement of working people in general and blacks in particular because they ascribe the causes of differences in educational performance to internal deficiencies in capacity. And based on this fraudulent claim, which is implicit in the structure and content of the test however much some psychologists may back off from asserting it, IQ tests partially result in and basically justify an educational system that builds in ine-

---

[17] H. J. Eysenck, *The IQ Argument: Race, Intelligence and Education* (New York: The Library Press, 1971), p. 57.

208

qualities through tracking within schools and classrooms as well as between schools . . .

A test constructed in the atheoretical common sense manner of the Stanford-Binet is bound to include items of moral opinion which reflect class biases, vocabulary reflecting racial and class bias, as well as items for which such types of particular bias have been eliminated.[18]

But Eysenck says:

The ability to reason, to abstract, to educe relations and correlates, is funda-mental to intelligent activity, to educational progress and to professional competence. The color of a man's skin has nothing to do with the truth or otherwise of these statements.[19]

The nature-nurture controversy surfaced anew and came to na-tional attention at the beginning of the decade of the 1970s. The compen-satory programs that were encouraged and funded by the federal govern-ment had been operating for a number of years, and, as has already been noted, their success had received mixed reviews, to say the least. In fact, the author of one of the most controversial articles published during this period began his article in the *Harvard Educational Review* with this sentence, "Compensatory education has been tried and it apparently has failed."[20] By this time, too, the results of the national survey, *Equality of Educational Opportunity*, known as the "Coleman Report," were being widely disseminated: funding and facilities differences between schools serving black children and those serving white children were not as exten-sive or as profound as had been expected; the academic achievement of white children continued to excel that of blacks; variables associated with the school itself had little effect on the academic achievement of the students who attended them. Also at this time a number of articles were published in the popular press as well as in professional journals having to do with the relationship or lack of relationship between social class and IQ and either implicitly or explicitly the relationship between social class-race-intelligence variables. Some of these articles were based on research, but many were entirely speculative. Many of them were simply

[18] James M. Lawler, *IQ, Heritability and Racism* (New York: International Publish-ers, 1978), pp. 83–84.

[19] Eysenck, op. cit., p. 75.

[20] Arthur R. Jensen, "How Much Can We Boost IQ and Scholastic Achievement?" *Harvard Educational Review* 39:1 (Winter 1969): 2.

209

pleas for social justice. Oftentimes the rhetoric was characterized by harshness and bitterness.

It is doubtful if this subject matter can be discussed in a sober, balanced, and scholarly way even today. Writers and researchers seem not to be able to separate their academic, presumably scientific, concern for these issues as legitimate areas of inquiry and research from their own personal social and political philosophies. Knowing an author's social or political orientation makes it possible to predict how he or she will perceive data—if there are any data to perceive. Thus, the Marxists-socialists interpret data from one perspective; the neoconservatives from another perspective; and both views are represented by spokespersons who have impressive scholarly credentials. The researchers Loehlin, Lindsey, and Spuhler make this cogent comment on this set of circumstances:

> When the questions are re-examined in the context of racial and social class differences in a society ridden with unresolved tensions in these areas, it is not surprising that the result should be a massive polemic in which personal convictions and emotional commitment often have been more prominent than evidence or careful reasoning.[21]

The major issues surrounding this controversy are these:

1. How much of one's intelligence—as measured by an intelligence test—is heritable? That is, what is the genetic contribution to intelligence? Some researchers put the figure as high as 80 per cent (A. R. Jensen); others believe that estimate to be much too high; at least one (L. Kamin) asserts zero heritability.
2. Does the IQ test measure intelligence? The question here is whether what is being measured is intelligence or a set of tasks that correlate with school tasks, and, therefore, strongly bias the outcome of the test in favor of children and adults from middle- and upper-class homes.
3. Are the differences in measured IQ between whites and blacks the result of racial genetic differences? The issue here is not the difference itself but the source of the difference. Some studies report a fifteen-point IQ difference favoring whites. Researchers

---

[21] John C. Loehlin, Gardner Lindsey, James N. Spuhler, *Race Differences in Intelligence* (San Francisco: W. H. Freeman and Company, 1975), pp. 2–3.

have interpreted this difference as resulting from genetic differences between the races; others say that the differences are largely environmentally related.

4. Is the IQ a fixed quantity, relatively stable throughout life, or is it amenable to change as a result of environmental stimulation, improved nutrition, restoration of physical conditions, and so on?

There is a considerable amount of evidence to link both measured intelligence and school achievement with social class. These differences have been observed consistently through numerous replications. The differences in intelligence begin to appear after the first year of life. Some would suggest that this means that children, therefore, begin life on an equal footing, but soon the debilitating effects of an impoverished environment begin to produce their inexorable effects. Others would say, simply, that except for gross developmental differences, the measuring instruments are so crude and the child's response so variable that it is not possible to get a reliable measure at such an early age. If intelligence is highly heritable, one could reason that through the years the process of natural selection has resulted in a less favorable endowment of genes that govern intelligence for low social class youngsters. If intelligence is largely the result of one's environment, one could argue that early intervention of experiences known to be intellectually stimulating would be efficacious to mental development. But if environmental circumstances for all children are brought up to par—that is, if differences between nurturing environments virtually disappear, but differences in academic achievement persist—the case for a genetic basis of intelligence is obviously strengthened.

When one considers mean differences between groups, whether those are aggregates of people in social class, ethnic, or racial groups, the variance within them is substantially greater than it is between groups. This means that (1) there is tremendous variation in the academic performance of children within *any* social class, ethnic, or racial group; (2) there is substantial overlap of achievement between groups being compared; and (3) the performance of an *individual* cannot be reliably predicted, that is, with a high level of confidence, from a knowledge of his or her group membership alone. In examining group differences of human traits in general, one can usually be sure that some members of the low-scoring group will distribute themselves above the mean of the high-scoring group. Likewise, some members of the high-scoring group will have scores falling below the mean of the low-scoring group. The within-group variance that results in the overlap of achievement, intelligence, or other traits from one human group to the next is one of the least well-understood concepts in education.

We close this section with an excerpt from the work of Loehlin, Lindsey, and Spuhler. A careful review of research relating to the problems discussed in this section led them to the following general conclusions:

1. Observed average differences in the scores of members of different U.S. racial-ethnic groups on intellectual-ability tests probably reflect in part inadequacies and biases in the tests themselves, in part differences in environmental conditions among groups, and in part genetic differences among groups. It should be emphasized that these three factors are not necessarily independent, and may interact.

2. A rather wide range of positions concerning the relative weight to be given these three factors can reasonably be taken on the basis of current evidence, and a sensible person's position might well differ for different abilities, for different groups, and for different tests.

3. Regardless of the position taken on the relative importance of these three factors, it seems clear that the differences among individuals *within* racial-ethnic (and socioeconomic) groups greatly exceed in magnitude the average differences between such groups.[22]

THE UNDERCLASS: POVERTY IN THE MIDST OF AFFLUENCE

The subject matter of this and the preceding chapter makes it clear that social power is closely associated with social class structure. In Chapter 6, reference was made to the lowest stratum of the social class structure, the powerless group sometimes referred to as the "underclass."

[22] Ibid., pp. 238–239.

It is appropriate here to return to a discussion of that group as we conclude our analysis of the effects of social class on schooling.

In 1969 the president's Commission on Income Maintenance stated that "the paradox of poverty in the midst of plenty causes many to ask why some people remain poor when so many of their fellow Americans have successfully joined the ranks of the affluent."[23] We do not have a satisfactory answer to that question. The status of the poor, the disenfranchised, and the underprivileged has stubbornly resisted all remedial efforts, which have included relocation, job training, health improvement services, compensatory education, community participation opportunities, direct income support, food stamps, welfare benefits, and others. It is a fact that efforts to remediate poverty, without exception, have been conceived, designed, and implemented by persons with middle- and upper-class orientations and values. This may explain, in part, some of their ineffectiveness because they are often based on faulty assumptions concerning the psychology of persons who occupy the underclass.

Those we identify as the underclass are underprivileged to the extent that they lack the knowledge and skills needed to develop psychological, social, and communication links with the rest of society. They are cultural outsiders, causing some authors to speak of them as being in a "culture of poverty." Individuals are socialized into that culture of poverty one generation after another. There are a number of recorded cases of three generations of the same family receiving public assistance (welfare) at the same time, leading some to conclude that poverty "runs in families." Of course, poverty does run in families but not for the reasons usually assumed. Whether one regards this group as living in a culture of poverty or simply in a subculture of the dominant culture, they are removed sufficiently far from the mainstream to be alienated and disaffected from the social system.

Not everyone who is poor can be classified as being in the underclass. Nor is everyone who is in the lower-lower class considered underclass. If we use income as a measure of poverty, we can identify a great number of persons who are poor but who lead responsible, stable lives. Many elderly persons living on low, fixed retirement incomes are of this

[23] President's Commission on Income Maintenance, 1969b, "Why the Poor Remain Poor," in *Poverty amid Plenty: The American Paradox* (Washington, D.C.: U.S. Government Printing Office), p. 194.

213

type, as are hundreds of thousands of persons who are in the work force occupying low-paying jobs. The underclass, on the other hand, is characterized by different qualities, and defining it requires another set of descriptors.

People of the underclass are generally unemployed or are irregularly employed at menial, low-paying jobs. They live on the outskirts of hope in circumstances that most would consider wholly unfit for human habitation. In past years this group was stereotyped with depressed rural life—Appalachia, *Tobacco Road, Grapes of Wrath*. Although some remain in rural areas, today the heavy concentration of the underclass is found in the ghettos of America's large cities. They include all races and ethnic groups but are predominantly disadvantaged urban blacks, urban Hispanics, migrant Chicanos, and some Indians (Native Americans). Crime, delinquency, drug addiction, alcoholism, prostitution, hostility, unemployment, and social alienation characterize the life of the underclass. Television and other direct contact with the rest of society have familiarized members of this subculture with the reality of their own meager circumstances as compared with the rest of society, and what they see has made them resentful and defiant. From time to time their antagonism bursts out in wild rampages of burning and looting, as it did in New York City in July of 1977. The underclass is at the same time a national disgrace and one of the most dangerous social realities facing this country today.

It would be a mistake to assume that everyone in the underclass leads a life of violent crime, is hustling on the street, or is looking for a quick fix. The fact that most of the persons do not lead such lives makes it possible for society to contain the condition. But the underclass has no sense of investment in, or ownership of, the larger society, and this leads to personal feelings of destitution and hopelessness. Little wonder that this should be true, considering the conditions under which these people live. The unemployment rate is constantly twice as high for blacks as it is for whites. For black teenagers, the unemployment rate is nearly three times what it is for their white counterparts, currently nearly 40 per cent.

Quite apart from the economic effects of unemployment, the direct psychological damage is devastating in terms of feelings of personal self-worth. Any job at all that is regular provides one with a feeling of accomplishment and makes for a sense of stability. It seems clear that if people living in this subculture are ever to develop any identity with the larger social system and build any sense of investment in it, employment opportunities for them will need to be expanded by monumental proportions.

What effect does such a life-style have on the schooling of children who come out of it? The answer is not at all encouraging. Many, perhaps most, of these children are not reached psychologically by the school at all. The school becomes largely a custodial center rather than an educational institution. Teachers have an incredibly difficult, stressful, and tension-ridden work environment. For many it is a challenge simply to survive in what is literally a dangerous place. Student absenteeism is high, and school officials make little effort to enforce truancy laws. Teachers usually breathe a sigh of relief when the troublemakers are absent. The school curriculum is based on values that have little meaning for children and teenagers who come from a world of strutting pimps, drug pushers, and apartment houses shared with rats and cockroaches. A child terrorized by a street gang can hardly be expected to be highly motivated to attend to what is being presented in the classroom.

Teachers, school officials, political leaders, legislators, and citizens generally must realize once and for all that the problems associated with the underclass cannot be solved through educational efforts alone. To suggest that public education can somehow provide solutions to a dangerous social condition of this magnitude is hopelessly naïve. Indeed, public education by itself is no answer at all to this serious cluster of problems. If this society is to overcome the problems of the underclass, it will have to mount a major rehabilitation effort, of which education would necessarily be a part. But national priorities are not so arranged at the present time, and there is little to suggest that they will be in the near future. Meanwhile, the most prosperous and highly educated nation on earth continues to sit on a social time bomb that will one day surely explode and create a major upheaval in social relations in this country.

What is being suggested should not be construed to mean that the school has no constructive role to play in helping children from the underclass. We are suggesting only that the school cannot do it alone. Successful strategies for dealing with the problems of the underclass will need to extend across a broad spectrum of social and health services, including social, psychological, economic, political, educational, vocational, and allied health spheres. Until society sees fit to tackle this problem on a broad front, teachers must do the best they can in making a conscientious effort to teach these children to read, write, and perform basic arithmetic operations simply as survival skills. Beyond that teachers need have that might impact positively or negatively on school achievement.

9. What evidence can you cite to support the idea that our society is basically meritocratic?

10. Why is the mother often a more powerful socializing agent in the *nuclear* family than in an *extended* family? What family conditions might alter the mother's influence in either case?

SELECTED BIBLIOGRAPHY

BLUMBERG, RAE LESSER. *Stratification: Socioeconomic and Sexual Inequality.* Dubuque, Iowa: Wm. C. Brown Company, Publishers, 1978.

BOWLES, SAMUEL, and HERBERT GINTIS. *Schooling in Capitalist America: Educational Reform and the Contradictions of Economic Life.* New York: Basic Books, Inc., Publishers, 1976.

EYSENCK, H. J. *The IQ Argument: Race, Intelligence, and Education.* New York: The Library Press, 1971.

HERRNSTEIN, RICHARD J. *IQ in the Meritocracy.* Boston: Little, Brown and Company, 1973.

HURN, CHRISTOPHER J. *The Limits and Possibilities of Schooling: An Introduction to the Sociology of Education.* Boston: Allyn & Bacon Books, Inc., 1978.

JENSEN, ARTHUR R. "How Much Can We Boost IQ and Scholastic Achievement?" *Harvard Educational Review* 38:1 (Winter 1969): 1–123.

JENSEN, ARTHUR R. *Bias in Mental Testing.* New York: The Free Press (Macmillan), 1979.

KAGAN, JEROME S., ET AL. "How Much Can We Boost IQ? A Discussion." *Harvard Educational Review* 39:2 (Spring 1969): 273–356. (This is a discussion of the issues raised in the Arthur R. Jensen article.)

KARABEL, JEROME, and A. H. HALSEY, eds. *Power and Ideology in Education.* Part 5: "Cultural Reproduction and the Transmission of Knowledge." New York: Oxford University Press, 1977.

LAWLER, JAMES M. *IQ, Heritability, and Racism.* New York: International Publishers, 1978.

LOEHLIN, JOHN C., GARDNER LINDSEY, and J. N. SPUHLER. *Race Differences in Intelligence.* San Francisco: W. H. Freeman and Company, 1975.

RAVITCH, DIANE. *The Revisionists Revised.* New York: Basic Books, Inc., Publishers, 1978.

REHBERG, RICHARD A., and EVELYN R. ROSENTHAL. *Class and Merit in the American High School.* New York: Longman, Inc., 1978.

REIMER, EVERETT. *School is Dead: Alternatives in Education.* Garden City, New York: Doubleday & Company, Inc., 1970.

ZIGLER, EDWARD. "Social Class and the Socialization Process." *Review of Educational Research* 40 (February 1970): 87–110.

chapter 9

Economic Influences on School Decision Making

Economic influences on the school are obviously one of the most powerful influences. Schools simply must have financial resources in order to operate, and funding restrictions or limitations have direct impact on the curriculum and personnel decisions school authorities can make. In addition to being a very potent force in shaping school decision making, economic factors are ones that are often easily manipulated at the local level. This is because of the system of school funding that prevails in this country.

To some extent schools throughout the United States depend on local property taxes for their support. The amount of school funding that comes from this source varies greatly from state to state, with the national average being about 44 per cent. Local funding is highest in those states where the state contribution to schools is low. State support is lowest in New Hampshire (6 per cent) and highest in Hawaii (100 per cent). The trend in recent years has been for states to increase the state contribution, and consequently they rely less heavily on local property taxes for school support. This change has been and is a slow process, and it doubtless will be several years before all states move to full state funding of schools.

There are many disparities in the economics of educational support in this country. First, there are enormous differences in the states' ability to finance education. Some of the affluent states have considerably higher per capita income than others do. Moreover, the tax structures in some states are such that relatively more income can be generated on the same taxing potential. For example, if a state does not have an income tax, the burden of securing an appropriate amount of tax dollars will fall on other taxable items, most likely property.

There is also great unevenness in educational needs. Some areas have a higher percentage of poor families. If a state has a large number of families living in poverty, educational costs are bound to be high. The disparity of need relates to a disparity in costs. Children of the poor are frequently hard to educate; to do an adequate job with them costs more than it does to educate children from moderately affluent homes. Ironically, it is often the areas that have the largest number of hard-to-educate children that also have the poorest financial resources.

As long as schools depend on local sources of revenue for their operating budgets, there will continue to be large differences in the amount spent on education from one place to another. We can also safely say that there will also be continued dissatisfaction with education so long as local funding structures prevail. There are fairly specific upper limits that a community is willing to tax itself for schools. Beyond that point taxpayer resistance will become so great that efforts to raise additional revenue will prove to be futile. It should also be noted that there are limits on the amount of tax funds that can be raised locally because of the value of local property.

Economic influences on school decision making can be studied from several perspectives. We will examine four: (1) personal income, (2) state and local financial support, (3) federal funding, and (4) the philanthropic foundations. We will discuss each of these separately, but it is important to keep in mind that there is an interaction among these four dimensions. For example, persons with high incomes can and often do influence legislation and policies regarding education at the state and local levels. Adequacy of state and local funding may influence the amount of federal dollars available because of the matching requirement. Therefore, as the reader analyzes each of these four dimensions of economic influence, he or she should also relate it to the other three.

PERSONAL INCOME AS A FACTOR IN EDUCATIONAL DECISION MAKING

Traditionally and historically, education has gone to those who could pay for it. In Chapter 1, we discussed the rise of compulsory education, and it is pointed out there that the idea of education for all the children of all the people is one of relatively recent origin. And even though we have made great gains in extending education to all, personal income still has a great deal to do with the kind and quality of education a child receives in this or any other country.

The selection of a private school is still an option—an educational alternative—that can be exercised by those who can afford it. The upper class and the wealthy typically send their children to the best private schools. This is done for several reasons, quality of education being one, personal security being another important one, and specific socialization expectations being still another. The attendance of a child at an exclusive private elementary and/or secondary school enormously increases the chances of social, political, and economic benefits that flow from one's school experience.

In the early growth of public education in the last century, social reformers and educators promoted the idea of the "common" school in part to discourage attendance at private schools. This was a democratic idea—that the public school should be a common experience for all. The concept of "common" was used to mean that the school was for everybody, not common in the sense of meaning "ordinary." Common as "the air we breathe is common" according to one enthusiast for the common school. Efforts were made to elevate the quality of public education.

But alas, even in the case of those attending the common schools, personal income makes a difference in their education. For one thing, if parents are seeking a good school for their children, it makes a big difference where they choose to live. Of course, where they live depends on how much money they have to assist with the choosing. Well-educated, affluent, middle-class families may not wish to send their children to a private school. They will, nonetheless, seek out homes in those neighborhoods where the people who live there value education and provide solid support for schools. This almost always means the preferred residential areas of large cities or the suburbs. One does not need to be a trained sociologist to locate such neighborhoods—they can be identified simply by driving in and around a city.

221

Personal income makes a difference because only affluent families are able to afford to purchase homes in such areas. An examination of achievement test scores of children from elementary schools throughout the city and its suburbs will show gross differences in means from one place to another. For example, in Seattle the mean score obtained on a basic skills test for children in one elementary school was sixteen; in another school it was eighty-seven. Of course, these differences reflect, in part, family social class differences, but they also say something about the quality of education in the two schools. Indeed, social class background of families in the neighborhood and quality of education in the local school are interacting variables.

When families purchase homes in those areas that provide well for the education of children, they buy a "packaged deal." Good schools are a part of that "deal." So is a degree of segregation—today based more on social class than on race, but the effect is the same in either case. Also a part of these tacit agreements is a tightly zoned residential area that restricts heavy commercial development and allows only residences of certain value on generously sized building lots. In return, the families agree to pay the exorbitant property taxes that usually characterize such areas. Quite naturally, these taxpayers, who are also parents of schoolchildren, expect to have their voices heard at the forums at which school policies are shaped.

But even families who live in other, not so privileged areas can greatly enhance their children's education if their personal income is sufficient. For example, parents can buy enrichment experiences for their youngsters—dancing, music, art, or drama lessons, camping in the summer, skiing in the winter, concerts and plays, travel, and so on. Or if the child finds him or herself in difficulty in learning to read in the elementary school or learning a foreign language in high school, the parent with the wherewithall can engage a tutor to help the child over the rough spots. Although one obviously cannot buy an education in the literal sense, there is no end to the stimulating and interesting doorways to learning that can be secured by those who can afford it.

The effects of personal income on the kind of education a person can receive is well summarized by Prichard and Buxton in the following excerpt:

> The Kennedy family serves as an excellent example of the life-style maintained by the members of the lower-upper class. The sons of the family

have been prepped at private nondenominational schools and most of the daughters have attended Catholic schools and colleges. At Harvard the late President John F. Kennedy served as chairman of the Frosh-Soph Party and threw a party in Memorial Hall still remembered by many. A Broadway musical show was flown in as part of the entertainment. Following his graduation from Harvard, he, at the insistence of his father, attended the London School of Economics, where he studied under the tutorship of Harold Laski, a prominent economist-sociologist. While members of the middle and lower class might opt to follow the same career pattern, few have the financial resources provided by a multimillionaire father to tide them over the difficult moments. Possibly, the informal education afforded the members of the upper class is more significant than the colleges and universities attended. Within the Kennedy family circle prominent actors, financiers, politicians, etc., were frequently dinner guests, and provided much cultural affluence for the Kennedy children.[1]

STATE AND LOCAL FINANCIAL SUPPORT OF SCHOOLS

Nationally, state and local taxing units provide approximately 91 per cent of the funds required to operate public schools. Using average figures, this is split with the state contributing 47 per cent and the local government 44 per cent. As has already been noted, this varies greatly from one place to another, and the trend of increased contributions by the state is likely to continue. There can be little doubt that one of the reasons why schools have been so roundly criticized in recent years is because they directly and visibly contribute to increased taxes at the local level.

The reliance of school support on the property tax has come to us out of the past, when wealth was associated with property. Historically, indeed until modern times, the wealthy person was one who had substantial holdings of land and property. Having an estate was a mark of wealth. Huge farms and plantations were owned by people of means. The concept of "landed gentry" reinforces the relationship between property and wealth. It is significant to note that corporate wealth, income, and stock holdings are excluded from this traditional concept of wealth.

Thus, in designing a system of taxation for schools, our forebears

[1] Keith W. Prichard and Thomas H. Buxton, *Concepts and Theories in Sociology of Education* (Lincoln, Nebraska: Professional Educators Publications, Inc., 1973), pp. 78–79.

Sources of Funds for Public Education 1979

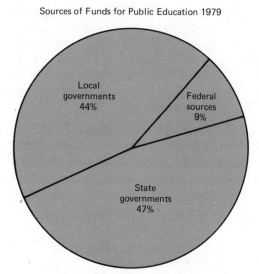

FIGURE 8. Which sources in this graph are likely to increase and which ones decrease in the next two decades? Why?

quite logically taxed property because property holders were persons who were best able to pay. There was also a sound rationale for the idea of having such taxes paid and collected at the local level. This was to serve two purposes. First, it would ensure prudent use of such funds. If local persons saw schools wasting money, they would be less willing to tax themselves for school support. Second, the system was designed to encourage monitoring of the school program at the local level. Parents and patrons would want to be sure they were getting their money's worth of education if they were reminded that their taxes were supporting the schools. This system never worked especially well and has broken down completely in recent years.

The Way in Which the System of Property Tax Works

Suppose you were to select a school district and make an analysis of it in terms of the value of all property within its boundaries. Let us say that you actually looked at every piece of land, every house, garage, barn, building, factory, store, and so on, and attached a fair market value to those items of property. This is precisely what assessors do in every county in the United States on a more or less regular basis. Such evaluations of property worth, known as assessments, result in a total *assessed valuation* of the school district. It should be apparent immediately that the assessed valuation will vary enormously from one school district to another. In one instance, there are many stores, factories, and expensive pieces of property. In another there are small, ill-kept houses, unproductive farmland, and abandoned business places. In some instances, such gross differences have been known to exist in adjoining school districts. These inequities, as one would expect, have been the source of conflict over school funding policies.

Of course, the amount of tax dollars a district needs to operate its schools depends on how many children reside within it. One measure of a school district's ability to support its schools has been the ratio between the assessed valuation and the number of school-age children. For instance, if one divides the assessed valuation of a district by the number of school-age children, one obtains the amount of taxable dollars "behind each child." In other words, this is a per pupil tax potential. Here again there are huge differences in these ratios. It has been estimated that these differences in actual dollar amounts vary as much as 10,000 to one!

These differences in property values have significant implications for funding at the local level because the ratio of taxable property to number of children determines the *rate* at which a district must tax itself in order to generate a specified level of funding. This is usually expressed in *mills*. A mill is one thousanth of a dollar (1/1000 or usually .001) or one tenth of a cent. When school officials talk about "millage" or "mill rate," they are referring to the rate at which property is to be taxed. It should be clear that a district with a *high level* of property value and *few* children will be able to get by with a low mill rate (low tax rate). Conversely, a district with a *low level* of property value and *many* children will need to have a high mill rate (high tax rate). These differences and relationships are illustrated vividly by the data in Table 3, which is based on two actual cases of school districts in the same state.

Notice that the two school districts shown in Table 3 enroll about the same number of students. Notice also that property owners in South Fork pay more than *twice* the rate of taxes as do those in Meadowvale (14.57 mills as compared with 6.90). This means that a homeowner of a $60,000 house in Meadowvale would pay $414.00 in school taxes each year, whereas his counterpart in a $60,000 house in South Fork would

225

TABLE 3.

	Enrollment	Per Pupil Property Valuation	Levy Mills	Levy Revenue	Per Pupil Revenue Generated
Meadowvale	8,192	34,060	6.90	$1,925,000	$234.00
South Fork	7,935	9,447	14.57	1,092,000	137.00
			Difference	$ 833,000	

pay $874.00. Yet, in spite of paying more than twice as much in taxes, South Fork has nearly $100.00 *less* to spend per pupil than does Meadowvale. By taxing itself at half the rate of South Fork, Meadowvale has $833,000 more to spend on its schools each year!

The differences in the financial situation between these two school districts can be accounted for by the differences in assessed valuation. Meadowvale is the site of the largest lumber operation in the world. The taxes it pays greatly relieves homeowners who live in the district. South Fork, on the other hand, is a typical suburban "bedroom" community. It has many residences, many children, but few commercial buildings that are high tax revenue-producing properties. This is typical of suburban residential communities, and until recently, at least, the people who live there have been willing to pay the higher tax rates in return for what they believe to be a higher quality of residential life.

State financial support for operating budgets of schools has generally taken two forms: (1) flat aid based on per pupil in average daily attendance and (2) a variable amount based on need. This second type of state aid is intended to compensate in part for the kinds of tax inequities we have been discussing. This has come to be known as the principle of *equalization*. It would be hard to argue, for example, that the additional $833,000 that Meadowvale has to spend each year does not affect the quality of education there. Therefore, on the basis of the principle of equalization of educational opportunity, states have attempted to supplement local budgets in terms of their needs. But no matter what is done by the states to shore up this type of local funding, inequities are bound to persist. Increasingly, states are recognizing this and are moving toward full state funding of schools.

Many tax specialists and economists believe that the property tax today is basically unsound as a reliable source of revenue for essential public services such as schools. The chief objections to it are these: (1) It is not a good money raiser. It does not come close to raising an adequate amount of money even in those areas where it is excessive. (2) It is irritating to taxpayers because it is direct (not hidden) and is one of the few taxes that can be controlled by the taxpayers. (3) In many ways it is unfair. For example, only property owners pay it. Others who work in the district—perhaps even work for the school district but live elsewhere— pay no tax. (4) It does not represent real wealth. Wealthy people today do not accumulate large holdings of property. Quite to the contrary, they keep their wealth fluid so that it can be moved about and invested appropriately. (5) It is too subject to the control by vested power groups locally. A small vocal minority at the local level is able to defeat tax issues to the disadvantage of the schools. (6) School personnel and the schools themselves are often blamed for an unsound tax system. (7) Increasingly, there have been questions raised concerning its legality.

Magnitude of the Educational Enterprise

Few persons appreciate or understand the massiveness of the educational enterprise in this country. For the past eighty years, about one-fourth of our population has been in school. Commenting on this statistic, Charles O. Burgess says,

> There has long been an interestingly near-static nature to that figure. Since the early 1900's our school-age population has grown older; but so has our general population. In 1900 there were 23 elementary schools for every secondary school, while in the 1970's there were only 3 elementary schools for every secondary school. But the one-out-of-four figure has held fairly steady even while the raw numbers of school students trebled.[2]

In the fall of 1979, nearly 42 million youngsters of ages five to seventeen years were in public schools. It cost American taxpayers over $67 billion to educate them. To this enrollment figure could be added approximately twelve million students who were enrolled in postsecondary schools, making a total cost of upwards of $80 billion. Smith and Orlosky point out that in 1970 the expenditures for schools "exceeded the combined revenues reported by General Motors, American Telephone and

[2] Charles O. Burgess, "Our Way of Educating." Paper prepared for the Ford Foundation (1978).

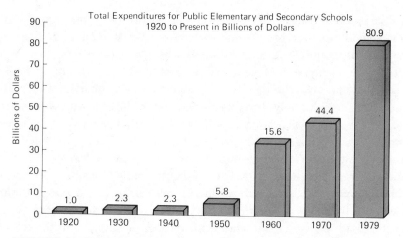

FIGURE 9. Compare this graph with the one in Chapter 1 showing trends in school enrollments. What effect do these trends have on the per-pupil cost of education? What factors have contributed to the dramatic rise in the expenditures for education during the decade of the 1970s? (Sources: National Center for Education Statistics and the NEA.)

Telegraph, Standard Oil of New Jersey, and the Ford Motor Company."[3] Education is the second most costly public service of our country, second only to national defense expenditures.

School expenditures nationally grew from slightly over one billion dollars in 1920 to just over $50 billion in 1972. Part of this escalation of costs can be accounted for by increased numbers of pupils in school, especially at the secondary school level. But perhaps more of the increase has occurred simply because of rising costs of education. People demand more educational services, and all of those services cost more than they once did. For instance, in 1920 the average annual salary paid teachers was $871; in 1972 it was $10,608; today it is $16,001. Inflation, of course, has also contributed to these rapidly rising school costs.

Legal Challenges to School Funding Practices

In recent years there have been numerous legal challenges to school funding policies, and, as a result, these policies are undergoing drastic revision in several of the states. The nub of the legal issue has been and con-

[3] B. Othanel Smith and Donald E. Orlosky, *Socialization and Schooling* (Bloomington, Indiana: Phi Delta Kappa, Inc., 1975), p. 267.

tinues to be inequity—inequity resulting from the expenditure of different amounts of money per pupil and thus allegedly violating principles of equal protection and equal treatment; inequity in different *rates* of taxation for essentially the same educational services; inequity in the quality of education as a result of an inequitable tax system. Many of the cases have been brought as "class action" suits, the claim being that not only a single individual has had rights violated but that *all* individuals whose circumstances are similar have had their rights similarly violated. The significance of class action suits is that when they are successful, they result in policy changes.

The movement of these disputes to the courts for resolution indicates that local officials and state legislatures have not addressed the issues responsibly. Litigants have found the local and state power structure unresponsive to their concerns and needs. Court action thus represents a way of going around or evading local and state political power. In the late 1970s state legislatures and local power elites have been more sensitive to the need for distributive justice, and consequently there has been less need for judicial intervention.[4]

The first case dealing with inequities in the way local and state governments finance schools that came to national attention was *Serrano* v. *Priest*. This case involved two California school districts—Baldwin Park and Beverly Hills—both in Los Angeles County. The issue in this case had to do with the difference in tax money available for school use as a result of the difference in value of real property in the two districts. More specifically, John Serrano found that his child attended school in a district that raised $577 per child per year, whereas in Beverly Hills, just a few miles away, the sum raised was $1,232. Moreover, Serrano discovered that his tax rate was twenty-three times that of what it was in Beverly Hills. Serrano took the matter to court, and it eventually reached the California Supreme Court, which on August 30, 1971, ruled California's system of financing its schools to be unconstitutional because it "invidiously discriminates against the poor because it makes equality of a child's education a function of the wealth of his parents and neighbors." Following this decision, courts struck down common school funding systems in Texas, Minnesota, New Jersey, Kansas, Arizona, and Michigan for the same reason. The Texas case, known as *San Antonio Independent*

---

[4] David L. Kirp, "Laws, Politics, and Equal Educational Opportunity: The Limits of Judicial Involvement," *Harvard Educational Review* 47:2 (May 1977): 117–137.

School District v. *Rodriguez,* turned out to be another precedent-setting case that came to national attention.

The city of San Antonio, Texas, has within its city limits several independent school districts. At the time this suit was brought, Demetrio P. Rodriguez lived with his family in a Mexican-American section of the city and attended the Edgewood School District. This area is poor in the sense of having few taxable resources. Young Rodriguez's father worked as a custodian in a school in another district in San Antonio. It was obvious to him that the children attending the school where he worked were receiving a more generously financed education than was his child, and he brought suit. In December of 1971, a three-judge federal panel ruled in favor of Rodriguez and declared the Texas system of school funding void. In so doing, the panel adopted the principle of "fiscal neutrality" derived from the Serrano decision. Fiscal neutrality means that the wealth of a child's school district should not determine how much money is spent on education.

The decision in the Rodriguez case was appealed to the U.S. Supreme Court. The Court reversed the finding of the federal panel on the basis that it was not a constitutional issue. Because education was not

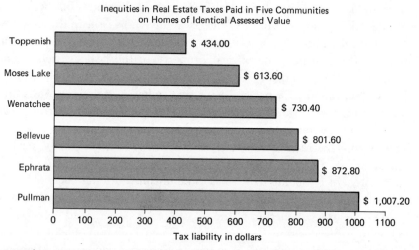

FIGURE 10. This example from Washington State is not unlike what is found in many states. In these six cases, tax amounts were calculated on actual 1977 tax rates for those six communities. The result is a tax liability difference of nearly six hundred dollars on homes assessed at identical value! Little wonder citizens are insisting on tax reforms.

defined as a fundamental right in the U.S. Constitution, the Court declared there was no constitutional obligation for equal expenditure. The Court did not deny the existence of inequities but declared that these were issues to be dealt with by the states. The significance of the Rodriguez decision was that it remanded the issue to the state courts and legislatures for resolution.

Some authors believe that the publication of the Jencks book *Inequality* may have influenced the thinking of the Court.[5] The book cites research that raises doubts about whether increased spending actually enhances the quality of education. The following excerpt is illustrative:

> the best way to appraise the likely effect of, say, doubling per pupil expenditures is to assume that schools now spending $400. per pupil will become like schools now spending $800., that schools now spending $800. will become like schools now spending $1600. and so forth.
>
> The evidence we have examined does not suggest that doubling expenditures would raise students' performance on standardized tests. A school's annual expenditure is, it is true, moderately related to the test scores of its alumni. But this is because affluent schools enroll students whose test scores are above average to begin with. When we compare schools with similar entering students, we do not find those with fat budgets turning out more skilled alumni than those with inadequate budgets.
>
> When we turn to elementary schools, the data is less conclusive but equally discouraging. EEOS (Equality of Educational Opportunity Survey) found no association of consequence between district-wide expenditures and mean achievement in elementary schools.[6]

John E. Coon points out that "the timing was perfect; Jencks's and related studies appeared early enough to influence the Supreme Court but too late for rebuttal by the plaintiffs."[7]

The Supreme Court decision in the Rodriguez case dealt school financing reform a stunning blow. It took several years to restructure reform efforts based on state laws and state constitutions. The Serrano case went to trial court in Los Angeles and reached the California Supreme Court a second time. In March of 1977 the California Supreme Court

[5] John E. Coon, "Financing Public Schools After Rodriguez," *Saturday Review*, October 9, 1973, p. 46.

[6] Christopher Jencks et al., *Inequality: A Reassessment of the Effect of Family and Schooling in America* (New York: Harper & Row Publishers, 1972), pp. 95–96.

[7] Coon, op. cit., p. 46.

231

ruled that, based on the state constitution, it *was* unconstitutional to finance schools on the basis of property taxes based on local property values. In a similar case in Washington State, a superior court judge ruled that the use of special levies based on local property values was not an adequate method of funding schools and charged the state legislature with (1) defining basic education (and stipulated that basic education today includes more than the three Rs) and (2) providing full state funding of such basic education.

Out of the litigation of the past decade, certain trends have emerged fairly clearly: (1) the principle of "fiscal neutrality" is well established; (2) school funding and equity issues surrounding it are matters for the states to resolve and are not federal constitutional issues; (3) school funding is a state rather than a local responsibility, meaning that states will pick up more of the cost of education than local districts will; (4) there are strong movements toward full state funding with ceilings or "lids" on the amounts local districts are *allowed* to contribute; (5) disparities in the amount spent per pupil are permitted in those cases where children are hard to educate, handicapped, or have other special needs.

FEDERAL ECONOMIC INFLUENCES

There are several reasons why the federal level of government is often disassociated from the funding of education in the United States: (1) the U.S. Constitution makes no mention of education, and, as we have seen in the foregoing section, this excludes education as a constitutionally guaranteed right; (2) we do not have a national system of education—education is the responsibility of the states; (3) there is strong resistance to federal control of education in this country; (4) the tradition of local control and local support is strongly entrenched in the mentality of the nation. The fact is, however, that the federal government has had a long history of direct and massive involvement in education. Many of the nation's Founding Fathers spoke out in support of education. Indeed, even during the Revolutionary War, soldiers were observed to be so deficient in basic learning skills that some instruction was provided.

If the Constitution does not mention education, how can the federal government involve itself in the education of its citizens? The rationale is usually based on one or a combination of three principles: (1) The "to promote the general welfare" principle of the Preamble to the Constitu-

232

tion. Presumably, one way the federal government can promote the general welfare is to see to it that its citizens are well educated. (2) The equal protection clause of the 14th Amendment. It is on the basis of this clause that numerous equity suits have found their way into the judicial process for resolution. (3) The principle of education as an arm of the national defense system. This principle was established as a matter of national policy when in 1958 the Congress passed the National Defense Education Act. When education is defined as a part of the nation's security system, it is legitimate for the federal government to provide funds to sustain it.

One of the earliest pieces of federal legislation dealing with education was the Land Ordinance of 1785. The federal government under this ordinance required that the sixteenth section of each township be reserved "for the maintenance of public schools within said township." It should be explained that a "section" is a piece of land measuring one square mile and containing 640 acres—a sizable piece of real estate by any standard. The Homestead Act, for example, only allowed the grantee to claim 160 acres—a quarter of a section. A township consisted of thirty-six sections in a square with six sections on a side. These were numbered from left to right, beginning in the upper left-hand corner of the plat. Thus, the sixteenth section fell near the center of the township.

This Land Ordinance of 1785 was very significant for the development of American public education. First of all, at that time in rural America the township was a meaningful unit of government. The local "town hall" was the seat of local township government. There were "town" roads, meaning township roads. By awarding the sixteenth section of each township to schools, the federal government strongly reinforced the concept of local governance of schools. Designating the sixteenth section meant that it was located at the geographic center of the township. What was to be done with this land was up to local authorities. In most instances, the timber rights were sold. In other cases, the land was rented. Sometimes it was sold and the money put into trust for school use. In some few cases, the land is still held for school use.

Another piece of federal legislation that spoke clearly about the national government's concern about public education was the Ordinance of 1787, which established the government of the Northwest Territory. Its meaning could hardly be misunderstood: "Religion, morality, and knowledge being necessary to good government and happiness of mankind, schools and the means of education shall forever be encouraged."

Since these early beginnings, the federal government has been involved in a great many educational ventures. A few of the best known are the following.

Military Academies

The U.S. military academies are these: army, West Point; navy, Annapolis; air force, Colorado Springs; Merchant Marine, Kings Point; Coast Guard, New London. These schools train officers for careers in the various branches of the armed forces, but they also provide the cadets with an accredited course of study leading to a bachelor's degree.

ROTC

The Reserve Officers Training Corps was authorized under the Morrill Land Grant Act of 1862. It made land available to state colleges if they offered part-time military training to young males. This program continues to this day and provides the armed forces with a substantial corps of male and female reserve officers. The officers ordinarily receive their commission upon graduation. Volunteers are paid a monthly subsistance for their participation in the program. The institutions also benefit financially by having the programs on their campuses.

Bureau of Indian Affairs (BIA)

The bureau was established in 1824 as a part of the War Department but was moved to the Department of the Interior in 1849. The BIA operates a broad spectrum of welfare and assistance programs, a major one being the education of Indian children. The BIA operates schools on reservations but also contracts with states, local educational agencies, and in the past even with religious schools for the education of Indian children.

Servicemen's Readjustment Act of 1944 (GI Bill of Rights)

The 1944 act was a massive program of direct financial aid to veterans of World War II and to institutions of higher education. The act was extended and revised a number of times to cover veterans of the Korean and Vietnamese Wars. In terms of numbers of persons served, the nation had not experienced anything like the magnitude of the education of GI's following World War II. Altogether over eight million vets participated in the program, averaging nineteen months of training taken in 20,500 schools and 400,000 training sites at a cost of $14.5 billion.

Vocational Education

Beginning in the latter part of the nineteenth century and continuing to the present time, the federal government has passed numerous pieces of legislation supporting vocational education. The major ones were these:

Morrill Act of 1862 It brought vocational education into the college curriculum and established land-grant colleges.

Second Morrill Act of 1890 It provided additional financial assistance to land-grant colleges.

Hatch Act of 1877 It established agricultural experimental stations.

Smith-Lever Act of 1914 It established agricultural extension and authorized the Commission on National Aid to Vocational Education.

Smith-Hughes Act of 1917 It provided aid for high school programs in agriculture and home economics.

Servicemen's Readjustment Act of 1944 The GI Bill of Rights provided for the education of returning World War II veterans.

National Defense Education Act of 1958 It contained a provision for vocational education.

Vocational Act of 1963 It introduced new concepts, new fields to vocational education and updated the field.

Revised Vocational Act of 1968 It extended and refined the 1963 legislation.

Elementary and Secondary Education Act of 1965

Passage of the Elementary and Secondary Education Act in 1965 represented the successful culmination of a twenty-year effort by the late Senator Wayne Morse of Oregon to secure major federal legislation for the support of education. The original bill contained five major sections or *titles*. Title I provided funds for compensatory school programs for children of the poor. Title II provided money for library books for all students. Title III provided funds for innovative programs for schools.

Title IV provided for research and development, and Title V provided funds to state departments of education to strengthen their administration of education. This act has been revised and extended since it was passed, and today it contains generous financial provisions for a broad spectrum of educational programs. In 1978 it was amended and extended for five years under PL95–561. It includes the following titles:

Title I Aid for Disadvantaged Children

Title II Basic Skills Improvement

Title III Special Projects (Special projects include innovative solutions to educational problems, energy conservation, use of the metric system, consumer education, environmental education, law-related education, and population education.)

Title IV Educational Improvement, Resources, and Support (Provides financial assistance to state and local educational agencies for local projects to improve educational practices, acquisition of instructional materials and equipment, and strengthening of guidance, counseling, and testing services in elementary and secondary schools.)

Title V State Leadership

Title VI Emergency School Aid Act

Title VII Bilingual Education

Title VIII Community Schools

Title IX Additional Programs

Title X Impact Aid Amendments

Title XI Indian Education

Title XII Administrative Provisions

Title XIII Revision of Other Educational Programs

Two major problems have always dogged federal aid to education. One of these is the religious issue of separation of church and state. The other is the fear of federal intervention in, if not control of, local schools. Let us examine each of these issues.

The Religious Issue

Children of this nation are served by a large number of private and parochial schools in addition to the public schools. The largest of these nonpublic schools (approximately 80 per cent) are those operated by the

Roman Catholic Church, which today enrolls some two and a half million elementary and secondary school pupils. This represents a substantial decline over the approximately five million who were enrolled in 1960.* Parents of children who attend private schools or religious schools are, of course, taxpayers, as is everyone else. Their tax dollars are used to support local public schools, and they must also pay for the support of the private or parochial school that their children attend. Through the years, they have worked actively to gain some relief from this financial burden, which amounts to the support of two school systems.

Those who oppose any support of private and/or parochial schools with public funds argue that such use of public moneys would be in violation of the First Amendment that calls for the separation of church and state. Moreover, they indicate that sending one's child to a private or parochial school is a choice freely made and that, therefore, one must expect to pay the additional costs. It would be unfair to use public tax money to support a private or parochial school for a favored few. Thus, whenever federal legislation has been presented to provide aid to education, lobbyists for private and parochial schools have sought to have those schools share in such financial benefits. This has usually succeeded in killing the legislation. The issue is far from simple, as is indicated in the following statement of the late Senator Wayne Morse:

> Suppose tonight every private school in America should be closed, and tomorrow morning the students of those schools should go to the doors of the public schools and ask for admittance. Would there then be imposed upon the taxpayers of America an additional tax burden? There is no question about it. It would amount to many millions of dollars.

> I think the American people will recognize the fact that our private schools, through their educational programs, are in fact performing also a public service. Hence, within the Constitution and in keeping with the doctrine of separation of church and state, I for one, feel that private schools are performing public services which entitle the children in private schools to some Federal-aid benefits.

> I do not know what kind of a compromise can be worked out in regard to giving aid to the child who attends a private school. For the superior child I suppose a scholarship could be worked out. However, I do not agree that it is

* The total enrollments in private elementary and secondary schools, both religious and secular for the years 1970, 1975, 1976, and 1977 in millions of students were 5.1, 4.5, 4.3 and 4.5 respectively. In 1980 the National Center for Education Statistics reported private school enrollments to be slightly over 5.0 million, which suggests a reversal in the downward trend in private school enrollments. Private schools enroll approximately 10 per cent of the nation's elementary and secondary school students.

not proper to provide students in the private schools with hot-lunch programs, transportation or textbooks. I think that to say that supplying Federal aid for such services only results in the private school being able then to use its own money for other purposes is stretching the point a bit. I say that because I think those who so argue are overlooking the fact that the strictly educational functions performed by private schools involve a great public service.[8]

The legal issue of direct financial support of parochial schools from public tax sources is settled. It is illegal. The opinion of Justice Black, speaking for the majority of the Supreme Court in a 1947 decision, could hardly be misunderstood.

No tax in any amount, large or small, can be levied to support any religious activities or institutions, whatever they may be called, or whatever form they may adopt to teach or practice religion. Neither a state nor a Federal Government can, openly or secretly, participate in the affairs of any religious organizations or groups and vice versa. In the words of Jefferson, the clause against establishment of religion by law was intended to erect "a wall of separation between Church and State."[9]

In order to deal with the constitutional prohibition against the use of tax funds to support church-related schools, the "child benefit theory" has been proposed. The rationale for the child benefit idea is based on the principle that individual children as citizens have a right to share equally with others in public benefits. Accordingly, the child attending a parochial school may be provided certain benefits and services that accrue to him or her but do not directly aid the school itself. On this basis, the U.S. Supreme Court has allowed transportation payments to parochial schools, rental and use of textbooks, library resources, and other instructional resources. In the case of *Wolman* v. *Walter*, the U.S. Supreme Court in 1977 upheld the loan of textbooks to nonpublic schools, the use of standardized tests, the provision of diagnostic services, the loan of instructional resources, the authorization of payment of transportation costs for field trips and related services, and expenditure of public funds for certain therapeutic services. Although the point may be arguable, these payments are considered legal by the Court because it is the *in-*

[8] Cited in Harold E. Morse, "An Analysis of the Published Statements of Senator Wayne Morse on Education," 1947–1965 (Ph.D. diss., University of Washington, Seattle, 1969), pp. 21–22.

[9] *Everson* v. *Board of Education*, 330 (U.S.) 1 (1947).

dividual child citizen who benefits from them, not the school. Because the state has a legitimate interest in assuring that all children receive an adequate education, it can legally provide appropriate resources and services to *individuals*.

Another plan that was suggested as a way of implementing the child benefit theory was the use of "school vouchers." Under this plan a voucher would be issued to a family for each of its school-age children. The voucher could then be used in payment for what amounted to tuition fees to any school—public or private—of the family's choosing. The school would then redeem the voucher and receive payment. It was claimed that this system would provide the pupils (clients) and their parents with greater choice of schools, would make schools more competitive and, therefore, improve their quality, and would also provide a way of paying for nonpublic school services from public funds. The voucher plan has not proved to be successful and, as far as is known, is at this time not in operation anywhere.

The most recent proposal for financial support for nonpublic schools is legislation that would authorize "tuition tax credits." Under this plan a family could apply a tax credit of some fixed amount on their federal income tax liability. The legislation originally proposed by Senators Packwood and Moynihan would have allowed up to $500 for the private school student. This was later reduced to $250. Supporters of tuition tax credits argue that nonpublic school education costs are so high that private schools and colleges are not able to survive. This can be documented by the declining enrollments in nonpublic schools over the past quarter of a century. Senator Moynihan reports that there were 2,246 *fewer* private schools in 1976 than there were a decade earlier. This means that the choice of a private or parochial school, for those who would wish to make such a choice, obviously cannot be made. This would have the undesirable effect of further strengthening the monopoly public schools have on the education of children and youth of the nation.

Opponents of tax credits claim that such a system amounts to little more than general financial assistance for private education. They argue that tax credits aid a few million private school students at the expense of the over 40 million who attend public schools. Moreover, they say that the plan clearly favors higher-income families because it is they who most often send their children to private schools. So far, the opponents have been the more convincing, for the Packwood-Moynihan proposal was defeated by the U.S. Senate in 1978 by a vote of fifty-six to forty-one.

239

The Issue of Federal Control

There is a long tradition of local involvement in the control and governance of elementary and secondary education in the United States. In spite of strong trends toward centralization in organization and administration of schools within the states, the insistence on local control remains strong. There is little doubt that the doctrine of local control has been badly eroded in recent years, and some see a relationship between that erosion and the increased fiscal intervention of the state and federal governments in educational affairs. "Whoever controls the purse strings has control over schools" is the guideline applied by those whose objection to federal aid to education is based on the control issue.

Do increased federal dollars to education result in greater federal control? If we use past experiences as an answer to this question, we would have to say definitely that it does. There can be no doubt that the guidelines issued by federal agencies in the awarding of funds have been used to shape and promote social policy. The implementation of Title VI of the Civil Rights Act of 1964 provides specific documentation of this assertion. Title VI stated that no person because of race, color, or national origin could be excluded from or be denied the benefits of any program receiving federal assistance. Under Title VI, federal agencies were required to establish guidelines to implement this antidiscriminatory policy and to terminate or refuse to grant federal assistance to institutions or projects that did not comply with the guidelines.

This was a significant departure from past policies of the U.S. Office of Education. Under this new policy, it would not only write the guidelines but also was responsible to see that they were enforced. Now it was necessary for local school systems to show proof of compliance with civil rights guidelines. Moreover, school districts and institutions of higher education now operated under the constant threat of having federal funds withdrawn if they were judged to be in noncompliance. Of course, local districts and institutions of higher education were not required to accept federal funds, but they had so grown to depend on them that to have them suddenly withdrawn would be to deal those institutions a nearly mortal blow.

The issue of whether or not federal aid to education brings increased federal intervention, therefore, seems clear. It does. The federal government simply does not disburse the tax dollars of the nation without attaching some conditions on how that money is to be spent. Most

240

Americans would agree that such accounting for expenditure of public funds is necessary. The extent to which such accountability is used as a powerful weapon to shape and implement social policy is another question—and a highly controversial one at that. This presents a philosophical and value question of profound magnitude: Can educational problems be best addressed at the grass roots level, depending on localism and voluntarism to effect needed reforms; or is it only at the national level of government, where we have the power to garner financial resources, the educational expertise, and the administrative skill to deal with national educational problems? The historian Henry Steele Commager argues convincingly that educational reform will require more, rather than less, federal intervention:

> The fact is that for a century and a half almost every major reform in our political and social system has come about through the agency of the national government and over the opposition of powerful vested interests, states, and local communities.[10]

Categorical and General Aid

One of the ways state and federal governments exercise control over local school decisions is by specifying in the legislation itself the exact purpose for which the money is to be spent. This is known as "categorical aid." Thus, there are allotments of moneys for designated purposes, and they can be spent for those and no other purposes. For example, funds may be earmarked for the handicapped, bilingual education, the disadvantaged, vocational education, basic skills, and so on. This ensures that local administrators are not able to shift those dollars to other, more needy or more popular, purposes. Categorical aid may be contrasted with "general aid," in which grants are made to local districts but have no strings attached to them as to how they are to be used.

There are, of course, advantages and limitations to both of these methods of school funding. The recipient groups, especially if they are in some way disadvantaged (that is, bilingual, minority, poor, handicapped, and so on), tend to favor categorical programs. This means that dollars so designated are protected from reallocation to other purposes

[10] Henry Steele Commager, "Only the National Government . . . ," *Today's Education* (October-November 1973), p. 47.

that may have more politically powerful advocates. Politicians like categorical aid because they can be identified with programs of interest to specific constituents. Administrators and local school officials tend to favor general aid programs because these give them greater freedom in shifting funds to programs that need support. Be that as it may, we are likely to continue to have federal funding of the categorical type, as is illustrated by the various Titles of the Amendment to the Elementary and Secondary Education Act, PL95–561. (See page 236.)

THE PRIVATE PHILANTHROPIC FOUNDATIONS

The private foundations represent one of the most powerful forces that shape educational policy in American schools. Indeed, it would be difficult to name a single significant reform thrust in this century that did not involve one of the major foundations. These tax exempt foundations have huge amounts of money that is made available as grants for approved projects. The best-known of the foundations are Ford, Carnegie, Sloan, Kellogg, Guggenheim, Danforth, and Rockefeller, but *The Foundations Directory* lists more than 6,000 such organizations.

The projects supported by the Carnegie Foundation provide good examples of the extent of the involvement and influence of a foundation in the educational policy formation:

The Carnegie Unit

At the turn of the century, high school curricula were in such disarray that there was little similarity in offerings from one place to another. In 1909 the Carnegie Foundation for the Advancement of Education standardized the high school curriculum by establishing the "Carnegie Unit." A Carnegie Unit consists of 120 clock hours per year in a subject and is widely used even today.

The American Dilemma

The American Dilemma is one of the two major sociological studies of American society (the other being the Coleman Study) having to do with race relations. The study was conducted by the Swedish scholar Gunnar Myrdal and was sponsored by the Carnegie Foundation.

The Comprehensive High School

The Carnegie Foundation supported the study of secondary education by the late James Bryant Conant. This study and the publication that flowed from it firmly established the comprehensive high school as *the* American institution for secondary education.[11]

Crisis in the Classroom

The Carnegie Foundation awarded Charles E. Silberman, then a member of the Board of Directors of *Fortune* magazine, $300,000 to do a survey of the status of American education. This "study" resulted in the popular publication *Crisis in the Classroom.*[12]

Inequality

In the Preface of his book on inequality, Christopher Jencks writes, "Money for our work came primarily from the Carnegie Corporation of New York."[13] This publication has been extremely influential in shaping educational policy during the decade of the 1970s. Some think that it might have been a factor in the decision of the U.S. Supreme Court in the Rodriguez case.[14]

These examples clearly illustrate the enormous influence that a foundation can have on the thinking of Americans about educational matters. If it can be assumed that these institutions operate on the basis of enlightened self-interest, it would follow that they are likely to support projects that are consistent with their view of the world. Because these institutions are tax-exempt, they enjoy certain privileges that should make their influence on public education a matter of public concern. They represent enormous wealth and, therefore, can exercise great power in promoting their pet projects and concepts. It is probably accurate to say that most Americans, even educators and teachers, are hardly aware of the power and influence of the private foundations in shaping educational policy and educational decision making.

[11] James Bryant Conant, *The American High School Today* (New York: McGraw-Hill Book Company, Inc., 1959).

[12] Charles E. Silberman, *Crisis in the Classroom* (New York: Random House, Inc., 1970).

[13] Christopher Jencks et al., *Inequality: A Reassessment of the Effect of Family and Schooling in America* (New York: Harper and Row, Publishers, Inc., 1972), p. vi.

[14] Ibid., pp. 95–96.

STUDY AND DISCUSSION

1. Identify and discuss some of the consequences to the American people of having an unreliable method of financial support for the educational system of the country.
2. Describe the sources of funds available to schools and some of the issues relating to the procurement of those funds.
3. What economic trends in society impact directly on the funding support of schools?
4. What effect do local taxes have on the participation of citizens in the affairs of the local schools?
5. Summarize the position the Supreme Court has taken on the issue of inequities in funding of schools.
6. What conditions in a local community might influence the outcome of a ballot measure dealing with a school levy or a school bond?
7. The National Education Association (NEA) has proposed that the federal financial contribution to public education should be on the order of 33 per cent. Many persons oppose this. Why would one be opposed to such a proposal?
8. Summarize the historical background of the involvement of the federal government in the education of Americans.
9. Explain why the Elementary and Secondary School Education Act of 1965 is considered a major turning point in the attitude of the nation toward federal support of public schools.
10. Identify and comment on issues arising from the involvement of tax-exempt philanthropic foundations such as Ford, Carnegie, and Sloan in public education.

SELECTED BIBLIOGRAPHY

GARMS, WALTER I., JAMES W. GUTHRIE, and LAWRENCE C. PIERCE. *School Finance: The Economics and Politics of Public Education.* Englewood Cliffs, N.J.: Prentice-Hall, Inc., 1978.

GORDON, C. WAYNE, ed. "The Role of the Federal Government in Education." *Uses of the Sociology of Education.* 73d Yearbook of the National Society for the Study of Education. Chicago: University of Chicago Press, 1974, pp. 411–502.

Johns, Roe L., and Edgar L. Morphet. *The Economics and Financing of Education*, 3d ed. Englewood Cliffs, N.J.: Prentice-Hall, Inc., 1975.

Hollings, Ernest F. "The Case Against Tuition Tax Credits," *Phi Delta Kappan* (December 1978): 277–279.

Miller, Harry L. *Social Foundations of Education: An Urban Focus*, 3d ed. Part 2: New York: Holt, Rinehart and Winston, Inc., 1978.

Moynihan, Daniel Patrick. "The Case For Tuition Tax Credits," *Phi Delta Kappan* (December 1978): 274–276.

Soble, Ronald L., Efrem Sigel, Dantia Quirk, and Patricia Whitestone. *Crisis! The Taxpayer Revolt and Your Kids' Schools*. White Plains, N.Y.: Knowledge Industries Publications, 1978.

chapter **10**

Political Influences on School Decision Making

In the previous chapter we took note of the fact that education is not a right guaranteed by the U.S. Constitution. In fact, that document makes no mention of education. The Tenth Amendment speaks of powers "reserved to the States" as those not delegated to the United States by the Constitution and not "prohibited by it to the States." The power to establish an educational system is, therefore, a power "reserved to the States." As a result, this country provides for the education of its children through state systems of education. Typically, this is achieved through the establishment of a state education agency, such as an Office of the State Superintendent of Public Instruction or an Office of the Commissioner of Education. The state education agency, in turn, provides for the establishment of local education agencies, usually school districts governed by a school board of directors or trustees. It is important to stress that a state is not obligated to provide free public education for its children, but if it provides it for *some*, it must then make education available equally to all in accordance with the equal protection provisions of the Fourteenth Amendment.

Until the early part of this century, school governance in this country was a patchwork of overlapping jurisdictions and diverse authorities. In large city school systems, conflicts between agencies having some responsibility for the operation of the schools were not unusual. Little wonder that this should be the case, considering arrangements such as the following in Buffalo: ". . . the mayor appointed janitors, the superintendent teachers; the city council bought sites for new schools, while the department of public works erected them."[1] Tyack continues, "Fights between school boards and city councils over appropriations and over school functions were commonplace from Providence to Los Angeles."[2]

At the turn of the century, school governance was thoroughly enmeshed in political activity at the local level. Corruption, graft, and less objectionable forms of political influence characterized hiring of teachers, purchase of textbooks, construction contracts, and the employment of noncertified personnel not only in the large urban areas but in smaller communities as well. The malaise that afflicted school administration was so pervasive that it became the object of a national reform movement, consistent with the progressive political ideology of the early part of this century. Highly respected and powerful scholars and educational leaders gave support and leadership to the effort to remove school governance from the grip of local politics. As a result, school districts came to be autonomous political units, independent of other local jurisdictions such as local county or city governments.

The efforts to reform the administrative structure of schools also initiated the movement to consolidate and centralize schools, a process that continued well into the 1970s. The consolidation and centralization of schools appealed to business-minded Americans because it resembled a corporation structure. The efficient corporate model was obviously attractive as compared to the decentralized, unbusinesslike way in which schools conducted their affairs. Indeed, the term *businesslike* is considered to be synonymous with efficiency. A major cornerstone of the school district reorganization effort was to eliminate wherever possible those districts that were too small to operate efficiently. At the end of World War II there were over 100,000 school districts in the United States. By 1960 that number had been reduced to 42,000; and by 1970, to about 18,000. Today there are approximately 16,000 school districts.

[1] David B. Tyack, *The One Best System* (Cambridge, Mass.: Harvard University Press, 1974), p. 88.
[2] Ibid., p. 88.

The legal governing body of a school district is the school board, known as the board of directors or as the board of trustees. School boards are given the power by state law to establish local school policies, consistent with guidelines and laws of the state. Their responsibilities include such matters as hiring the superintendent, approving curriculum documents, setting the school calendar, negotiating contracts with employees, receiving and expending funds, establishing a budget, and developing and maintaining facilities. The school superintendent is the chief executive officer of the board, and it is through the office of the superintendent that the board policies are actually implemented. School board members have authority only when sitting as a board; that is, an individual school board member, on his or her own, has no more authority to direct the affairs of the school than any other citizen in the community has. This is often not understood, and, as a consequence, sometimes board members will attempt to usurp responsibilities that are more appropriately those of the superintendent, principal, teachers, budget director, curriculum director, or other professional staff.

Many studies have been made of the nature and composition of school boards. Typically, boards consist of five to nine members who are elected for a period of from three to six years. Their level of education tends to be above average, which means that school policies in most places are being set by persons who have themselves succeeded in school. Most board members are white males who are proprietors, businessmen, executives, and professionals. Tradition and public policy hold that school board members should give their time and talent as a public service; that is, they should serve without salary or only at a token salary, they should be nonpartisan in their political affiliation, and they should be elected at large. These requirements are intended to reduce the more objectionable political aspects of board membership.

ATTEMPTS TO REVERSE
THE CENTRALIZATION TREND

In recent years there have been renewed efforts to halt or even to reverse the trend toward centralization. This has been promoted by minority groups, especially blacks, living in the large urban areas. It would be a mistake, however, to associate this movement only with inner-city blacks. Other groups such as Indians and/or Native Americans, Latinos, and Asians have also been active in working toward greater local control of schools. The disadvantaged minorities have not been satisfied with the way schools have served their children and feel that, if they had more to say about setting policies and making decisions, they would be better served. As a consequence, there has been considerable pressure to get what is called "community control" of schools.

The issues that are involved in centralization-decentralization represent value conflicts having to do with keeping decision making close to the grass roots while at the same time having an efficient administrative operation. Because it is essentially a question of values, there is no way that it can be resolved entirely on the basis of expertise. What is being sought is a system that will maximize both democratic control over decision making and also one that will maximize efficiency in governmental operations. Most advocates of centralization would not go so far as to push for a nationally centralized system of education. Similarly, most advocates of decentralization would not want to return to the days of a school district at every crossroad in the land. Most feel that schools should accommodate the educational needs of local constituents.

Two ways have been suggested to achieve school decentralization. One might be called *political* decentralization. Under this system, large consolidated school districts now operating under the direction of a single school board would be split into smaller districts. This, essentially, would reverse the consolidation trend that has been taking place for the better part of this century. Each of these newly created administrative units would be autonomous, have its own school board, and be under local community control. As such, it would set its own policies, hire personnel, approve the curriculum, set its own budget, and so on.

Although this type of political decentralization has a certain nostalgic attraction, it is really not a practical or feasible alternative to what is done today. Public services for today's communities require such complex and costly delivery systems that a metropolitan-wide effort is required to have them become a reality. This is true in the case of public transportation, water and electrical services, fire and police protection, sewer and garbage services, and, to some extent, health care. Increasingly, such service districts include all, or a good part, of the entire metropolitan region. The move toward political decentralization of school districts would take communities in the opposite direction of metropolitanism, a very unlikely development.

250

A more realistic approach to preserving or restoring some semblance of local control is to handle it through *administrative* decentralization. Under this arrangement, the large district boundaries are maintained, and there is a central governing board. An effort is made to separate functions in a way that will maximize both efficiency and democratic control. Thus, such activities as purchasing, budgeting, and personnel services are handled at the central administrative office level. This provides the district many advantages in terms of cost and efficiency. For example, payrolls and bookkeeping can be computerized for the entire district, thereby eliminating the need to duplicate the operation several times. The district can exercise economies by making purchases on bid and making them in such large quantities that suppliers are willing and able to offer them at a lower price. Whereas the district centralizes functions such as those just described, it decentralizes functions that involve curriculum and instruction. For instance, the district might be divided into several areas, each of which is headed by a regional administrator. Such areas might even have school councils that consist of local parents who advise the school authorities with respect to school policies. Although such school councils may not have any legal basis, they do, nonetheless, have credibility and can have considerable power. Parent and student involvement at the local level helps to ensure a meaningful curriculum for children attending local schools. Because administrative decentralization preserves the advantages of both a centralized and decentralized system, it has been implemented in many large city school districts in recent years.

LOCALISM AND LOCAL CONTROL

In a decentralized administrative organization the authority and responsibility for education is dispersed. For example, in our system, authority and responsibility for education is shared by local communities, larger school districts, and states. The assumption is that when there is such dispersion of authority and responsibility, the system will more adequately take care of local needs. A further assumption is that this system will reduce the amount of arbitrariness in decision making because the farther away from the effects of a decision that the decision is made, the more likely it is to be arbitrary. Another assumption is that local involvement in decision making will result in greater interest in schools. All of these assumptions and others like them that surround the complicated issue of local control are open to much question. They are partially true; perhaps in some instances, altogether true. In other cases, they may not be true at all. Certainly, local control of schools does not necessarily mean a better quality of education.

Individuals usually favor local control of schools for some combination of the following reasons:

1. Advocates of local control feel that the schools belong to the people.

This view argues that schools are literally owned and operated by the taxpayers of the local community. School administrators, teachers, and other personnel associated with the school district are employees of the local community. As such, these employees should be accountable to the citizens of the local community. Because the schools belong to the people of the local community, it follows that local citizens would inform the school as to the kind of educational program they want for their children and would supervise the work of the school to ensure that it was being carried out. Teachers who are unable or unwilling to perform in accordance with the mandates of local citizens would be dismissed. Naturally, organized teacher groups believe otherwise, namely, that they do not work well when they are under such close supervision and that as professionals they must be permitted a considerable amount of autonomy in the exercise of professional decision making.[3]

2. Local control reflects local needs.

Advocates of local control often state that they do not need bureaucrats in the central office many miles away or officials in the state education office to tell them what kind of education their children need. They insist that the persons who can best decide on local education needs are local citizens. Obviously, this point and the foregoing one are closely related. There are convincing arguments against this point of view that are discussed in the section that follows.

[3] Robert F. Lyke, "Political Issues in School Decentralization," *The Politics of Education at the Local, State, and Federal Levels*, Michael Kirst, ed. (Berkeley, Calif.: McCutchen Publishing Corporation, 1970), pp. 111–132.

3. School management and curriculum will be more closely monitored when control is at the local level.

If school administrators and teachers are accountable to local constituents, parents will more likely monitor school activities themselves rather than rely on representatives from the central office to do it for them. Who is the first to know if a teacher is not doing his or her job responsibly and adequately? Local control advocates say that it is the parents of the children with whom the teacher is working. Consequently, they are able to call such a situation to the attention of the school authorities and have it corrected. But this can happen only if such decisions can be made at the local level. Parents are not likely to be very effective if they have to register their concerns at some anonymous bureaucratic office many miles away. It follows, too, that the schools would be more responsive to such local criticism and suggestion. In order to get this type of responsiveness, local authorities must remain vigilant and alert to what is going on in the schools. This assumes that local citizens have the time, the motivation, and the expertise to be so involved in the work of the school.

4. People who are affected by decisions should be involved in making them.

Of course, those who support local control believe this is more likely to happen if decisions are made at the local level. The fact is that in representative governments we are more often than not involved only indirectly in decisions that affect us. Even though participatory democracy has become a popular concept in recent years, it is simply not possible for us to be involved in everything. Local control advocates would say that one is not asking to "be involved in everything"—only in the education of one's children. The education of one's children is an extension of parental responsibility and cannot and should not be relinquished to a state agency such as the public schools. Democratic decision making under a representative system is based on the concept of "consent of the governed," and in this case, the governed are not willing to give consent.

5. People will be more interested in schools if they are controlled locally.

If local people perceive schools as belonging to them, they are more likely to pride themselves on having good schools and will be more interested in supporting what they do. Schools are more than educational institutions; they are symbols of the community. They contribute to community solidarity and unity. The high school football or basketball game is not only an athletic event; it is an expression of community loyalty and esprit de corps. Thus, the school has important socialization functions for a community beyond fulfilling educational needs that are served when the school is controlled and operated locally. Often communities are very upset about a school closure, not because this will do violence to the education of children locally but because such a closure says something about the community itself.

Individuals usually *do not* favor local control of schools for some combination of the following reasons:

1. *Localism promotes parochialism, narrowness of vision.*

Opponents of local control do not deny many of the arguments made in its favor. Indeed, they would say that is precisely what is wrong with local control. Whatever biases and prejudices exist at the local level will be reflected in the school when schools are controlled locally. "If desegregation, for example, were left in the hands of local citizens, we would still be at the stage we were in in the early 1950s," say opponents of local control. Opponents also say that children may get their early educations at the local neighborhood school, but they do not usually spend a lifetime in that community. They grow up and move away. Therefore, they must have a familiarity not only with the local area but with the world beyond.

2. *School expenditures will work to the advantage of local elites and to the disadvantage of low socioeconomic status (SES) families.*

It is further argued that the social class composition of the community has little to do with contradicting this principle. However the local community is constituted with respect to income, occupation, race, ethnic groups, or social class, *some* group can be identified as being most influential in decision making. That group of elites will see to it that school funds are expended in accordance with its views of what constitutes a good education. The net effect of this is a replication of social class structure at the local community level from one generation to the next. Local control ensures that the "haves" will continue to get in generous amounts and the "have-nots" will continue to be shortchanged by the schools.

Opponents argue that if it is equity of education that is being sought, one does not get it through the mechanism of local control. They would say that policy formation has to take place beyond the local community—where local elites cannot dominate and control the decision-making process.

3. *When education is controlled locally, it does not address itself to large societal needs.*

The world of today's children does not begin and end at the boundary of the local community. People and places interact with each other. A community has many interlocking social, political, economic, and geographic links and bonds with other places. As a nation, we are heavily involved in international relations. "We cannot educate children only in terms of the needs of the local community," the opponents to local community control tell us. Every school in the country has to be concerned with those broad social issues that concern us as a nation. Today's children not only need a community perspective but also need to see the world from the perspective of the region and the nation.

4. *Localism works contrary to the integration of neighborhoods into the larger community.*

Too great an emphasis on the local community can promote separatism just at a time when society is stressing integration. If one community is black, another is Chicano, another all white, and so on, the local operation of schools in those communities accentuates the racial and ethnic variable. Very substantial efforts have been made in recent years to avoid such homogeneity of racial and ethnic composition of schools; indeed, they are required by law to be otherwise constituted.

5. *The improvement of education is too complex, too sophisticated, and too large to be handled adequately at the local level.*

What is really being said here is that what is needed is not localism but metropolitanism. The concern should be spread over a wider rather than a narrower area because social and educational problems are usually pervasive to a large region, not limited to a neighborhood, according to the opponents of local control. To believe that local persons, who are often poorly educated themselves, have the wisdom and the expertise to make sound decisions about the education of their children approaches incredible heights of naïveté. Such procedures might have been adequate in the day of the hoosier schoolmaster and his little rural school, but not for children who will spend most of their lives in the twenty-first century.

6. Funds for special projects are often used poorly.

Guidelines for the funding of federal education projects have required that projects be governed by local executive boards consisting of members of "the community." Modeled after self-improvement programs in Communist countries, such involvement is supposed to develop skills of participatory democracy and at the same time ensure the project's relevance to the group involved. Of course, it rarely works that way, according to opponents, because the money is squandered on worthless projects or otherwise misappropriated. Persons who have been totally unaccustomed to handling anything but trivial amounts of money in their personal lives, now find themselves in charge of huge amounts of money, a responsibility for which they are totally unequipped either by personal experience or professional expertise.

7. It is more difficult for professional personnel to engage in negotiated contracts.

It is obviously easier for a union to negotiate with a single school board of a large city than it is to deal with all units at the local level. But supporters of localism would take the opposite view. They would want to bargain with teachers at the local level. They would want to hire, fire, or reward teachers. This issue, therefore, is one that places the teachers' unions and local community advocates on opposite sides.

8. Localism defeats high priority social goals such as integration, cultural pluralism, and metropolitan coordination.

Great strides have been made in the last quarter century in achieving these broad-based social goals. Localism seems to fly in the face of these trends. It is difficult to support school integration and desegregation, for example, and at the same time support the separatism that is suggested by local control. The revitalization of communities cannot occur through efforts of the local community alone. The problems are too complex and their resolution too costly to be handled by such a limited effort. Good social policies are made by persons who are competent to make them. To suggest that people at the local level have such competence by themselves is probably expecting too much.

As was noted earlier in this section, the issue of local control of schools is not one that can be resolved entirely on the basis of objective data and expertise. It is obvious that the problem is enmeshed in different and conflicting value orientations. This means that opponents as well as advocates are likely to overstate their particular point of view. For instance, let us take the matter of professional autonomy. Should teachers be accountable to, and supervised by, local laypersons? The answer to this question cannot be a clear-cut yes or no. The truth is that teachers *are* accountable to local citizens and parents, but this does not mean that teachers are or must be under the constant supervision of parents. Teachers *do* exercise a considerable amount of freedom in carrying out their duties and responsibilities, yet they are not completely autonomous in performing their professional roles. This same type of compromise position characterizes most of the specific points of conflict regarding local control of schools. There are valid claims that can justify differing perspectives on this issue.

POLITICAL POWER GROUPS AND THE SCHOOLS

When we speak of "politics" in the context of education, we obviously are not talking only about the Democrats and Republicans, national political conventions, state legislative sessions, and political campaigns. These traditional views of politics are too narrow for our purposes. Instead, we will take a broad view of politics. The definition of Professor Harold Lasswell will suit our purpose: "The study of politics is the study of influence and the influential."[4] Politics in education, therefore, may take many forms because individuals and groups are always trying to influence the views of others. In Chapter 2, we discussed critics of the schools and, in that setting, talked about various pressure groups. Such groups might also be considered political power groups that attempt to, and often do, influence school decision making. In this sec-

[4] Harold Lasswell, *Politics* (New York: McGraw-Hill Book Company, Inc., 1936), p. 1.

tion, we will examine some of the more powerful of these political action groups.

School personnel have been slow in recognizing the political dimensions of the educational decision making in this country. Teachers and even administrators have held securely to the belief that schools somehow are outside the realm of politics. Despite the fact that the most important decisions affecting schools, namely, how they are financed, are wholly political, school people insist on clinging to the naïve belief that "schools are above politics." As a result, persons most closely associated with school decision making often have the least well-developed political skills.

The time has come for those associated with school decision making to set aside the romantic notion that schools are not involved in politics. Schools are and always have been influenced by local, state, and federal political power groups. This is so because schools serve many constituent groups, each of which has its own set of priorities for the schools. They are not all mutually exclusive, of course, but neither are they wholly alike. The efforts to influence decisions in accordance with a group's own enlightened self-interests often involve the use of political power.

The Education Establishment

The education establishment consists of an interlocking network of schools, education officials, and agencies that have to do with the operation of the public schools. The more obvious components of the education establishment are public elementary and secondary school officials—boards of education, superintendents, principals, and other administrators. To these primary groups should be added the officials associated with the chief state school officer's operation with its many divisions and offices—curriculum and instruction, supervision and administration of schools, pupil personnel and accounting, school finance, teacher certification, and others. Tied closely to these schools and agencies are college and university departments of education who conduct and monitor teacher preparation, school administrators, counselors, and other personnel associated with professional roles in schools.

In the past the so-called professional associations were considered a part of the educational establishment. In recent years an adversary relationship has developed between these organized teacher groups and certain segments of the education establishment. Therefore, groups such as the National Education Association (NEA) and the American Federation of Teachers (AFT) and their state and local affiliates are not really a part of the education establishment even though individuals may find themselves in both groups. It is correct to think of such professional groups as the National Council for the Social Studies, National Science Teachers Association, National Council of Teachers of English, International Reading Association, Association for Supervision and Curriculum Development, and the National Association of Mathematics Teachers as part of the educational establishment because their primary concerns have to do with teaching procedures, curriculum development, and teacher education. They, thus, are allied with other components of the education establishment.

Graduate and Professional Schools

Graduate and professional schools are among the most powerful and influential groups that have an impact on educational decision making. This is because they control admission to the prestigious professional occupations, they set standards and requirements for admission and certification, and they sort and select society's intellectual and professional elite. This means that the graduate and professional schools train the men and women who will be the major shakers and movers in the community, in the state, and in the nation.

When graduate and professional schools set requirements for admission, they have a profound effect on the entire curriculum from the preschool upward. This is true even though only a small fraction of those who start kindergarten ever enter, to say nothing of complete, a program of graduate and/or professional education. Because these advanced schools teach, train, and socialize society's elite, their requirements strongly influence the definition of what an education is. All of the egalitarian rhetoric concerning education notwithstanding, the preferred type of education in this or any society is one that the elite obtain for themselves. In this society this means an education that is basically intellectual, dealing largely with abstract concepts and ideas, one that requires a high level of verbal and linguistic capability, one that is based on competitive goal seeking. Little wonder, therefore, that vocational and industrial education cannot establish itself on a parity basis with conventional academic education that is rooted in the liberal arts. The graduate and professional schools epitomize the notion that knowledge is power because they have it, husband it, and decide who the privileged few are to be who will have access to it.

Teacher Unions

In recent years teachers' unions, specifically the National Education Association (NEA) and the American Federation of Teachers (AFT), along with their state and local affiliates, have become the most powerful political action groups influencing American education. Even though these organizations like to refer to themselves as "professional associations," they must be regarded as teachers' unions that work for the material benefits, welfare, and the extension of political power of their constituents. In many states, the state teachers' union is one of the most powerful lobbys in the state legislature. Having the authority to negotiate contracts at the local level, as is the case everywhere today, puts the local teachers' union in a position of power that equals or even exceeds that of the school board, who are the elected representatives of the people of the community. Teacher unionism has become such an important force in the political arena of educational decision making that the entire next chapter is devoted to it.

Student Groups

Student groups have not been a particularly potent political force in education in this country until relatively recently. Teachers taught, professors professed, administrators administered, boards of regents set standards for admission and completion, and students could pretty much take it or leave it. The adults made the rules and regulations; students were expected to comply with them. Students could involve themselves in so-called student councils and student governing bodies at the high school and college levels, but these were frequently controlled by the institutional establishment. The governance of institutions was rarely challenged seriously on any issue of substance.

All of this began to change dramatically at the college and university levels with the return to the campuses of the veterans of World War

II. Attending under the GI Bill of Rights (Servicemen's Rehabilitation Act of 1944), these men and women invaded the campuses of the country by the hundreds of thousands. They had already had their career plans delayed because of the war, most were several years older than the conventional college student, and most were highly self-directed in terms of their career goals. Also, many were fed up with the bureaucracy and seemingly senseless regulation of military life and were not about to put up with it as civilians. The students, then for the first time, began putting real pressure on colleges and universities to reform their procedures and to provide a sympathetic ear to the demands of the students. Institutions had little choice, really, for they could not survive without the income these potential students could provide.

Thus, the World War II veterans of the period between 1946 and 1956 paved the way for student involvement in educational decision making at the college and university levels. Institutions had been accommodating student demands for nearly two decades before the extreme student activism of the 1960s and, therefore, should have been able to cope with it. Nonetheless, when student activism reached its peak in the late 1960s, these institutions found themselves in complete disarray and, in some instances, became practically ungovernable. These developments had the effect of dramatizing the political power of student groups in campus decision making. As a result, students have become active participants in the processes of decision making on college and university campuses. There is an awareness of the rights of students and a sensitivity to the need to involve students in decision making. Today we find student members on many committees that deal with the academic and institutional affairs not only on college and university campuses but in secondary schools as well.

The Courts

Historically, the courts have not been heavily involved in educational decision making in this country. This, of course, changed with the landmark decision of *Brown* v. *The Board of Education of Topeka, Kansas*. The resolution of the Brown case in favor of the litigants not only outlawed the separate but equal principle, but it also ushered in a whole new era of the involvement of the courts in educational policy formation. This came about, in part, because of changes in judicial procedure that made "class action" suits easier to file. A class action lawsuit means that the outcome of the case will affect not only the individual litigant but also all others who are similarly grieved or affected. Thus, a class action lawsuit has the effect of establishing policy. David L. Kirp has noted that this relaxation of the procedures in filing class action lawsuits, along with the expansion of the substantive meaning of the Equal Protection Clause of the Fourteenth Amendment, were instrumental in the judicial system's becoming a vehicle for efforts to secure distributive justice.[5]

As was explained in Chapter 6, for a period of nearly twenty years following the Brown case, one case after another found its way into the courts. Clearly, this was done in order to achieve justice when local institutions were unable or unwilling to provide it. One might say that the unresponsiveness of traditional institutions to human needs encourages judicial involvement in policy formation for public education. But this development was greatly slowed by the U.S. Supreme Court decision in the Rodriguez case in 1973 and the Bakke decision in 1978 (see the section on judicial intervention in school policy formation in Chapter 6 for both cases). The judicial success in recent years has not been as predictable as it once was, making potential litigants more wary in becoming involved in a lengthy and costly lawsuit that might eventually have adverse class action consequences. Nonetheless, the courts remain a potent political component in educational policy formation in this country.

State Legislative Bodies

Changes in school funding practices, with a greater share of the costs of education being paid by the state, coupled with citizen concern over student achievement, have given ascendance to state legislatures as powerful political forces in educational decision making. Another reason for the growing potency of the state legislature is the increased strength of other politically influential groups. For example, the local school authorities can no longer deal effectively with the powerful teachers' unions, business groups, and taxpayers' associations. These local authorities cry for help from the state legislatures in setting down policies having to do with contract negotiations, funding, student rights, tax

---

[5] David L. Kirp, "Law, Politics, and Equal Educational Opportunity: The Limits of Judicial Involvement," *Harvard Educational Review* 47:2 (May 1977): 118.

rates, and many other complex issues. The same forces that have reduced the influence of the judicial system on educational policy formation have *increased* the role of the state legislatures.

There is little doubt that the state legislature today is the most powerful political body affecting educational decisions. Increasingly, political groups are recognizing this and are taking their problems directly to the state legislature. This applies no matter what the problem might be—curriculum, school finance, personnel, affirmative action, minority group education, and so on. Local political units are not able to deal with these complex problems, and the federal government either refuses to or cannot legally become involved. Consequently, it is the state legislature that has become the educational unit of first and last resort in resolving educational issues.

Business and Corporate Groups

Business and corporate interests have traditionally been among the most powerful influences on educational decision making. This is because they represent the governing elite of the community. If there is a "power elite" who is responsible for all of the major decisions of a substantive nature in a community, it would be this group. Business and corporate interests organize themselves around such organizations as the chamber of commerce, Kiwanis Club, the Rotary Club, and the local taxpayers' association. These men and women are likely to have many social contacts at local private clubs, at business luncheons, at community affairs, and even in each other's homes.

The business and corporate interests have been stereotyped as bedrock political, economic, and social conservatism in this country. There is, however, growing evidence that there is not as solid agreement among leaders of these groups that there once was. Everett Ladd, Jr. sees these differences as essentially *generational* and refers to them as representing "moderate" and "orthodox" conservatism.

> moderate conservatives accept the service state and the governmental intervention that accompanies it. Even though they may inveigh against it at Rotary luncheons and convention banquets, back in the privacy of the boardroom they try to shape its uses, especially in promoting economic development and in advancing the immediate interests of the business middle class. Orthodox conservatives, in contrast, remain profoundly and genuinely

263

uncomfortable with the New Deal state. As practical politicians, such con-servatives usually understand full well the limits on how far they may reasonably expect to cut back government. But still, their objective is to pro-duce a situation where government taxes less, spends less, and regulates less.[6]

Business groups have often been represented as opposed to good ed-ucation. This is simply not true. Increasingly, the business community is recognizing that schools are vitally important to the quality of life in a community. If young families are to be attracted to the city as a place to make their homes, they will do so only if those communities provide op-portunities for a quality education for their children. In an effort to ar-rest or even reverse the flight to the suburbs trend, many young business leaders have become centrally involved in the revitalization of education in America's cities.

Religious Groups

Religious groups have been active politically in the formation of educational policies dealing with school finances and with curriculum issues. Some of the issues surrounding religious groups and school funding were discussed in the previous chapter. At the time of this writing, the In-ternal Revenue Service is challenging the tax-exempt status of some religious schools. As a result, those groups are marshaling their political troops.

Public education and religious groups often encounter value con-flicts. The issues become political when pressure is brought to bear on the school to *do* something that it is not now doing or to *stop* doing something that it is doing. Examples of the first concern is to persuade schools to engage in prayer recitation and/or *Bible* reading or to teach the creation theory. Examples of the second concern are pressures to get schools to stop using inquiry procedures, and to refrain from including sex educa-tion or evolution in the curriculum. The extent to which religious groups are powerful political agents depends largely on the community. In those places where the entire community is of a single religious persuasion, the religious influence can be, and usually is, very strong. If a community is

[6] Everett Ladd, Jr., "The New Lines Are Drawn: Class and Ideology, Part II," *Public Opinion* 1:4 (September–October 1978), p. 15.

heterogeneous in its religious composition, no one group is powerful enough to dominate the public school decision making.

Minority and Ethnic Groups

Minority and ethnic groups have become political forces of consequence since the beginning of the Civil Rights Movement in the early 1950s. By the late 1960s, hardly any school decision could be made without taking into account the effect it might have on the minority and ethnic component of the community. These groups gained considerable strength as a result of several favorable judicial decisions and because of federal and state legislation. Although these groups are not as powerful politically as they may have been a decade ago, they still wield formidable political power. For instance, political analysts suggest that the black vote was responsible for the election of President Carter in 1976.

The political and social climate of the period between 1960 and 1970 encouraged self-determination for minority and ethnic groups. Guidelines for federal projects not only encouraged the involvement of minorities and ethnics but required it. The Civil Rights Act of 1964 opened many doors to opportunity for these groups and enhanced their political strength. The formation of human rights commissions in states, affirmative action programs, and a growing public awareness of discrimination also strengthened minority and ethnic groups politically. By the mid-1970s, representatives of visible minorities were found in a great many positions of influence in schools, colleges, universities, and throughout the educational establishment in this country.

Organized Labor

Organized labor has not been the powerful influence on public education that one might expect it to be. It is true that labor played an important part in securing educational opportunity for all American children and youth. Also, labor was instrumental in promoting compulsory education legislation, but this was done as much to protect itself from the competition of a youthful labor force as it was out of humanitarian concern. In general, it can be said that the public school authorities of this country have marched to the beat of drummers other than that of organized labor. Organized labor remains a largely untapped but potentially very powerful political force for education.

265

WEAPONS IN THE ARSENALS OF POLITICAL ACTION GROUPS

It should be stressed that the influence of political and pressure groups is not necessarily detrimental to the cause of education. Indeed, these groups have been important forces in promoting much needed educational reforms. The schools' harshest critics are often the ones that produce the most beneficial results because they force school officials to examine and defend publicly what they are doing. What strategies do these groups use to achieve their goals? Here are some of the most common:

1. Reduce the amount of money available to education, as, for example, limits on taxes.
2. Lobby for the passage of legislation favorable to their point of view.
3. Publish material relating to specific issues and concerns.
4. Force public disclosure of data embarrassing to school authorities such as expenditures, drug use in schools, achievement scores, and so forth.
5. Take legal action to force specific issues.
6. Seek public support through the initiative process.
7. Elect school board members who support a particular position.
8. Serve on textbook review and/or selection committees.
9. Attend school board meetings.
10. Establish and serve on citizens' advisory panels.
11. Seek redress of grievances by way of human rights commissions.
12. Engage in public protest—picketing, sit-ins, marching, occupation of buildings, and so forth.

SHIFTS IN POLITICAL INFLUENCE

For the first two-thirds of this century, the dominant political voice in education at the state level was the chief state school officer, and at the local level it was the school superintendent. It is abundantly clear that

that is not the case today. Today political power is highly dispersed, but certain trends seem to be emerging:

1. The power of the state legislatures is ascending and is likely to continue for the foreseeable future.
2. The power of organized teacher groups, that is, teachers' unions, is growing in strength.
3. Disenfranchised groups seeking redress in the courts through class action lawsuits are likely to be less successful than they were in the two decades of 1954 to 1974.
4. Federal control of education is not likely to be expanded even under the new federal Department of Education.
5. Greater decentralization of certain aspects of curriculum decision making with involvement of parents at the local level is likely to continue.

STUDY AND DISCUSSION

1. Discuss the advantages and disadvantages of having school governance and operating authority separated from, and independent of, other units of government at the local level.
2. Describe the difficulties parents sometimes face in being effective in dealing with the school bureaucracy. Suggest ways these obstacles can be overcome.
3. What do you see as the most powerful and persuasive arguments for and against local control of school policies and programs?
4. Provide examples of incidents or situations in which the values *social integration* and *localism* conflict.
5. What are the advantages and disadvantages of using *efficiency* as a criterion for judging the effectiveness of a school system?
6. Provide five examples to illustrate that groups *other than* school boards are profoundly influential in school decision making.
7. How do you account for the fact that organized labor has been less influential in shaping public school policies and impacting

the school curriculum than have business and professional groups?

8. Some individuals and groups have been opposed to public preschool education (ages 3 to 4) on the grounds that young children would be too susceptible to political socialization by the school. Do you believe this to be a legitimate and valid concern? Provide reasons to support your response.

9. What are some of the implications for school desegregation if school districts move toward large, metropolitan administrative structures? Is this likely to encourage or discourage metropolitanism?

10. Provide specific examples from a community with which you are familiar of action (or lack of action) by local authorities that has encouraged state legislative involvement in school decision making.

SELECTED BIBLIOGRAPHY

BROOKOVER, WILBUR B., and EDSEL L. ERICKSON. *Sociology of Education.* Chapter 3: "The Control of Education." Homewood, Ill.: The Dorsey Press, 1975.

COHEN, DAVID K. "Reforming School Politics." *Harvard Educational Review* (November 1978): 429–447.

CUSHMAN, M. L. *The Governance of Teacher Education.* Bloomington, Indiana: Phi Delta Kappa, 1977.

DOMHOFF, G. WILLIAM. *Who Really Rules?* Santa Monica, Calif.: Goodyear Publishing Company, Inc., 1978.

———. *Who Rules America?* Englewood Cliffs, N.J.: Prentice-Hall, Inc., 1967.

KARABEL, JEROME, and A. H. HALSEY, eds. *Power and Ideology in Education.* Part 4: "The Politics of Education." New York: Oxford University Press, 1977.

KATZ, MICHAEL B. *The Irony of Early School Reform.* Cambridge, Mass.: Harvard University Press, 1968.

MILLER, HARRY L. *Social Foundations of Education: An Urban Focus.* 3d ed. Part 2. New York: Holt, Rinehart and Winston, Inc., 1978.

MOSHER, EDITH K., and JENNINGS L. WAGONER, JR., eds. *The Changing Politics of Education: Prospects for the 1980's.* Berkeley, California: McCutchan Publishing Corporation, 1979.

ORNSTEIN, ALLAN C. *Race and Politics in School/Community Organizations.* Pacific Palisades, California: Goodyear Publishing Company, 1974.

PETERSON, PAUL E. *School Politics Chicago Style.* Chicago: University of Chicago Press, 1976.

SHER, JONATHAN P., ed. *Education in Rural America: A Reassessment of Conventional Wisdom*. Boulder, Colorado: Westview Press, 1977. (A volume of readings.)

SPRING, JOEL. *The Sorting Machine*. New York: David McKay Company, Inc., 1976.

WIRT, FREDERICK M., and MICHAEL W. KIRST. *The Political Web of American Schools*. Boston: Little, Brown and Company, 1972.

ZIRKEL, PERRY A., ed. *A Digest of Supreme Court Decisions Affecting Education*. Bloomington, Indiana: Phi Delta Kappa, 1978.

chapter **11**

The Influence of Organized Teacher Groups on School Decision Making

In 1977, when the Seattle teachers were negotiating their contract with the school board, School Superintendent David Moberly identified the prime issue as "control of education—whether the union controls or the school board controls it."[1] Many believe that control of education is also the prime issue nationally—whether boards of education and state legislatures will control it or whether the organized teaching profession will control it. At this writing, the issue is in considerable doubt. The fact that it is a problem of national concern was underscored by an article in the November 1978 issue of *The Reader's Digest* entitled "The NEA: A Washington Lobby Run Rampant." A lead into the title of the article states, "The drive for power, nationwide, by this huge and aggressive teachers union provides a classic study of how special-interest politics can overwhelm the public interest."[2]

[1] *Seattle Post-Intelligencer*, June 4, 1977.
[2] Eugene H. Methvin, "The NEA: A Washington Lobby Run Rampant," *The Reader's Digest*, November 1978, p. 97.

TEACHER ASSOCIATIONS AS POLITICAL POWER GROUPS

The National Education Association

The National Education Association of the United States (NEA) enrolls nearly 2,000,000 members and is the largest professional association in the entire world. Ten state associations of teachers called a convention in 1857 and founded the National Teachers Association, the purpose of which was "to elevate the character and advance the interests of the profession of teaching, and to promote the cause of popular education in the United States." Women were admitted to membership in 1866. In 1870 the association united with the National Association of School Superintendents and the American Normal School Association to form the National Education Association. It was incorporated in the District of Columbia in 1886 and was chartered by an act of Congress in 1906 as the National Education Association of the United States. The original purpose of the NTA was preserved intact in the NEA charter. When the association moved to Washington, D.C., in 1917, its membership was only 8,500. It reached a million in 1966 and has almost doubled since then. The power and influence of the NEA has escalated in recent years, just as has its membership.

The NEA has made the concept of "a united profession" one of its guiding principles. This has meant that every teacher would participate in the professional association at all three levels—the local, state, and national. The NEA, therefore, has worked hard to build the strength of its local and state affiliated units. Today in some states there is a unified dues structure that requires that one hold membership in the state and local units as a prerequisite to membership in the NEA. The "unified teaching profession" concept has also meant that persons in professional roles other than classroom teaching could be members—central administrators, supervisors, principals, college professors, and so on.

The broad membership umbrella has had deep-seated consequences for the development of the NEA as an organization representing the interests of classroom teachers. It is clear that superintendents, principals, curriculum specialists, and supervisors would have to be a small minority in an organization of teachers enrolling a million or more members. Ironically, however, it was from this group of what amounted

272

essentially to school managers that the NEA and its state and local affiliates were selecting much of their leadership. The conflict of interest created by this type of organizational structure reduced the effectiveness of the NEA and its state and local affiliates in dealing with issues concerning the welfare and conditions of employment of teachers. The administrators who were the influentials in the policy-making group of the "professional association" were really the representatives and executives of the school boards in any contract negotiations! Little wonder the NEA had developed a reputation as being a relatively impotent organization when it came to hard-nosed, adversary-oriented collective bargaining on salary, status, fringe benefits, retirement benefits, and similar issues.

It was common knowledge that the teachers' unions such as the American Federation of Teachers (AFT) were more productive organizations in achieving status and welfare benefits. The NEA was unable or unwilling to do anything about changing the situation, however, until the early 1960s. At that time the New York United Federation of Teachers, under the leadership of Albert Shanker, secured the exclusive right to engage in collective bargaining with the New York City Board of Education for the 44,000 teachers of that city. The defeat of the local NEA affiliate on this important issue and the success of the UFT represented a major setback in the influence of the NEA. This event was the capstone of a whole series of member dissatisfactions with the leadership and organizational structrue of the NEA. At its annual meeting in Denver in 1962, the NEA took the first steps to remove and disallow nonteaching personnel from leadership positions in the organization. The leadership that followed up to the present time has been much more aggressive, much more militant, much more adversarial in its posture—so much so that it has clearly outdistanced its only competitor for membership, the AFT.

The NEA gains its strength as a political action organization from a unique combination of characteristics. First of all, its intellectual resources are probably unmatched by any similar group. All of its members are college graduates, many have advanced degrees, and a growing number have doctorates. Second, its size is enormous. In terms of numbers, only the Teamsters' Union has a larger membership than the NEA. Third, it reaches into every congressional district, indeed, into every *precinct* in the entire nation. No other union can make that claim because most unions are to some extent regional. Fourth, it has huge financial resources available to it. Fifth, it is a politically skillful and sophisticated organization, with nearly 1,500 professional field organizers and thousands of teachers who have been through the NEA political action workshops.

It is apparent that great changes have taken place in the NEA since 1960, when it was mainly a broadly based professional fraternity lacking in political clout. In the 1976 national election, the NEA endorsed Jimmy Carter, the first time ever that it had made an endorsement of a presidential candidate. Following President Carter's election, his campaign manager, Hamilton Jordan, was reported as saying, "The massive support from teachers was crucial to our winning. We turned to the NEA for help and it delivered nationwide."

The American Federation of Teachers

Teachers' unions existed in this country for several years before the American Federation of Teachers (AFT) was formed in 1916. In fact, it was teachers' unions in Chicago that took the initiative in forming a national organization of classroom teachers, an action precipitated by arbitrary action taken against them by the Chicago Board of Education. As a result of the Chicago organizational meeting, charters were given to teachers' unions in Chicago, Gary, New York, Oklahoma City, Scranton, and Washington, D.C. The application of the AFT for affiliation with the AFL was approved on May 9, 1916.

In terms of percentage of gain in membership, the AFT grew very rapidly in the first few years. Indeed, by 1920 it had more members than the NEA. That soon changed, however, and its growth through the years has been rather slow. Its most dramatic gains have been in recent years. For instance, in 1950 its membership was just over 40,000; by 1960 it had grown only to 50,000. Efforts by the AFT to organize teachers in the nation's big cities during the 1960s, however, paid large dividends. By 1969 AFT membership had risen to 175,000; by 1975 there were 450,000 members. The AFT has always been most attractive to the urban, male, secondary school teacher. A very high percentage of AFT membership—80 per cent or more—comes from the nation's largest cities: New York, Chicago, Detroit, Philadelphia, Cleveland, Boston, Washington, D.C., Baltimore, Pittsburgh, and Kansas City.

274

It is fair to say that there has always been a strong anti-union bias among teachers. This can be accounted for in several ways. School teachers in the past have been products of lower middle-class or working-class families with strong aspirations for upward social mobility. Their fathers as truck drivers, miners, carpenters, plumbers, or factory workers were members of unions. Teacher aspirants were conditioned to associate unionism with trade school vocational training or apprenticeship training that would lead to a job in the skilled or semiskilled labor market. People who were college-trained or who went to university professional schools did not belong to trade unions—they were professionals! As professionals, they should belong to professional associations, as, for example, the way doctors belong to the American Medical Association. It is significant that the literature of education is replete with medical analogies. Even today we do not have student teachers; we have *interns.* We have *clinical* professors; we *diagnose* difficulties; we *prescribe* remedial instruction; we speak of *clients* when we mean students; and so on. This fondness of educators for medical jargon is another example of the obsession of people in the teaching field with so-called professionalism.

There seems to be no doubt that the NEA used these latent anti-union attitudes of school teachers to its own advantage. It created the impression that belonging to a union was not professional. Moreover, the NEA successfully persuaded teachers that they should not be "identified with one segment of society." This meant that if they were members of a union themselves, their teaching of social issues would thus be tainted. Evidently, this same principle did not obtain if they were identified with that segment of society known as professionals! Finally, the NEA made a big point of associating unionism with the strike, a weapon the NEA considered "unprofessional." The fact is that the AFT had adopted strong, no-strike policies on many occasions and had always rejected the strike as a method of achieving its goals, whereas the NEA had no such policy. Of course, all of this is now moot because both groups have been involved in the "withholding of services" in recent years.

The AFT has always defined itself as an organization that worked for the benefit of teachers. In 1966 an amendment to the AFT constitution was approved specifically excluding from membership administrators holding the rank of principal or higher. This simply formalized existing conditions because few administrators and supervisors had union membership. The AFT assumes that school systems are organized along

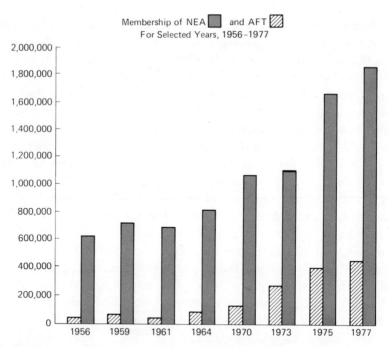

Membership of NEA ■ and AFT ▨
For Selected Years, 1956–1977

FIGURE 11. What reasons can you suggest for the much larger membership of the NEA as compared with the AFT? What conditions might contribute to an increased growth of the AFT in the future? (Sources: *Encyclopedia of Associations* and the NEA.)

the lines of a management and labor operation with administrators and supervisors being a part of the management team. This is compatible with an adversary or confrontation-type model of conflict resolution. The AFT perceives teacher-school board negotiations as basically a conflict of power to determine how resources are to be allocated. In recent years the NEA has operated along the same lines exactly.

The AFT has never made any secret of its use of confrontation strategies in seeking to attain its objectives. It has always maintained a militant, aggressive posture. Thus, in communities where year after year teachers were frustrated in dealing with school boards, they turned, often in desperation, to the AFT. The AFT has had a good track record in serving the needs of its members. Being an affiliate of the AFL–CIO, it has the combined power of organized labor that it can bring to bear on educational issues.

276

Curriculum and Subject Matter Associations

The NEA and AFT are explicit in their goal statements concerning the improvement of the quality of education in American schools. In actual practice, however, most of their efforts have been along the lines of bread-and-butter issues that have to do with improving the status, salaries, and working conditions of teachers. As a result, other professional associations have been formed that address themselves to the curriculum and teaching of specific subject areas—mathematics, English, social studies, science, music, art, and so on. Other organizations are not tied to a specific subject area but deal more broadly with curriculum, supervision, or instructional issues. Organizations such as the Association for Supervision and Curriculum Development and the American Education Research Association would be examples of the latter type. At one time many of these organizations either were departments of, or were affiliated with, the NEA. Gradually, however, most of them have dropped their NEA affiliation and are autonomous professional associations.

These curriculum and subject matter groups do not, of course, have the same political power that the NEA and AFT do. They can be, and often are, very influential, however, in affecting curriculum and instruction procedures and education legislation. Many of these organizations publish guidelines for the curriculum, and these guidelines become standards that are used by school districts all over the country in building instructional programs. Most of them have a publications program that informs the educational community of trends and developments in that particular subject field. The state, regional, and national conferences of these organizations also provide an important means of communicating and disseminating ideas. In some instances, these groups have established standards for the preparation of teachers. Very often they take some responsibility for in-service education at the local level.

The publications program of groups such as the National Council for Teachers of English, National Council for the Social Studies, and National Science Teachers Association are very impressive. Typically, they include a professional journal published monthly during the school year, a yearbook, bulletins, research reports, newsletters, occasional papers, pamphlets, and other literature. Because these publications represent the views of leaders in the field and because they are marketed nationally, they have a strong impact on the curriculum development and teaching practices of the nation's schools. These organizations, and particularly some of their publications, help to standardize the curriculum throughout the country.

AREAS OF CONFLICT BETWEEN TEACHERS' UNIONS AND THE COMMUNITY

In a perceptive article entitled "Political Issues in School Decentralization," the political scientist Robert F. Lyke addresses himself thoughtfully and analytically to three fundamental conflicts implicit in the power struggle between teachers' unions and communities for the control of schools:[3]

1. The conflict between *democratic control and professional autonomy.* Advocates of community control insist that as public employees, educators must be accountable to local constituents. That is to say, educators are the employees of the local community and, therefore, it has the authority to determine and monitor policies regarding personnel, budget expenditures, curriculum, and instruction. Educators, on the other hand, insist that as professional practitioners they cannot function under such close supervision. Moreover, laypersons lack the knowledge and the expertise to direct the work of teachers.
2. The conflict between *procedural values and substantive values* in policy formation. Teachers and educators usually take the position that questions and policies having to do with curriculum, instruction, and other school matters are technical, substantive matters that ought to be resolved on the basis of expertise. For instance, if one were instituting a new reading program in a school system, the persons who should have the most to say about policies and procedures relating to such decisions ought to be reading specialists. These are substantive matters, and laypersons lack the knowledge and expertise to deal with them effec-

[3] Robert F. Lyke, "Political Issues in School Decentralization," in *Challenges to Education,* ed. Emanuel Hurwitz, Jr. and Charles A. Tesconi (New York: Dodd, Mead & Company, Inc., 1972), pp. 155–177.

tively. Supporters of the community argue, however, that the *procedures* used in coming to those decisions are at least as important in the final outcome as are the substantive elements involved in the issue. Needless to say, part of those procedures includes parent and community involvement. Parents are likely to say that although reading specialists may know the field of reading, they do not necessarily know their children. Experienced curriculum specialists know very well the importance of "taking the parent along" with any proposed curriculum change. Indeed, if they are not involved at every step along the way, the curriculum change often falls flat for lack of community support. Procedural values are obviously critical to such policy decisions, but so are substantive values. The issue is joined on the *amount* of importance each is to be given.

3. The conflict between *community development and societal integration*. Those who support community control argue that citizen involvement in the operation of local schools is important to the revitalization of neighborhood communities. If communities are to deal effectively with such problems as drug traffic, crime, housing, and employment, the remedial measures must begin at the local level, or so it is claimed. Because the school is not only an educational institution but also a symbol and instrument of community cohesion, it is crucial to the transformation of a community. The other side of this issue argues that most of the problems that plague the ghetto community are simply too complex to be dealt with adequately at the local level. In order to attack such problems as drugs, health, crime, housing, and discrimination, a metropolitan, regional effort is required. Dealing with these problems demands expenditures of vast sums of money and the application of expertise, neither of which is in abundance at the local level. Moreover, it is argued that there are overarching societal values that transcend the local community. People who are educated in one place often spend most of their lives somewhere else, and, therefore, educational programs should focus on societal integration rather than on local values and local concerns alone.

These three areas of conflict between teachers and communities identified by Robert F. Lyke provide a good general context within which to examine specific areas of contention that occur between these groups. Let us now examine some of those.

Freedom to Teach

Issues that surround the freedom to teach involve such things as deciding what is taught and how it is taught and also the right of parents to decide what ideas their children will be exposed to and what books are to be used as opposed to the teacher's right to make these decisions as a matter of professional judgment. These problems often fall under the rubric of academic freedom. An occupation that is to have the status of "profession" requires that practitioners exercise a great deal of autonomy in performing their tasks. Little wonder, therefore, that teaching, which is striving to establish itself as a profession, would seek to increase the teachers' freedom to exercise professional autonomy, that is, to increase the scope of independent judgment allowed teachers in carrying out their work.

Many, perhaps even most, persons would agree that in an open society teachers should as a matter of principle be free to teach, and students should be free to learn. As a society we reject the idea of censorship; we believe that a free people must encounter divergent ideas and learn how to deal with them. We are repulsed by the practice of having forces external to the school, no matter how well intentioned, selecting textbooks, determining curriculum, or demanding that teachers teach in certain ways. The problem is now and always has been one of determining *whose* values and standards are to prevail. In her book *Bare Boobs in the World Book*, Patricia Ryan tells of the teacher who kept Volume 1 of *The World Book Encyclopedia* locked in her closet because she did not want the children to see the pictures of the African dancers with their bare bosoms![4] What one constituency finds admirable, another may find objectionable. Rather than try to attach preference to competing value systems, this society, as a matter of public policy, has taken the position of an open forum in the free marketplace of ideas. There are many examples of this principle that is based on the rights guaranteed by the First Amendment: "Congress shall make no law respecting the establishment of religion, or prohibiting the free exercise thereof; or abridging the

---

[4] Patricia Ryan, *Bare Boobs in The World Book* (New York: Vantage Press, 1978).

freedom of speech, or of the press . . ." The courts have been very reluctant to find in favor of censorship of ideas in any form whether these be in print, the spoken word, films, or other media. These rights are considered the foundation of our free society.

Yet the rights guaranteed by the First Amendment are not absolute. The government, for instance, may abridge freedom of speech when there is a "clear and present danger" to the state. Repeatedly, courts have stressed the *context* within which an action takes place. A bawdy dance hall might be permitted in an offbeat section of the waterfront but would be ruled inappropriate in a fine residential section of the same city. This principle applies precisely to education and is often the source of difficulty for teachers. What would be entirely appropriate—indeed, may even be *required* for a fair treatment of an issue at the college level— might be out of place at the elementary or secondary school level. There is such a thing as maturity, and social norms dictate that some matters are best left for persons who are older and, presumably, more mature. In most cases with which this author is familiar that have involved an academic freedom issue, teacher behavior represented questionable judgment regarding the selection of subject matter, a learning resource, or an instructional process as related to the maturity of the learners involved. For reasons not too hard to understand, parents of upper elementary school and junior high school pupils and even some of high school age students simply do not want to have their children reading schoolbooks that are sprinkled generously with crude obscenities. If teachers make foolish judgments in the selection of subject matter, in the selection of books and other learning resources, and in the selection of learning activities, they can expect parents of pupils K–12 to express their concern, as they should. Of course, this does not mean that teachers should knuckle under to the parent pressure groups who want to make decisions about the school program that should properly be made by teachers and other professionals.

It is obvious that some areas of the curriculum are more vulnerable to outside interference than are others. Physical education, music, industrial arts, mathematics, chemistry, physics, foreign languages, and geography have been relatively free of external pressure. Social studies, literature, general science, biology, home economics, health, and sex education are the curriculum areas where the teacher's judgment and actions are most frequently challenged. As reliably as the changing seasons, one can predict that each year somewhere in the country some school district will have parents who are concerned that their children are required to read certain books (*Catcher in the Rye* is a perennial favorite even though it is badly dated today), that the science classes or social studies teachers are teaching evolution, that sex education is included in the curriculum, that Thomas Jefferson is made out to be a champion of freedom but actually kept slaves himself and fathered at least one child by a slavewoman, that children are being taught through inquiry whereas they should learn what is in their science and social studies books, and so on and on. The social studies field is particularly susceptible to this type of external pressure because it deals with so many potentially controversial matters. And, of course, if one stays away from such topics, one cuts the heart out of the social studies curriculum.

From time to time there is a national concern for the security of basic beliefs and basic institutions because of a threat from some outside force or ideology. Patriotic groups who had a fear of Germany and German culture before and during World War I were instrumental in not only removing the German language from the school curriculum but in doing violence to all foreign language instruction. Similarly, in the decade of the 1950s, there was national fear of communism, and this caused superpatriotic groups to question the loyalty of many teachers. After all, what could be more threatening to the nation's security than a subversive teacher charged with the responsibility of shaping the minds of young children? The hysteria caused by these events resulted in a great number of states' passing laws that required teachers to take loyalty oaths as a condition of employment. These requirements were challenged in court, and in most cases such requirements were struck down, removed voluntarily, or modified to meet legal requirements. Loyalty oaths may be required of teachers even today if they call for clearly stated positive affirmations that do not otherwise violate the teacher's civil rights. But even relatively harmless loyalty oaths are an abridgment of academic freedom because they represent a loss of freedom of conscience by the teacher in this sensitive area. The National Council for the Social Studies, a national organization of social studies teachers, takes a strong position on the matter of academic freedom:

> It is the prime responsibility of the schools to help students assume the responsibilities of democratic citizenship. To do this, education must impart

the skills needed for intelligent study and orderly resolution of the problems inherent in a democratic society. Students need to study issues upon which there is disagreement and to practice analyzing problems, gathering and organizing facts, discriminating between facts and opinions, discussing differing viewpoints, and drawing tentative conclusions. It is the clear obligation of schools to promote full and free contemplation of controversial issues and to foster appreciation of the role of controversy as an instrument of progress in a democracy.[5]

Teachers would like to think that the freedom to teach at the elementary and secondary school levels is or ought to be the same as it is at the college and university levels, where professors have traditionally enjoyed a great deal of, but not total, academic freedom. But the situations are not the same and probably never will be. Children of elementary and secondary school age are minors, living at home, and parents are legally responsible for taking care of them. Time after time the courts have affirmed the parents' rights in determining the upbringing of their children. A home situation has to be very bad—some think much worse than it should be—before a court will remove the children from the custody of their natural parents. Precedence clearly shows that the parents' rights over the lives of their children extends beyond the physical and health needs of children. It is the *parents* who have a great deal to say about how their children are to be educated; by whom; what religious beliefs, if any, they are to embrace; and whether or not and how or if they are to pray. The parents' responsibility and rights relating to the upbringing of their children, when kept within reasonable limits, is inviolable.

Tenure and Dismissal

Today teachers everywhere in the nation are protected from arbitrary, capricious, and unfair dismissal by so-called tenure laws. This means that following some period of probation, which usually ranges from one to three years, the teacher's contract cannot be terminated without showing cause, that is, without showing that the teacher is not

[5] National Council for the Social Studies, "Academic Freedom and the Social Studies Teacher" (a policy statement of the National Council for the Social Studies), *Social Education* 35 (April 1971): 378.

performing his or her duties satisfactorily. During the hiring and probationary period, it is up to the teacher to demonstrate that he or she is able to perform well enough to justify employment. Once the teacher is on tenure, however, the burden of proof shifts to the school officials if they want to dismiss the teacher. The tenure principle is one of the least well-understood concepts by teachers and by the public.

Tenure laws were established in the first place because of the high-handed way school authorities dealt with teachers. For example, a teacher would always be hired at the minimum salary. During each year of service, the teacher was often given a salary raise. After a period of seven to ten years or more, the school district could save a substantial amount of money if it were to fire the experienced teacher and replace him or her with a newly trained teacher who could be hired at the beginner's salary.

In order to fire a teacher not protected by tenure, a school district can easily find an excuse if not a reason. When a teacher works with children day after day for several hours each day, evaluating their conduct, trying to teach them something they often resist learning, putting up with their mischievous behavior, the teacher is very likely to offend some parents. It could hardly be otherwise if the teacher had any strongly held convictions. A teacher's job might very well be placed in jeopardy because he or she gave a well-deserved low grade to the son of an influential family in the community. Teachers, like governors and mayors, are often forced to make unpopular decisions simply because of the nature of their positions. Their ability to make such decisions would be greatly compromised if their jobs were in constant jeopardy. They could not even touch controversial issues, let alone discuss them. They could not evaluate student's work honestly. They would constantly be faced with conflicts of conscience in doing what is professionally needed, yet knowing that they place their jobs on the line each time they do. Such a situation would be intolerable.

The tenure principle represents a type of social contract in which society protects the position of the teacher and the teacher has fewer remunerations and perquisites than would be available in higher-risk positions. A teacher with a master's degree may earn a lower salary than a similarly trained person who works as an engineer for an aircraft company. But when the aircraft company falls on hard times and does not sell its planes, the engineer may lose his job, but the teacher will not. Or the

284

aircraft company may transfer the engineer to another part of the country against his or her wishes, but the teacher cannot be so transferred. The engineer may also be fired at age fifty-five because he or she has not kept abreast of his or her field, whereas this rarely happens to teachers.

This last point brings us to the abuses of tenure by teachers, abuses of which there are many. It is a sad fact that teachers and the unions and associations that represent them have used the tenure principle to protect the jobs of marginally competent and, in some cases, even incompetent teachers. The positions of the teachers' groups (AFT and the NEA) are clear: If a teacher is not doing his or her job satisfactorily, the district should document a bill of particulars and initiate dismissal procedures; if the school district cannot document a case that would support dismissal, the district probably does not have adequate grounds for releasing the teacher. This seems to be a fair enough policy on the face of it, but it presents incredibly complex problems when one tries to implement it. The AFT and the NEA officials know this. Short of the most flagrant violations of social norms—drunkenness on the job, sexually molesting a student, conviction on a felony charge, and similar conduct, *if* it can be documented—it is virtually impossible to dismiss a teacher. To fire a tenured teacher solely on the basis of doing a poor job in the classroom probably cannot be achieved in America today, and, if it could be, not many school superintendents would want to risk trying it.

Merit Pay

If there is one issue that infuriates parents and teacher association officials more than teacher tenure, it is merit pay. The position of parents on this issue is that teachers who are more effective should be appropriately rewarded. They point to the private sector of society to illustrate that those who are more productive, more diligent in their performance, and/or are more competent get more pay. This is seen on the one hand as a reward for doing a good job and as an incentive to others to encourage them to improve their performance. Teacher associations on the other hand, argue that peoples' perceptions of good teaching vary from one person to another, and, therefore, it is unfair to impose a uniform set of expectations on all teachers.

285

The issue of merit pay usually raises the question of whether or not teaching can be evaluated. The argument is often made that teaching involves such a complex array of skills that the process cannot be effectively evaluated. Furthermore, it is said there is not even agreement among experts as to what teaching really is. How can one evaluate something that cannot even be defined by experts in a way in which there will be consensus among them?

Children and their parents, however, are not concerned about making uncontestable definitions of teaching in order to advance the scientific study of education. All they know is that the teacher they are encountering this year is much less effective than the one they had last year. To claim that teaching cannot be evaluated is ridiculous. It would be hard to think of anything in society that is more frequently evaluated by so many people of such varied age groups and diverse backgrounds than is teaching, unless it would be the weather! *Everyone* evaluates teaching! The kindergarten child comes home and tells his or her parent, "Boy, do I have a good teacher!" Years later as a college student the same person comes home during the winter break and reports, "Boy, did I have a lousy prof this last quarter!" The teaching profession may not like the kinds of evaluations that are made of the work of teachers, but that does not stop the public from making them.

School principals, who are the ones usually tagged to evaluate teachers, are understandably reluctant to support merit pay. After all, they have to work closely with teachers on a day-to-day basis. If they give a teacher a low rating that results in a low pay raise, it is difficult to get the best and most cooperative performance from such a teacher. They are willing to evaluate teachers; in fact, their jobs call for them to do so, but those evaluations are for the purpose of improvement of instruction—not rating for salary purposes. So the administrators also beg the question of making qualitative distinctions between the performance of teachers. Yet, in confidence, a principal can direct the visitor to the two or three best teachers in the building.

It would seem that sooner or later the teaching profession itself must face up to the challenge presented by the merit pay issue. Like it or not, some persons are simply more effective teachers than others. Parents are always going to be unhappy, and rightly so, about the marginally competent teacher who draws the same salary as the outstanding teacher. The profession itself must police its own ranks and would make a commendable contribution to American education by doing so.

Salaries and Working Conditions

Salaries and working conditions are standard bread-and-butter issues that school districts face everywhere each year. Traditionally, teachers' salaries have been abysmally low. Many reasons can be given for this tradition—until relatively recently, a low level of training was required; the field was largely dominated by women, especially at the early grades; teaching was considered a "stepping-stone" profession; it was associated with social service, much like the ministry; there was a lack of organization among teachers; teachers were timid in demanding power and status; teachers' salaries depended on local tax support. But during the past three decades, this situation has changed dramatically. Teachers may still not share adequately in the social rewards of society in the measure that they contribute to it, but the picture has improved and continues to improve. Because these changes have come about just within the past few years, persons look at teachers' salaries today and can hardly believe "the outlandish amounts of money paid for nine months [of] work!"

As was indicated earlier in this chapter, teacher groups have developed some degree of sophistication in the collective bargaining process and are much more militant than they once were. They are less reluctant to assume an adversary role with their administrators and their boards of education. In fact, they prefer it that way. They have no hesitancy in employing professional negotiators. Albert Shanker, president of the AFT, is quoted as follows:

> Power is never given to anyone. Power is taken, and it is taken from someone. Teachers, as one of society's powerless groups, are now starting to take power from supervisors and school boards. This is causing and will continue to cause a realignment of power relationships.[6]

Thus, teachers have the *power* to demand greater equity on the salary

[6] Alan Rosenthal, *Pedagogues and Power: Teacher Groups in School Politics* (Syracuse, New York: Syracuse University Press, 1969), p. 20.

issue. Communities, on the other hand, are faced with taxpayers' resistance of unprecedented magnitude. The result is increasing conflict each summer and fall over salary matters. Little wonder the number of teachers' strikes increase each year. They are likely to continue.

Administrative Costs

On the issue of administrative costs, we often see some realignment of bedfellows. Both the community *and* teacher groups object to the increase in the administrative staffs of schools. Parents often voice the opinion that they do not object to increased school budgets if such funds are used to reward the teachers who work with the children. What they *do* object to are increased numbers of principals, vice-principals, associate superintendents, directors, department heads, counselors, accountants, supervisors, and other mid-management personnel. They argue that the main job of the school is to teach children and that a large number of supporting personnel is not needed to deliver such services.

On the face of it, the position of parents is logical and persuasive. The reality of present-day school operations, however, makes such a sensible approach to education impossible. The school bureaucracy has been growing for the past one hundred years, and it is highly unlikely that much will happen to change that trend. First of all, schools today operate within a strict legal framework. This means that precise record keeping is essential. Funding from the federal and state levels carries with it certain requirements having to do with accounting. Such accounting not only has to do with how the money was spent but also with the racial, ethnic, and sex makeup of the student population, the community, the faculty, and so on. The social and ethnic composition of the school has to be closely monitored to make sure the district is in compliance with affirmative action and desegregation requirements. Due process legal procedures have to be followed in the promotion and dismissal of staff. Contract negotiations have to be conducted in accordance with set procedures. The performance of staff and faculty members have to be evaluated regularly and reported in ways that will stand up under a legal challenge. Institutional activity has become highly regulated, and undoubtedly much of the regulation serves useful purposes. By the same token, the implementation of regulations does not take place by itself; it requires personnel. Consequently, for schools to do what they are required to do by law means that a continuing escalation of administrative staffs can be expected.

Teacher Education

Teachers' unions and associations have been vigorous in promoting their own involvement in the education of teachers. This movement was started in the decade of the 1960s and has been building ever since. In some cases, teachers' professional associations have been made full partners in a teacher-education consortium along with the institution of higher education and the school district. As teacher education programs have moved toward competency-based and performance-based approaches, teacher groups have become more concerned about the implication of these thrusts for in-service teachers; that is, if the performance of teacher candidates can be evaluated on some basis of competence, why cannot the same procedures be projected upward to the in-service level? This bothers teachers.

All signs point to stormy times ahead in the relationships between teacher organizations such as the NEA and its affiliates and those institutions that have anything to do with the training of teachers, setting standards for entry into the profession, conducting in-service education, and selecting teachers and their placement. It is clear that the NEA wants to control these processes because, from its perspective, it views such activities as legitimate professional functions. Naturally, state certification officers, boards of education, and, most particularly, institutions of higher education take a different view.

The potential for serious conflict between institutions of higher education and the organized profession is particularly severe. Both groups have strong weapons in their arsenals. For instance, the institutions of higher education have charge of the "coin of the realm," so to speak, the college credit. They also have a strong claim on the research arm of education and its related expertise. The associations, on the other hand, have control of the training sites in the field. They also have the credibility that is associated with on-the-job practice.

At the time of this writing, this conflict is being played out in the establishment of so-called teacher centers. The teacher center idea is one that was brought to this country from England in the 1960s, where such units had been established as in-service centers. The teacher center there was a place where a teacher could go to prepare materials, interact with other teachers, review instructional resources, engage in idea exchange, and so on. Teacher centers are supposed to be a grass roots effort by teachers to enhance their professional development. Properly conceived, they are to be by and for teachers. The NEA has insisted that the majority of any policy board of a teacher center be teachers. In the actual governance of teacher centers in this country, often a loose consortium is formed consisting of teachers, administrators, supervisory staff, and representatives of institutions of higher education. These boards are usually advisory, but in some instances they are involved in setting policy.

The U.S. Office of Education* at the urging of the NEA has sought and received federal funding for the establishment of teacher centers nationally. The purpose of these centers is to take over responsibility for a part of the in-service teacher training at the local level. This, of course, puts them into direct competition with local colleges and universities that have been established by the states for that purpose. Although teacher centers are not able to award college credit for their in-service programs, in at least one state non-college in-service centers can award credit for certification and salary increments (Pennsylvania). Because teacher centers are being established *outside* the traditional institutionalized frames of reference, it is doubtful that they will become a permanent part of the structure of teacher education in this country. But until their future is resolved, a considerable amount of controversy will be generated surrounding them.

THE FUTURE OF PROFESSIONAL ASSOCIATIONS

All signs point to an increase in the strength and vigor of teacher unions and associations. In the past fifteen years, they have made great strides in establishing themselves as powerful political forces. Such success has the effect of encouraging them to become even stronger. There is

* Now the Department of Education

no question that the organized teaching profession has the potential for becoming the most powerful lobby in the entire nation, simply because it has a ready-made network that extends into every hamlet and crossroads in the country. The history of groups such as this is (1) growth in power, (2) abuse of power, and (3) regulatory legislation to curb power. At this point, it appears that the organized teachers are at stage one, but some believe the NEA has already entered stage two.

In the early 1970s, there were strong signs that the AFT and the NEA would merge into one massive teacher organization. Experts were predicting such a union to occur within a decade. There would be some obvious advantages to the organized teaching profession if such a merger took place. Because of some deep-seated philosophical and political differences, however, the two groups could not get together, and by 1975 the talks had broken off completely. The AFT attaches great importance to its affiliation with the AFL–CIO, which the NEA regards as an anathema. Whether or not these two giants will one day join forces as a single association is impossible to predict at this time. Meanwhile, teachers, at least in the urban areas, have a choice of the type of organization they think best satisfies their professional needs.

STUDY AND DISCUSSION

1. What are some questions and problems surrounding the growing social and political power of organized teacher groups?
2. What evidence could be presented to document the claim that stronger professional teacher organizations have resulted in improved education for the schoolchildren of America?
3. Explain why the greatest strength of the AFT is found in the large urban areas of the Midwest and East.
4. Analyze and compare the potential for social power of both the NEA and the AFT, using the dimensions of power discussed in Chapter 7 in the section entitled, "Social Stratification and Community Power Structures."
5. What persuaders do the NEA and the AFT have in recruiting members that are not available to curriculum and subject matter associations such as those representing the fields of mathematics, science, English, and social studies? Why is it im-

portant for teachers to belong to these latter organizations?

6. If parents of high school students find the content of a book objectionable, should such a book be removed from a list of required reading? Should such a book be removed permanently from the high school library? Can you think of specific books that should *not* be in a high school library? What reasons do you have for your answer?

7. Suppose you were a teacher who was unfairly and undeservedly dismissed from your job ("let go"). How can your membership in a professional organization such as the AFT or NEA (and their local affiliates) be of assistance to you at such a time?

8. Parents and other citizens of the community often favor merit pay for teachers whereas teacher groups oppose the idea. If you were selected to argue *against* merit pay at a local forum of parents and teachers, what points would you be sure to make?

9. What are the pros and cons of having organized teacher groups control the admission of applicants to teaching and have a major role in the professional education of prospective teachers?

10. Many teachers and other professional educators believe that all teachers should be required to be members of the local association that represents teachers in contract negotiations. They argue that those who are not members are simply "freeloaders" who share in the benefits obtained by the organization at the bargaining table, yet contribute nothing to the process. The other side of the matter is that membership in *any* organization should be a matter of personal choice simply on the basis of an individual's right to belong or not. What are your views on this issue?

SELECTED BIBLIOGRAPHY

BRAUN, ROBERT J. *Teachers and Power: The Story of the American Federation of Teachers.* New York: Simon & Schuster, Inc., 1972.

CRESSWELL, ANTHONY, and MICHAEL MURPHY, eds. *Education and Collective Bargaining.* Berkeley, Calif.: McCutchan Publishing Corporation, 1977. (A volume of readings.)

DONLEY, MARSHALL O., JR. *Power to the Teacher: How America's Educators Became Militant.* Bloomington, Indiana: Phi Delta Kappa, 1976.

LANG, THEODORE H. "Teacher Tenure as a Management Problem." *Phi Delta Kappan* 56 (March 1975): 459–462.

MYERS, DONALD A. *Teacher Power: Professionalization and Collective Bargaining.* Lexington, Massachusetts: Lexington Books, 1975.

LIEBERMAN, MYRON. "Eggs That I have Laid: Teacher Bargaining Reconsidered." *Phi Delta Kappan* 60:6 (February 1979): 415–419.

ROSENTHAL, ALAN. *Pedagogues and Power: Teacher Groups in School Politics.* Syracuse, N.Y.: Syracuse University Press, 1969.

SHANKER, ALBERT. "Why the Merit-Pay Idea Lacks Merit." *American Teacher* 59 (April 1975): 4.

STINNETT, T. M., and RAYMOND E. CLEVELAND. "The Politics and Rise of Teacher Organizations." In *Policy Issues in Education.* Edited by Allan Ornstein and Steven Miller. Boston: D.C. Heath & Company, 1976, pp. 83–94.

chapter 12

Managing Educational Change

The most significant thing that can be said about change in the contemporary world is the *rate* at which it takes place. The changes of which we are most aware are those that take place in the physical and material things that surround us. Cars that are a few years old look out-of-date. Clothes that were in style a decade ago look old-fashioned today. The airplane flown by the Wright brothers at Kitty Hawk seems to belong to the world of Leonardo da Vinci rather than to the twentieth century. Nearly all of the changes that occur with such swiftness are the result of the application of scientific thought systems to problem solving, which results in a technology that creates a virtual cornucopia of things that add both to the comforts and to the problems of modern life. This process started with the Industrial Revolution of the nineteenth century and continues at an ever-accelerating pace. Knowledge begets more knowledge, creating a growth rate that is exponential rather than a simple linear extension of the present.

Changes have not been limited to the technological and material realm. Profound social changes have also taken place, but they seem to occur at a slower pace. We can more easily adapt to changes in the physical world than we can to those in the social world. For instance, churches equip their places of worship with modern heating and lighting systems, electronic sound amplification, and other appointments to make the surroundings modern; but changes in the rituals or liturgy may take many decades, perhaps even hundreds of years.

But social changes obviously do occur. When the movie *Gone With the Wind* was released in 1939, the sensibilities of some viewers were offended when Clark Gable as Rhett Butler closed the film by saying to Scarlett "Frankly, my dear, I don't give a damn!" Today such language would not draw comment, even from the most straight-laced among us. Also, it should be said that sequences in that film that had to do with racial references, which were acceptable to the viewing public in 1939, were found to be offensive when the film was released for television in the 1970s.

In the field of education, changes are occurring constantly. Some of these changes are minor, as, for example, when a school decides to lengthen or shorten its school day by fifteen minutes. When such a change is compared with a change calling for school desegregation by busing, we see a vast difference in the significance of the two events. But whether we examine those changes that are trivial or those that are profound, changes often displease those affected by them. For some, changes in school practices come too slowly. Those individuals and/or groups who have been traditionally poorly served by the schools are often impatient with the slowness of school change. They believe that schools are not doing enough to accommodate the educational needs of the constituents they represent. Others believe schools are changing too rapidly and, for the most part, to the disadvantage of quality education. They feel that children and youth were better served by schools of the past, before many of the changes and innovations took place.

It is clear, therefore, that whatever position the school authorities decide to take regarding educational changes, some groups and individuals will be displeased. In Chapter 2 we discussed the critics of the schools and pointed out there that if the schools accommodate one group of critics, they often alienate another group. The same applies to the management of change. This is precisely why simplistic solutions to educational problems that begin with the stem "If the schools would just . . ." are bound to fail. The problems are too complex and the dissatisfactions too diverse to be handled by simple change strategies.

Educational change relates directly to conditions in the larger soci-

296

ety. Educational reformers often take an approach of childlike innocence toward this reality. Many decisions regarding schools simply cannot be made by the school authorities because the decision is controlled by someone else—the state legislature, federal regulations, taxpayers, national mood, and so on. Successful management of school change requires that school authorities examine social conditions and realities in the whole of society rather than work with education alone.

Educational institutions that have pursued an overall strategy for the reconstruction of their programs have been rare. More often than not, there is a piecemeal effort. We see a little in-service education activity, much of it of dubious value. We see a project here and another there that was able to get federal funding and will doubtless terminate when the federal funds run out. Perhaps there is an effort to operate an alternative classroom or two in order to placate a group of parents who are interested in such a facility for their children. Here we see a school building constructed for open education, but the district did not bother to do the necessary curriculum and staff development, so it operates along conventional lines. There we see a new school building just completed, but it cannot be opened because the district lacks money to operate it. Little wonder parents and communities lack confidence in educational planners!

The position taken here is that educational change and the reform of schools require an overall, coordinated effort that involves the total community over a period of several years. Education is very susceptible to faddism, and, therefore, one is well advised to regard simplistic change formulas with caution. The educational scrap heap contains a mountain of innovations that someone believed would be the answer to America's educational problems. In his cogent history of American urban education, Professor David B. Tyack makes the point that from the earliest years of the Republic, we have been searching for "the one best system of education."[1] We continue to search for "the one best system," and as a result we flail away by responding to every fad that educational opportunists create:

Many of these movements are *tours de force*—an amazing display of energy in pursuit of inordinate ends. They appear like comets and sweep through the schools periodically, sapping the energy of the personnel and leaving lit-

[1] David B. Tyack, *The One Best System: A History of American Urban Education* (Cambridge, Mass.: Harvard University Press, 1974).

297

tle residue to mark their path. The activity movement and child-centered movement of the 1920s are good examples. Today one sees the open classroom, behavioral objectives, performance contracting, alternative schools, alternatives to schooling itself, and neo-humanism as potential *tours de force*. These displays of energy exact a heavy penalty in the shape of bewildered school personnel, exhausted from activities extraneous to their daily problems and arrested in the development of their ability to cope with the problems of teaching.[2]

STAFF DEVELOPMENT

When a teacher completes the preparation program for initial certification, the presumption is that the individual is competent to engage in the professional practice of teaching. Neither the training institutions nor the state certification officials, however, regard such entry level competence as adequate for a lifetime of teaching. Accordingly, teachers are expected to continue their education, possibly through a fifth year of preparation, a master's degree, or even more. The concept of a lifelong program of career development for teachers is widely supported. Incentives in the way of salary increases are provided to encourage teachers to continue their professional development.

A variety of terms is attached to the professional preparation of teachers beyond the initial certification: in-service education, staff development, professional development, continuing education, retraining. These terms do not all mean the same thing; that is to say, they are not synonymous. The appropriate term to use depends on the purposes to be served by the activity. Purposes also help define the extent to which such activity is solely the responsibility of the teacher and the extent to which it should receive district and state support. For instance, a teacher may be performing satisfactorily but is seeking to improve professionally for personal satisfaction and/or to increase his or her salary. The school district is placing no new demands on the teacher that would require additional professional preparation. In such cases, many would agree that the teacher should bear the expense of such training. If, on the other hand, the state is mandating instruction involving mainstreaming of the handicapped, something a substantial number of practitioners have not been trained to do, it is reasonable to expect that the state and local

[2] B. Othanel Smith and Donald E. Orlosky, *Socialization and Schooling: The Basis of Reform* (Bloomington, Indiana: Phi Delta Kappa, 1975), p. 9.

school districts will have to make the financial, human, and material investment to provide necessary staff development opportunities.

Perhaps the most commonly used term applied to this activity is *in-service education*. It can be defined very broadly as follows:

> Inservice education of teachers (or staff development, continuing education, professional development) is defined as *any professional development activity that a teacher undertakes singly or with other teachers after receiving her or his initial teaching certificate and after beginning professional practice.*[3]

Or it can be more narrowly defined as follows:

> [in-service education is] A cooperatively-planned program of job related activities designed to increase the competencies of K–12 school employees in the performance of their assigned responsibilities.[4]

Clearly, from the standpoint of using in-service education as staff development, a more focused definition, such as the one from the Washington State Superintendent's Task Force, is preferred. If the training program is to result in the achievement of prespecified outcomes that relate to educational change at the local level, the program will need to focus on job-specific needs of the teacher *and* the district. The first definition cited earlier could include education to satisfy the personal needs of the teacher, which would not necessarily result in changes in the teacher's classroom performance or in the instructional program for students.

The research on in-service education as related to the management of educational change indicates that such programs are most productive when the following conditions prevail:

1. The program is the result of a collaborative effort.

Collaboration in this sense means that the relevant constituents have contributed in a significant way to the in-service activity. The relevant constituencies would ordinarily be such groups as these: (1) the teachers, (2) the school district central administration, (3) the agency providing the service such as a college or university, (4) the state agency,

---

[3] Roy A. Edelfelt and Margo Johnson, eds. *Rethinking Inservice Education* (Washington, D.C.: National Education Association, 1975), p. 5.

[4] Superintendent of Public Instruction Inservice Task Force Report, Olympia, Washington, 1978.

(5) professional associations, (6) supervisory personnel, (7) curriculum directors, and (8) program developers and specialists. The specific groups to be involved will, of course, vary from one location to another, depending on the local tradition, power alignment, personnel relationships, and so on. The essential point, however, is that in-service programs that are targeted to produce educational change should not be planned and implemented *only* by one group (administrators) to be participated in by another group (teachers).

2. *The program should be focused on the development of specific knowledge and skills.*

In-service programs that deal with general concerns of teachers have not proved to be very effective in promoting change either in the teacher's behavior or in the school curriculum. What seems to be a more productive approach is to zero in on specific knowledge and skills: how to be more skillful in involving learners in the instructional process, how to conduct inquiry episodes, how to ask more effective questions, how to use some newly produced piece of instructional material, how to deal with student disruptive behavior in the classroom, how to teach children who read poorly, and so on. If these programs are to be effective, they must be problem- or skill-specific.

3. *Programs are more effective when conducted on site.*

Just why this is so is not altogether clear. Perhaps the instructor and the program take on greater credibility when the instruction takes place in the school environment. When it takes place on a university or college campus, it takes on a theoretical rather than a practical focus from the point of view of the teacher-participant. Teachers, understandably, have a difficult time making the intellectual leap from the campus to the real world of the classroom. Also, when instructors are forced to work on the home turf of the teacher, they, too, develop a greater sense of appreciation for that real world of the teacher. Naturally, the closer the newly learned knowledge or skill is to the reality of where it will actually be applied, the more likely it is to be meaningful to the learner, in this case, the teacher.

4. *The in-service program should be an extension of preservice.*

Preservice programs for teachers are usually highly structured, well organized, and specific in their requirements, which are to be followed in a particular sequence. Typically, in-service programs have been just the

300

opposite. They are often poorly organized, piecemeal—an incoherent collection of summer sessions, evening and Saturday courses, district workshops, in-service "days," and, in general, a haphazard conglomeration of credits, courses, and workshops.

One of the persistent problems of in-service education has been and continues to be the practice of teachers' holding one professional role while preparing themselves for another. For example, a teacher may be faithful in attending summer sessions year after year, earn a master's degree, and be well down the road toward a doctorate. Yet the advanced work this teacher takes may have little to do with his or her work as a high school science teacher because the person is preparing for a principal's position or some other administrative role. Often the advanced work is not taken to make the person a more effective practitioner in his or her present teaching position, but rather to become qualified for another post, presumably perceived to be a promotion.

Perhaps the only way the in-service and preservice programs will be coordinated will be through state certification requirements that call for a systematically planned program in order to become qualified for a *lifetime* or a *continuing* certificate. Quite clearly, salary incentives should not be allowed when the in-service work does not relate in some obvious way to the job being performed by the teacher. Colleges and universities should also be more responsible in career-counseling teachers and in providing coordinated programs of study. The individual teacher must, of course, assume major responsibility for the continued growth in his or her professional competence.

5. *Programs that are based on a needs assessment and are individualized are perceived as being most effective.*

This characteristic of in-service education means that it must be planned from a research base. There should be data to show that a program is actually needed. Little is to be gained in promoting in-service that does not address itself to known deficiencies or what have come to be called "needs." Perhaps this is why the studies made of the effectiveness of in-service courses show that they have little impact on changing teacher behavior or in changing the curriculum.

A school district must have a competent data-gathering arm that is able to identify strengths and deficiencies in the instructional program. These data can be used to show that the curriculum needs shoring up, for example, in reading, mathematics, or some other area of study. Or perhaps the data show that the graduates of the district high schools are not

301

well enough qualified to enter the best colleges and universities. No one can identify what problems a school, a teacher, or a school district will encounter because they are all different. Consequently, in-service programs, if they are to be effective, must take these differences into account. This is not likely to happen unless some type of deficiency-detecting process is undertaken.

6. *Programs that are teacher-involving in planning seem to be more effective than those that are not.*

Traditionally, a well-defined vertical line relationship existed between teachers and the top administrators. With teachers on the bottom and the school superintendent on top, other school personnel found their place in this pecking order. Principals, obviously, were higher than teachers; supervisors higher still, as were curriculum coordinators, associate and assistant superintendents, and so on. In practice, this administrative relationship had the effect of generating innovative developments at the top and passing them down the line. Only rarely did the flow of ideas go in the other direction. Thus, curriculum development was produced at the top and handed down to teachers. Similarly, in-service ideas were thought of by supervisors, principals, curriculum specialists, and other mid-management types and were arranged for teachers. There may have been some basis for this years ago when teachers had only a year or two of college preparation. But those conditions no longer obtain, and teachers today are demanding a greater voice in the management of activities that affect their professional lives.

If the school district takes the attitude that in-service is something that we (the school leadership) are going to do to them (the teachers), there is little opportunity for the teachers to develop any sense of ownership of the activity. The teacher will probably go along with the program but take the position that "this dark cloud will also pass"—and then they can go on doing what they have always done. The result is little or no change in practices. When teachers do have the opportunity to be involved in planning in-service activities and when they do share responsibility for its success, the results are generally more productive.

7. *There needs to be a long-term effort of in-service rather than a "one-shot" program.*

When school districts have their annual "in-service day," the usual procedure is to engage a specialist, a university professor, or some other speaker to address the group on some relevant subject. This may be followed by a few section meetings, at which time teachers share ideas, see a demonstration, or participate in a workshop. Publishers may have exhibits at such a conference, at which time the newest instructional materials are on display.

The type of in-service activity described in the foregoing paragraph is often roundly and unjustly criticized as being ineffective. Activities of this type may be very productive in many ways. They are often inspirational, teachers share ideas and socialize with their colleagues, and they may pick up valuable ideas about teaching strategies and instructional materials that they may apply in their classrooms. There is an important place for such activities in the total spectrum of in-service education.

Such once or twice a year efforts, however, cannot substitute for an ongoing, long-term in-service effort by the teachers or by the school district. It is important to recognize that these two types of programs, that is, the "in-service day" and the ongoing effort serve different purposes. In order to build new teaching skills or improve existing ones, a teacher will need to be involved in a concentrated in-service program that will extend over a period of several weeks, perhaps even months or years. Teaching includes both scientific and artistic dimensions, and just as competent scientists and artists in other fields strive to improve their work, the improvement of teaching requires a career-long obligation.

PARENT AND COMMUNITY EDUCATION

If one discounts the routine, procedural matters on which schools make decisions, it is safe to say that they rarely are able to make decisions on substantive matters entirely on their own. Other persons and groups are involved, and the success of the action based on a decision will depend on the support it gets from these affected constituencies. One of the most important of these, of course, are parents and others living in the local community. A school district concerned about managing educational change and shaping and directing that change will engage itself in a continuing program of parent and community education. We are speaking specifically of *procedural* values associated with the change process; that is, policy decisions calling for significant changes, regardless of their merit, are likely to encounter resistance or rejection unless those affected by them contribute to their formation. Several avenues useful for this purpose are available.

1. Public Relations Activity.

A public relations program is an essential component of a modern educational system because of the need to inform the public of fast-changing developments in the schools. Various media can be used for this purpose, of course, depending on the size and nature of the community. In small districts, the local weekly newspaper is often used for announcements and other publicity. From time to time during the school year, the district may purchase space for a school supplement. In large urban areas, schools operate sophisticated public relations and provide a continual flow of news releases, radio and television appearances of school personnel, and other appropriate information-providing events.

2. Advisory Committees, Boards, Task Forces, and Commissions.

At one time school administrators and school boards felt secure in conducting their business without much attention to the involvement of the citizens of the local community, but that would not be possible—nor even desirable—today. The use of special groups has a number of values, two of which are (1) to provide the decision makers with expertise that they do not have and (2) to educate a significant segment of the public as to the nature and extent of the problems faced by the schools. There is no question that schools have often co-opted the critics and silenced their voices by making them a part of the school establishment. For this reason, a few "outsiders"—critics—refuse to accept assignment to groups of this type because to do so would compromise their positions and credibility as critics. We are not suggesting that the co-option of critics is a good use of such committees, boards, task forces, and commissions; we are simply pointing out that schools, like other complex bureaucratic organizations, will often use such mechanisms to neuter resisters.

3. School Publications.

Most school districts publish some types of documents that are intended to inform the public, and especially parents, about the school. These are often curriculum documents—what the school is doing about the teaching of reading, mathematics, social studies; why mainstreaming has become a necessity; why certain grouping arrangements produce good results; why the school is required to desegregate, and so on. These publications may, of course, be a part of the overall public relations effort.

4. *Curriculum Development.*

Curriculum development provides an excellent channel for parent and community education. Making surveys and documenting the need for change produces data that can and often should be publicized. Parents and members of the community can be asked to respond to curriculum issues and indicate how well they believe the schools are serving local needs. As the curriculum development progresses, parents can be asked to serve on committees to review documents and to offer suggestions. The trial of experimental units affords another point of contact for parent and community education.

5. *Community Service.*

A school that is concerned about parent and community education is one where things happen that provide service to the local area. The local school then becomes more than an educational institution for children and youth but is a genuine community center. This is the traditional role of the public school in rural America, and when those schools were closed through consolidation, their closure had a far-reaching social impact on the community. This does not mean only that the community makes use of the school *building*. It means that and more. It means that the school is perceived as an institution that provides unity and cohesiveness for the community. It is a place where people from all walks of life gather to address themselves to common problems of the human family. It is where all of the problems of the local community intersect.

CURRICULUM AND ADMINISTRATIVE REARRANGEMENTS

There is some question whether curriculum and administrative rearrangements promote change or simply reflect changes that have already taken place. The experiences of curriculum developers during the past twenty-five years show quite clearly that curriculum and administrative changes are not very productive unless there is an accompanying and intense program of staff development (in-service). All over this coun-

305

try are school buildings constructed in accordance with the so-called open concept of education that are functioning as conventionally designed schools. Curriculum committees adopt textbooks written along the lines of new curriculum concepts in the subject matter fields, but teachers use them in traditional ways. The problem in both cases is that there was not an adequate amount of developmental staff in-service prior to the time the changes were made. Even *with* such staff development, the changes may not be significant or long lasting.

Changes in educational practice are most apparent when they take the form of curriculum and administrative rearrangements. Here are a few examples that have surfaced in modern times:

nongraded schools	performance contracting
middle schools	storefront schools
junior high schools	magnet programs
community colleges	educational parks
comprehensive high schools	open classrooms
basic schools	flexible scheduling
free schools	modular programming
alternative schools	year-around schools
voucher plans	school camps

In an earlier period in this century these innovative programs often took the name of the place or school that generated them, such as the Dalton Plan, the Winnetka Plan, the Oswego Plan, Pueblo Plan, and so on. It would seem that it is impossible to exhaust the capability of the education profession for creating one fad after another to deal with the complexities of human learning. The field has become a fertile territory for opportunists, entrepreneurs, and carpetbaggers of every stripe who are long on promises and short on delivery. For of all of the so-called innovations in education of the last twenty-five years, few have had any profound and long-lasting effect on educational practice other than creating a credibility gap between the education profession and the public.

Curriculum restructuring and administrative modification are critical to the process of managing educational change. In the past three decades there has been a vast amount of developmental work in curriculum, much of it heavily funded by the federal government and by the foundations. Additionally, the rhetoric surrounding the need for curriculum change has been extensive. But when one looks at the changes that have actually taken place, one would have to say that the rhetoric greatly exaggerates accomplishments. Nothing even remotely resembling a revolution has taken place in American education, even though the reformers of the 1950s and 1960s often spoke in those terms. The main reason the proposed changes never came to fruition was that they were not institutionalized in the curriculum and administrative structures of the schools. When the experiment ended, the idea died; when the outside funding was withdrawn or expended, the project was shelved. Not enough of the *total system* was involved in the process to produce any long-lasting, significant impact.

One of the important lessons that should have been learned about managing educational change from the experiences of the past three decades is that curriculum and administrative changes should be based on empirical studies at the local level. These have come to be called "needs assessments." This undoubtedly means that schools need to make a greater investment in research than is typically the case today.

LEGISLATIVE AND JUDICIAL ACTION

The most profound changes in educational practice in the twentieth century have come about as a result of legislative and judicial action. A few examples of the kinds of problems and issues that have concerned state and federal legislative bodies and courts are these:

1. Inequality of educational opportunity based on race and ethnicity.
2. Inequality of expenditures for education from one district to another.
3. Inequality of tax burden from one place to another.
4. Defining educational objectives and requiring accountability for the attainment of those objectives.
5. Defining basic education.
6. Providing more appropriate education of the handicapped.
7. Providing funds for training and retraining of teachers.
8. Providing funds for special programs, curriculum development, and innovation.
9. Requiring the desegregation of schools.

10. Setting standards for the preparation and certification of teachers.
11. Procedural and substantive rights of students and teachers.

This is, of course, but a very brief list of the concerns and issues that have been touched by these bodies.

Traditionally, it has been the state legislatures and the local school boards that have set policies for the operation of schools. The state legislatures established broad authorization for education, provided funding, and set general guidelines for curriculum. Local school boards developed their specific programs within the frameworks established at the state level. As local school boards would choose to ignore the wishes of certain constituents, these groups sought to go directly to the state legislature to have their grievances attended to. As a result, educational issues have become politicized, which has resulted in highly specific legislative requirements regarding what local schools can and cannot do. One regulation follows another, and soon the state legislature finds itself in the business of legislating the curriculum. State legislative bodies are less likely to become involved in curriculum legislation if school boards at the local level are responsive to the concerns of constituents.

The courts have come into the picture in recent years for somewhat the same reason. If neither the local school board nor the state legislature is responsive to the needs of groups, the issue can and often is taken to the courts. The Fourteenth Amendment was added to the Constitution following the Civil War, but distributive justice and equal treatment in education did not become a reality for many individuals and groups until the landmark Court decisions of the 1950s and 1960s. The judicially mandated reforms that flowed from such cases as *Brown* v. *Board of Education, Hobson* v. *Hansen, Serrano* v. *Priest, Lau* v. *Nichols,* and *PARC* v. *Commonwealth of Pennsylvania* have had national precedent-setting effects on American education.

The high-water mark in judicially mandated reforms in education seems to have been reached with the *San Antonio Independent School District* v. *Rodriguez.* (The issues in this case are described in Chapter 6.) This case demonstrated that there are limitations to the judicial process in resolving social issues. It proved to be an excellent case to illustrate that there are risks in pursuing a judicial, as opposed to a political, solution to reform. The court may not even be competent to resolve some issues because a fact pattern cannot confidently be pursued. David L. Kirp cites yet another reason for the "recent demise in judicial activism":

> Concerning educational-equity issues other than school finance, aggrieved groups have obtained through legislation much of—and in some instances more than—what they sought through litigation. This legislation has addressed the demands of women, the non-English speaking, and the handicapped; and, with respect to these last two groups, moneys which no court could order expended have been made available to meet their needs.[5]

It would seem that once the courts had set the direction that social reform was to go, Congress and state legislatures were less reluctant to pass legislation to extend and support such policies. Consequently, as Kirp notes, there is less need to seek retribution through the courts.

THE PROVISION OF ALTERNATIVES AND OPTIONS

Early in this century school authorities were attracted by the efficient management and production operation of the business and industrial sector and began applying many of those practices to education. Increasingly, schools took on the appearance of factories—strict time schedules, standardized equipment, movement of children along an "assembly line," an hierarchal administrative organization, a standardized curriculum, reference to the "products" of schools, standardized tests, standardized texts, and so on. The extent to which schools adopted business and industrial practices and the impact of this development are cogently addressed in Callahan's book *Education and the Cult of Efficiency*.[6]

In order to increase efficiency, one has to standardize operations as much as possible. Assembly-line production is efficient in terms of time and motion because each task is performed in the same way. Whether the task is done by a human being or by a computerized machine makes no difference; the essential characteristic is its sameness. Thus, the worker

---

[5] David L. Kirp, "Law, Politics, and Equal Educational Opportunity: The Limits of Judicial Involvement," *Harvard Educational Review*, 47:2 (May 1977): 121.

[6] Raymond E. Callahan, *Education and the Cult of Efficiency* (Chicago: The University of Chicago Press, 1962).

can be trained to do a single operation with a high degree of proficiency. Similarly, a machine can be programmed to do a job in exactly the same way time after time, indefinitely. What upsets efficient operations of this type are idiosyncratic or unique events. A custom-built product is put together using less efficient production methods, but the result is a "one of a kind" product. The analogy to education would be a child educated with a group going through a standardized curriculum as opposed to an individually designed curriculum for a single learner who would be individually tutored.

As the cult of efficiency took hold of schools, educators prided themselves in the extent to which their practices were standardized. Thus, it is understandable why a superintendent of a large city school is reported to have boasted that at any particular time of day he could tell a visitor precisely what was going on in every classroom in the city!

The Progressive Education Movement along with the Child Study Movement were the first significant thrusts to challenge the cult of efficiency and the emphasis on standardization. These movements placed the emphasis on the individual learner. The educators who were identified with these developments stressed the need to individualize study programs for learners. These educational leaders were very influential, and their philosophy had a powerful impact on American schools. By 1950 the concept of individual differences among learners as an educational reality in the classroom and the need to make curricular modifications in terms of such differences were generally accepted. For the most part, however, the adjustments had to do with such variables as the time, amount, and complexity of the tasks rather than with constructing new programs that were philosophically different from the mainstream curriculum.

The contribution of the decade of the 1960s was the introduction of the concept of alternative schools. The demand for alternative schools came out of the activist, antiestablishment efforts of the so-called radical New Left. These schools were established under a variety of rubrics, the most common being free schools, alternative schools, open schools, and storefront schools. Usually, they were started by a committed group of activists who were willing to donate their time and effort to the movement. The schools were often poorly housed, sometimes in abandoned business buildings—hence the name "storefront" schools. They had little or no financial resources and predictably were short-lived.

The alternative schools spawned during the social unrest of the

310

1960s existed long enough to present the public school establishment with a challenge. The public schools decided not to oppose the movement openly but to work with the advocates of alternative education to incorporate them within the school establishment itself. Of course, this did not happen everywhere. In some places, the alternative movement was simply ignored, or the school officials resisted it publicly. But in the majority of instances, the alternative idea was accepted grudgingly, and some accommodation was made to its supporters. School authorities soon learned that if advocates of the alternative school were allowed to organize and operate their school within the existing school system, it could be made educationally defensible. Besides, having their own school kept them busy and off the backs of the school officials on other issues.

In Chapter 3 we discussed in detail various perspectives on the purposes of education. It is clear that people vary greatly on what they think education should accomplish and the best methods of achieving those goals. These differences often represent deep-seated philosophical and psychological conflicts that are not reconcilable. For instance, one simply cannot accommodate in the same classroom the views of a behaviorist who wants precision teaching aimed at the achievement of prestated behavioral objectives and the needs of a humanist who wants open, unstructured learning experiences. That is as impossible as designing a square circle. The questions are, "Who will referee these conflicts, and how can the needs of various constituents be served?"

One way of dealing with these differences is to break the standardization of school experiences further and provide for alternative programs within the regular school establishment. For many years, we have had alternative schools, on a limited basis, but they have been outside the public school enterprise. For example, we have had parochial schools, traditional private schools, Montessori schools, experimental schools, campus laboratory schools, and others. If a family was fortunate enough to live in a community where these schools were available, it did have an opportunity to make a choice as to where to enroll its children, providing, of course, that the parents could also afford the additional cost. But the idea of providing an alternative school that differs philosophically and psychologically from the regular school, yet have it as an integral part of the public school system, is a rather recent innovation and one that seems quite well established.

There is little doubt that the majority of children can be well served by the conventional school program—especially so when teachers are sensitive to individual differences and make programmatic adjustments in terms of those pupil differences. Nonetheless, there are many children who would be better served by some other approaches. School districts could, and most *should*, make other options available to learners. For example, most districts could have at least one or more classrooms in which instruction is conducted along informal, "open" lines; some with cross-age groupings; others that use behavior modification procedures; and perhaps still other options. Then those parents who wished to do so could choose the school whose practices are in accord with their child's educational needs or their own personal beliefs about education. What is more, most school districts have teachers who are competent to work in a variety of educational settings and would welcome the opportunity to become engaged in innovative efforts of this type. If such choices were available, undoubtedly most parents would opt for the regular, conventional program. Parents' choices seem overwhelmingly to favor not only conventional but *traditional* programs.[7]

Providing alternatives and options is an essential strategy for the management of educational change. Rarely will a school district be willing to convert its total program to a new and untested idea. Nor should it. Changes in schools should evolve gradually, with some opportunity to field test those ideas at the local level, in the home environment. This can be accomplished by setting up small, experimental units that serve as alternatives to the regular program. From these will come ideas and practices that show such promise that they will be institutionalized as a part of the entire school program. Other less productive efforts will be phased out. The school district that is on the cutting edge of the profession, the one that is keeping abreast of social and educational change is the one that has well-defined avenues for new ideas to flow into the mainstream of local school practice.

STUDY AND DISCUSSION

1. In many communities the school is the largest employer. It operates the biggest transportation system in the community

---

[7] John Jarolimek, "Social Studies and the Elementary School in the Years Ahead: Some Critical Issues," a lecture delivered on the occasion of the centennial observance of the College of Education of the University of Wisconsin-River Falls, February 13, 1975.

and has the largest food service program. Its athletic, drama, and music programs entertain more people than all of the other entertainment facilities combined. How do these realities impact on the ability of the local authorities to make changes in school programs?

2. This chapter provides both a narrow and a broad definition of in-service education. Are teachers likely to support one or the other of these definitions? Would the same apply to school boards? State departments of education? Supervisors and curriculum directors? Why do different groups perceive in-service education differently?

3. Have there been fewer changes in the elementary school curriculum or in the secondary school curriculum in this century? Why do you think so?

4. Describe strategies schools have used to implement a change in a curriculum area such as mathematics or social studies. What components of such strategies contributed to the overall success *or* failure of the change effort?

5. Suppose a teacher who retired in 1950 returned to the teaching service today, some thirty years later. What things about the school environment would impress the person as having changed *most?* Having changed *least?* In which of the subject matter fields would the person be *most* comfortable teaching? *Least* comfortable? Why?

6. What evidence can you secure to show that the U.S. Office of Education (now the Department of Education) either has or has not been effective in promoting educational change in the public schools of this nation during the past two decades?

7. Do you believe that legislative and judicial intervention in school policies since 1950 has resulted in improved intergroup relations? What reasons can you give to support your belief?

8. What are the main objections to highly specific, state-mandated curriculum requirements?

9. What educational values are sacrificed when a school is overly concerned with efficiency? Cite specific examples to illustrate your points.

10. Identify five instances of needed educational change that will present American education with its greatest challenges between now and the turn of the century. Explain and defend your choices in the context of the subject matter of this text.

313

SELECTED BIBLIOGRAPHY

ADAMS, DON. *Schooling and Social Change in Modern America.* New York: David McKay Company, Inc., 1972, Part 5.

CARNOY, MARTIN, and HENRY M. LEVIN. *The Limits of Educational Reform.* New York: David McKay Company, Inc., 1976.

CAVE, WILLIAM M., and MARK A. CHESLER, eds. *Sociology of Education: An Anthology of Issues and Problems.* New York: Macmillan Publishing Company, Inc., 1974, Part 3.

FANTINI, MARIO D. "Toward a Redefinition of American Education." *Educational Leadership* (December 1977): 167–172.

GOODLAD, JOHN I. and ASSOCIATES. *Curriculum Inquiry.* New York: McGraw-Hill Book Co., Inc., 1979.

KARABEL, JEROME, and A. H. HALSEY, eds. *Power and Ideology in Education.* Part 6: "Social Transformation and Educational Change." New York: Oxford University Press, 1977.

KATZ, MICHAEL B. *Class, Bureaucracy and Schools: The Illusion of Educational Change in America.* New York: Praeger Publishers, 1975.

LEVINE, DANIEL, and ROBERT J. HAVIGHURST. *The Future of Big-City Schools: Desegregation Policies and Magnet Alternatives.* Berkeley, California: McCutchan Publishing Corporation, 1977.

ORNSTEIN, ALLAN C. *Education and Social Inquiry.* Itasca, Ill.: F. E. Peacock Publishers, Inc., 1978, Chapter 10.

REITMAN, SANDFORD W. *Foundations of Education for Prospective Teachers.* Boston: Allyn & Bacon Books, Inc., 1977, Chapter 17.

Sources and Resources: An Annotated Bibliography on Inservice Education. rev. ed. Prepared by the staff of the National Council of States on Inservice Education. James F. Collins, Director. Syracuse, New York: Syracuse University School of Education, 1979.

Index

315